Negotiating
Lesbian
&
Gay
Subjects

Negotiating Lesbian & Gay Subjects

edited by

Monica Dorenkamp

and Richard Henke

Routledge | New York and London

Published in 1995 by

Routledge
29 West 35 Street
New York, NY 10001

Published in Great Britain in 1994 by

Routledge
11 New Fetter Lane
London EC4P 4EE

Copyright © 1995 by Routledge

Printed in the United States of America.

Library of Congress Cataloging-in-Publication Data

Negotiating lesbian and gay subjects / edited by Monica Dorenkamp and Richard Henke.
    p.   cm.
Contains essays from the Fifth Annual Lesbian and Gay Studies Conference, held at Rutgers University in 1991.
Includes bibliographical references.
ISBN 0-415-90832-9   —   ISBN 0-415-90833-7 (pbk.)
1. Homosexuality—Congresses. 2. Gays—Congresses.   3. Gay men—Congresses.   4. Lesbians—Congresses.   I. Dorenkamp, Monica.   II. Henke, Richard.   III. Lesbian and Gay Studies Conference (5th: 1991: Rutgers University)
HQ76.25.G378   1995   94-9173
305.9'0664—dc20   CIP

Contents

1

Introduction

Monica Dorenkamp
and Richard Henke

THE FIFTH ANNUAL LESBIAN AND Gay Studies Conference, from which these essays are taken, seemingly marked a new era in Lesbian and Gay Studies. With over sixty panels attended by two thousand people, the Rutgers-Princeton Conference was the largest event of its kind to date, an indication of the strength of this newly emerging academic discipline. However, over the course of the conference's three days, it became clear that even as Lesbian and Gay Studies was being affirmed as a coherent discipline, the papers presented were revealing that it continues to splinter and divide, creating a potentially huge field of discourse as well as an enormous problem of definition. We might even ask: what is Lesbian and Gay Studies? Who are and what are its subjects?

The impossibility of neat answers to such questions has become increasingly evident as we recognize that the privileging of (homo)sexuality as a category of critical understanding must not exclude consideration of other markers of identity by which we situate ourselves and are situated in the world. *Negotiating Lesbian and Gay Subjects* foregrounds this belief that discussions of homosexual identity and subjectivity cannot be considered at all (though they too often have been) outside of always overdetermined contexts. That is, while it may be possible to be a lesbian or gay man, it is never possible to be only a lesbian or gay man.

In this sense, the construction of homosexuality in opposition to heterosexuality—the well-worn "gay/straight divide"—has missed the point. Katie King has noted that, like most binaries, this one is a bit too neat for its terms, and unable to contain them. As it gets problematized by Diana Fuss in her refiguring of it as an "inside/outside" struggle of always potentially collapsable terms, it gets revealed as a troublesome twosome, erasing some differences by foregrounding others, stubbornly ahistorical. As King points out, "Other differences that cannot be imagined as opposites may be as salient or more salient: race, class, nationality, language, religion, ability. All suggest that sexualities are too plural, too politically granulated to be named in a gay/straight division."[1]

In our hierarchizing of "differences," we risk losing the specificities of experience and ignoring the historical and cultural contexts which shape them. But to trace the process of the construction of subjectivity is, as Teresa de Lauretis has noted, to map those specificities and contexts. Lesbian and gay subjects are constructed only through a "process" of experiences, which in turn come to be identified as "lesbian and gay." The temptation, and the danger, is to claim *my* lesbian experience as yours; *my* gay subjectivity as yours.

> Experience is the process by which, for all social beings, subjectivity is constructed. Through that process one places oneself or is placed in social reality, and so perceives and comprehends as subjective (referring to, originating in, oneself) those relations—material, economic, and interpersonal—which are in fact social and, in a larger perspective, historical.[2]

Examining the processes by which any given lesbian or gay subject gets defined and/or identified as such, then, should stear us clear of the threats of (re)constructing any fixed experience that could be said to be "lesbian" or "gay."

It could be argued that Lesbian and Gay Studies has long challenged and rejected the notion of a monolithic homosexual identity—of a marginalized, deviant, and often criminal figure constructed by religious, legal, and psychiatric institutions and discourses. However, in the very process of articulating such challenges, a series of paradigms of homosexual identity have been posited which may have emerged at particular historical moments in particular places, yet which often have been adopted with little qualification transhistorically and transculturally. Through widespread (mis)appropriations of such work, its original subtlety and complexity has gotten elided, and theories that may have worked to challenge orthodoxies of identity have threatened to give way to the construction of a new orthodoxy—one that ultimately reifies monolithic homosexual subjects.

The writers in this collection sense this in one way or another as they resist complacent notions of lesbian or gay subjectivity. For each, the way that lesbian and gay studies is constructing its subjects seems inadequate for their experiences and observations, as these reveal the process of becoming a specifically lesbian or gay subject as one of negotiation.

What does such negotiation involve? On the one hand, it requires some consideration of preconceived and articulated positions that have been available, whether in the end these are rejected completely or accepted with adjustment. On the other, it requires an awareness and consideration of those social and historical relations of which de Lauretis speaks: those relations which are perceived as subjective. Throughout, negotiating subjectivity is an extraordinarily complex and mobile process, and the product will necessarily not be fixed but simultaneously unified and in parts, coherent and incoherent.

Necessarily written from a variety of cultural positions, in some ways the essays in *Negotiating Lesbian and Gay Subjects* then are in radical disagreement with one another. Such discord is not a bad thing, however, as it continually forces us to critically rethink the ways in which we negotiate lesbian and gay subjectivity—both for ourselves and for others.

For this reason we have chosen to reject the often false divisions that such collections usually rely on. Because the essays attempt a more relational understanding of lesbian and gay subjectivity, even while one essay may privilege the site of the body, another the site of language, over other sites, none is so fixed as to "belong" to one division more than another. One of the points of the volume is that even as such divisions get constructed to help us better grasp and organize our ideas, too often they tend to de-emphasize the multiple and necessary interconnections between them. And it is precisely these that we want to foreground.

Such interconnections are inevitable of course, if we believe that negotiating a lesbian or gay subjectivity also necessarily requires negotiating one's experience(s) of being lesbian or gay (or one's observations as a lesbian or gay man) with the mediating forces (e.g., language, visual discourses, history) which allow for and/or obscure the articulation of such "being." Each of the writers of these essays is involved in such negotiation.

Presented as a keynote address at the conference, Samuel Delaney's "Aversion/ Perversion/Diversion" preserves the moment of the actual talk even as it creates a new moment within the context of this volume. Through a series of autobiographical "troubling" tales, Delany points to the necessity and impossibility of putting sexuality, and sexual experience, into language, for once put into language, sexuality becomes highly coded and therefore heavily policed. It is not, then, simply enough to point to experiences and assert that these are what collectively have produced this gay subject. Instead, Delany urges us to look as much at the processes by which these experiences themselves get constructed, by ourselves and others, through (in this instance) language. Ultimately, for him, gay identity "is an object of the context, not of the self."

The other writers in this volume are engaged in similar processes of negotiating gay or lesbian subjectivity in relation to specific contexts. Since these contexts diverge widely—from Marcia Ian's world of the bodybuilder's gym to Simon Watney's "queer diaspora"—the subjectivities which develop and get identified as gay or lesbian diverge widely as well, even perhaps to the point where they are not so explicitly identified as gay or lesbian at all, but understood as dependent on the negotiation of gay or lesbian subjectivities in establishing their own. This is the case with Sylvia Molloy's consideration of fin-de-siècle Latin America's reception of certain homosexual literary figures, particularly Oscar Wilde, as central to the construction of national (masculine) identity. Through an awareness of the specific cultural imperatives of this place and time Molloy concludes that although the homosexual may have ultimately been deemed "unhealthy," it was only through such a figure that a national sense of *modernismo* was established. In that way, the homosexual is in fact not other but integral to the cultural production of a national identity.

While in Molloy's essay such negotiation is provoked by the explicitly homosexual figure of Wilde, Eve Sedgwick looks at Wilde's contemporary, Henry James, who has come to represent the classic figure of the repressed homosexual. Examining the highly idiosyncratic language of James's later essays, Sedgwick considers the centrality of an anal preoccupation in his life and writings. In doing so, she challenges the pervasive supposition that James could not have been aware of his own "exhibitionistic enjoyment and performance of a sexuality organized…around shame."

The mediating force of language and of its role in constructing subjectivity is examined in other contexts as well, including those of Richard Fung and Julia Creet. Taking her own coming-out story as a starting point, Creet reexamines the seemingly stabilizing effects of its retelling to reveal the stakes involved in identity politics in general. An understanding of the "psychic crisis" of lesbian identity as "fully grounded in historical and political contexts" is central to her argument. Fung examines the "burden of representation" that accompanies his choosing, and having chosen for him, various identificatory labels. Fung focuses on the simultaneous but distinct processes of his becoming gay and Asian. An independent video- and filmmaker, he notes that these concerns are important in his work, but realizes too that the need for such negotiating does not disappear when the mediating element is visual rather than linguistic.

This is further explored by Richard Meyer, Joseph A. Boone, and Marcia Ian. Meyer looks at the highly charged homoerotic aesthetics in Andy Warhol's work of the sixties in relation to the gay male clones of the seventies, and analyzes how each "prized the surface of desirable sameness over the depth of (humanist) subjectivity, each valued 'wanton consumerism' above expressive 'indiviuality.'" Boone considers different cinematic versions of *Thousand Nights and A Night* to show how the homoerotic elements of the tales have not been part of their visual existence. When he focuses specifically on Pasolini's version, he notes that even as the complex framings of the male nude seemingly challenge a dominant Eurocentric culture they do so within a broader context of a colonializing ethos which has structured Western perceptions of the Arab "other." Finally, Ian considers how her own body may be a sort of visual representation, a symbolic field where the problems of the Cartesian split of body and mind are played out and contested in a vivid way, the significance of which, she believes, neither psychoanalysis, feminism, nor even Lesbian and Gay Studies has adequately accounted for.

As a discipline, Lesbian and Gay Studies—and specifically as it has been developing in the U.S.—is critiqued by Simon Watney for its failure to sustain active intellectual engagement with issues concerning HIV/AIDS. Since Watney believes that homosexuality and identities founded upon homosexual desire have been reconstituted specifically as a result of the HIV/AIDS pandemic, he critiques further a resistance to consider the cultural specificity of the experience of HIV/AIDS and the failure to address the disparate needs and strategies which countries with necessarily different types of epidemics require.

Watney's essay shares with many others in this volume an awareness of the anxieties that were emerging in Lesbian and Gay Studies at the time of the Rutgers-Princeton conference, and which are still much in evidence. Such anxieties indicate an increased understanding of the diversity and complexity of the issues that concern lesbians and gay men, and the impossibility of ever fixing "our" subject(s).

NOTES

1. Katie King, "Producing Sex, Theory, and Culture: Gay/Straight Remappings in Contemporary Feminism," in *Conflicts in Feminism*, Marianne Hirsch and Evelyn Fox Keller, eds. (New York: Routledge, Chapman and Hall, 1990), 83.
2. Teresa de Lauretis, *Alice Doesn't: Feminism, Semiotics, Cinema* (Bloomington: Indiana University Press, 1984), 159.

2
......

Aversion/Perversion/Diversion

....

Samuel R. Delany

[After an introduction by George Cunningham, this talk was delivered at Scott Hall, Rutgers University, 8:00 p.m., Friday night, November 1st, 1991, at the Fifth Annual Lesbian and Gay Conference on Gay Studies.]

AVERSION, PERVERSION, DIVERSION— the topics of my talk—present us at the outset with their intensely overlapping euphony, their entwined etymologies—sharing much with the Latin "*prover-sus*," source of "prose," "verse," "verb," and "proverb." Certainly they start with the suggestion of three very inter-confused topics. Nor is that confusion allayed by my further explaining that my talk tonight will be about neither "inversion" nor "reversion"—that is, it will not be about "homosexuality," female or male, considered as some notion either of the masculine or of the feminine inverted, negated, turned inside out or upside down to produce the "lesbian" or the "gay male," a production presumably recoupable by the simplest uncritical reversion to its former state—no matter how violent the effort needed, a violence too often justified by the very simplicity of the move.

But whatever confusions I bring you this evening, I shall assume that basical-ly you have asked me here as a storyteller. So let me say that, true to my triplet topics—aversion, perversion, and diversion—the tales I shall tell are tales that trouble me. Something about them makes me want either to turn away from them, or to turn their telling away from the pattern the tale made when it was presented to me.

There is, of course, a tale I would very much like to tell. The protagonist of that story is without sex. He or she is wholly constituted by gender—female, male, gay male, lesbian. What's more, our protagonist is unaware of any contradictions in the constitutive process, so that his or her blissfully smooth, seamless self may be called "natural," "unalienated," "happy"—or what-you-will.

Our hero—for certainly she must be a hero—never does anything that is ego-distonic, that does not please here. All her actions—purposeful, habitual, gratuitous—are ego-tonic. They *feel* good.

The only unpleasant things that befall her inevitably originate outside the self. Whether she is defeated by them or triumphant over them, their external origin is a knowledge she is secure in. I hope we can all recognize in the basic situation here the story of that most glorious political comedy that we have yet been able to erect in the name of liberation.

I adore it as much as anyone.

But it worries me; for while it can make me thrill, rejoice, and wildly applaud, it never makes me weep—other than in joy…and from what I know of the world, that is something to worry about. That is *why* I'm worried.

There was a movie theater in New York once, called the Cameo, whose screen provender was heterosexual commercial porn, whose clientele was overwhelmingly male, and whose management encouraged a high level of homosexual activities in its corridors, stairwells, side seats, and—to a lesser extent—its bathrooms; and, in its upper balcony, a somewhat lower level of drug commerce and use.

Of the many hundreds of men with whom I had sex there over more than a decade, from a dozen or so regulars with whom I had a settled and comfortable routine to a cavalcade of one-, two-, or three-time encounters, a number stand out. One such was a young man, white, with dark hair, of about twenty-five, who usually wore a suit jacket—in a population largely black and Hispanic and usually in jeans and sport shirts. Sitting on the right-hand side of the theater, a seat apart, we had exchanged some five or ten minutes of furtive eye contact, when he motioned me to sit beside him.

As we began to touch each other, he leaned toward me to whisper, in a light, working-class accent associated with the outlying boroughs of the city, "you know, I've never done anything like this before. All the other sex I've ever had has been with women. But somebody told me about this place. So I just thought…" He shrugged. And we continued, easily enough considering his virgin status, to some satisfaction for us both.

Three months later, visiting the theater once more, after a stroll down one aisle and up the other, I noticed the same young man, again sitting off on the side. Recalling our last encounter, I slid in immediately to sit a seat away from him, smiled, and said softly, "Hi!" This time, he motioned me to the next seat right away, grinning and saying hello. As we began to touch each other, again he bent forward to explain: "You know, I've never done this before—with a man, I mean. I've had sex with women, sure. But this is my first time doing it with a guy…"

I thought better of contradicting him. We went on as before—with the same results.

Some months later, when I met him there again, he actually began talking to me by saying, "Hello! Good to see you. How've you been?" quite ready to acknowledge that we knew each other. But when, in a moment, we started to touch, again he whispered: "You know, this is the first time I've ever done this—with a man, I mean…"

What troubles me in the memory of these encounters is, of course, how much of myself I can see in this fellow. His litany, like some glorious stutter, recalls that dictum of Freud's: repetition is desire.

But I have no way, at this date, to ascertain whether he experienced that desire as sexual predilection or as social fear. Was his endlessly renewed homosexual virginity (with its corresponding claim of heterosexual experience) part of the person he felt he must be to be sexually attractive? Or was that portable closet, that he was perpetually just stepping out of, merely some silly and encumbering excuse that could have been dispensed with by the proper enlightenment—the simple revelation that, other than himself, no one at the Cameo he was likely to run into really cared.

The fact that the latter represents, however, a certain level of common sense is what suggests that the fantasy itself might be part of the sexual order of his desire. But the social marginality of the situation, and the extreme behavioral range in that margin—for the breadth of human experience generally remaining outside one sub-language or another is far greater than what, from time to time, over-spills into the centers of articulation—militates for a social interpretation.

What was he averring socially?

What was he averring sexually?

And certainly it does not take much to see the two diverge dramatically.

But it was precisely my lack of concern with these questions, plus a general sympathy for the eccentric (and he was good-looking), that let me move with him through the labyrinths of mutual desire without questioning such contradictions.

The first time I taught for a full term at an American university, I had my thirty-second birthday while there as a Visiting Professor. As sometimes happens when a writer comes to a new school, a handful of the brighter students attached themselves to me, and soon I felt that some of those students had even become my friends. Among them was a brilliant young Hispanic woman, who, for the sake of the telling, I'll call Carla, and who, while I knew her, had her nineteenth birthday.

Full-figured, with black hair and astonishing gray-green eyes, Carla turned a questioning energy on everything about her. She was an attractive personality for anyone who enjoyed the pleasures of thinking for its own sake.

That term I came out to my students as soon as it flowed from the material we were dealing with. If it did not put them at ease, it made me feel more comfortable. But I was clear about announcing the fact that I was gay within the first two weeks of classes.

The isolation of a visiting professor moving onto a new campus—and, in my case, it was also my return to the U.S. after two years in England—can be extreme. The few people, including Carla, who helped alleviate it, I was grateful to. One day, however, when she was walking with me across the campus, she confessed, somewhat jokingly, that she was sexually interested in me and would have pursued it with some passion had I been straight. "I'm just a slave to my body," was her comment; it has remained with me for years from that afternoon. I know the feeling. But I reiterated that I wasn't straight; still I hoped we could stay friends. A notable current of my adult social education—and I feel it's very near the core of what I sometimes characterize as what it means to be a "responsible gay male"—is not to be irrationally terrified either by female anger or by female desire. I enjoyed Carla's friendship and hoped she could still enjoy mine, even if she had to suppress an overt sexual component—a relationship I have had and have enjoyed with many men. I decided to make no effort to distance myself from her, but give her the opportunity to reconceive the friendship in non-sexual terms—an opportunity a good number of men, both straight and gay, have given me.

Classes ended, and, about a week before I was to return to New York, Carla, an older male student (a carpenter we'll call Fred, an aspiring poet in his late twenties, whom, I confess, I was attracted to; but Fred had made it as clear to me as I had made it clear to Carla that he did not want to pursue a sexual relationship, even though, in his own words, the possibility flattered him), and another woman student who was Carla's close friend, invited me out with them for an evening. The specific suggestion came from Carla. She explained I was to be their guest for the night, and that dinner and dancing afterward were their way of showing their gratitude for my term's teaching.

A very pleasant night it started off. Somehow, however, I ended up with several more drinks than I wanted—twice when I came back to the table from a trip to the john, my half finished drink had been replaced by a full one; and at least three other times a round I didn't really want at all was brought over my protests.

But we were dancing, having a good time—and there was much talk of "drinking up."

In Fred's van, we returned from that very loud Buffalo dance bar which, in 1975, claimed to be the original home of the Buffalo chicken wing; and when we reached the double tier of motel rooms in which the university had housed me that term, Carla announced she would give me some help upstairs to my room—I only realized, perhaps, I needed some when I was halfway there.

In my room, she pushed me backward onto the bed, grabbed my arm to keep me from falling onto the floor, and proceeded to pull off first my clothes, then hers.

She climbed on top of me.

Then, at her insistence, we made love. I had the presence to ask if she was using any birth control. She answered: "What do you think I am? Crazy?" The only other interruption was, once, when I pulled away to race into the bathroom to be messily ill in the toilet. Solicitously, she brought me back to bed. The next morning, it was a while before anyone felt like moving. And, in the haze of my hangover, I recall her rising to dress and leave.

Some time later that day, she returned. I answered the door. She entered, and immediately began to undress.

"Wait a minute," I said. "Let's talk."

And so, for a while, we did.

It seems, she confessed, her plan from the beginning had been to take me out for the evening, get me drunk, bring me home and, in her words, "Fuck your brains out."

"Yeah," said Fred on the phone a little later. "But I told her she probably wouldn't succeed. I don't think you can really *do* that kind of thing to a guy, can you…?"

I pointed out to Carla that, one, this just was not what I wanted our relationship to be. Two, if I had done the same thing to her—or to any of her undergraduate friends—she would have been justifiably furious. "Didn't you just tell me, about a week ago, about some male professor here who tried something rather like this on a young woman that you knew? As I recall, you were pretty pissed off at him."

"Yes," she said. "But it worked when he did it, too."

"Carla," I said. "If we're going to be any sort of friends, you're going to stop this—*we're* going to stop this."

"Yes," she said. "I guess we are."

And she left.

And left me wondering if, indeed, we *could* be friends any more.

I hope you find this story, so far—for it is not over—troubling in all its resonances. I certainly did.

My term was up at the university. Three years later, when I was living in New York with my then-lover, I received a call from Carla. She was now in her second year of law school, there in the city. I said, quite sincerely, that it would be nice to see her again.

I mentioned that I had been living with a lover for more than a year.

She sounded very pleased. And about a week later, she came by. Her dark hair was cut very short and she wore very tight white jeans. "I want you to know," she told me, as we sat and talked in my study, "that I took your advice."

"Advice?" I asked. "What advice?"

"I'm a lesbian now."

"This," I asked, "was advice I gave you? I can't imagine my advising anyone to 'become' a lesbian—or a gay man. Although I hear it happens, I wasn't particularly aware that it was any more common than becoming straight."

"Well," she said, "what I meant is that I followed your example."

"What example?" I asked, totally lost.

"Well, you were married for thirteen years or so, weren't you, before you became gay?"

"Ah!" I said. "No, I've been pretty aware that I was gay since I was eleven or twelve—though, yes, I did get married. But now, at least, I have some idea what you're talking about. But 'advising' someone to become gay—that's like advising someone they'd be better off black than white. Sure, in anger, you could suggest someone might learn something if they experienced some oppression. But no one who's part of an oppressed group, who's really thought about the nature of that oppression, is going to *advise* someone else to join in."

Now it was her turn to say, "Ah." She went on: "Well, it's true; you never said it in so many words. But I thought that's what you were doing. Anyway, whether you gave it to me or not, it's been the best advice I've ever taken!"

"I'm very glad it was," I said. "But, next time you think I'm giving you advice, *do* ask me to tell you directly what it is. I'll feel better about it, even if you don't."

Two years later, Carla passed her bar exams. And on another visit, in which she came by to tell me both of her new job working as a civil rights lawyer and of her new and most satisfying relationship with another young woman, she said: "You must have been very angry at me, back at school. I have a very different take on all that now—we handle sexual harassment cases. That must have been quite dreadful for you."

"For whatever it's worth," I told her, "I wasn't angry. I don't know whether it has anything to do with it or not, but at least once in my life I've been held down by two men and raped. It was a lot less pleasant than what you did."

"Well," she said, "I'm glad you still let us be friends. I've gotten a lot from it."

"I'm glad too," I said. "So have I."

I have no way to be sure, of course, what that experience meant to Carla—or, indeed, how often it returned to her. Here we are speaking, and I feel it's important for me to say it clearly, of a situation where laws were violated, where the kinds of moral and ethical concerns Carla herself was now working with in her job were, on both sides, mine and hers, called sharply into question.

Were I asked what tales *were* characteristic of my young manhood as a gay male, what comes to mind are those nights circumstance put me beside some other man, peacefully asleep, whom I knew I could *not* touch—and so lay sleepless the night in a paroxysm of desire. But all the tales I shall be telling tonight I've chosen precisely because they are *un*characteristic.

So, another tale—in this case of a muscular Puerto Rican, with curly black hair, whose workshirt bore a name we'll say was "Mike" in yellow stitching across the gray pocket. He wore a green jacket with a green and yellow knitted collar to the same theater where I met the first young man I spoke of. Across the back, yellow letters spelled out "Aviation Trades High School," from which, I presume, he must have graduated sometime over the three-and-a-half years I knew him.

Mike was as regular a visitor to the theater as I was. He was handsome, in a bearlike way. From a couple of quiet approaches, however, I'd gathered he was not interested in me. From time to time, I would see him sitting in various seats in the balcony or orchestra. Nearly as frequently, as I walked up or down between the lobby and the balcony, I would pass him, sitting on the stairs, toward the top, sometimes leaning forward, forearms across his knees, sometimes leaning back, elbows on the step two above and behind.

Once, after I'd stopped paying much attention to Mike, I was sitting a few seats away from another black man, in green work clothes and dilapidated basketball sneakers. Knees wide against the back of the seat in front of him, he was slouched low in his chair, watching the film.

Mike, I noticed, was slouched equally low in the row ahead, one seat to the right.

Then something moved near the floor.

I glanced down—to see a hand. Under the seat and behind the metal foot of the ancient theater chair, it looked rather disembodied. But the fingertips now and again brushed the rubber rims and black cloth uppers of the man's right sneaker. Glancing at the top of Mike's head, then down at the man's foot—the man seemed oblivious to what was happening—I realized Mike had reached down between the seats and was playing with the man's shoe.

"Ah…!" I thought, in all the self-presumed sophistication of my own sexual experience. "So *that* explains it!" And, four or five times over the next few months, I noticed Mike, now in the balcony, now in the orchestra, at the same practice with different men.

This was back in the years when today's ubiquitous running shoe was just emerging as *the* casual fashion choice. As is more usual than not, I was at least a year behind most other people; and it was only that week that I broke down and got my first pair—in which, I confess, I never ran in my life.

They were a conservative gray.

One day I stopped at the Cameo and, on my way to the balcony, passed Mike sitting on the steps. Several people stood near the top, watching the movie; I stopped behind them, largely to watch them.

Minutes later, I happened to glance down. Mike's hand was on the step, the edge of his palm against my shoe sole. I was surprised, because till then I had considered myself outside his interests. My first and most innocent thought was that his hand's straying to that position had been an accident, even while more worldly experience said, no. Precisely because of what I knew of him already, while it might have been an accident with someone else, *his* hand's resting there could *only* have been on purpose—though his attention all seemed to be down the stairs.

I tried to appear as though I was not paying any attention to him. He continued to appear as though he was not paying any attention to me. I moved my foot —accidentally—a quarter of an inch from his hand. His hand, a half minute later, was again against my shoe. Again—accidentally—I moved my foot a quarter of an inch closer, to press against his fingers—and two of his fingers, then three—accidentally—slid to the top of my foot.

In ten minutes, Mike had turned to hold my foot with both his hands, pressing it to his face, his mouth, leaning his cheek down to rub against it.

To make the point I'm coming to in all this, I must be clear that I found his attention sexually gratifying enough so that I continued to rub his hand, his face, his chest, his groin with my shoe until, at last, genitals loose from his gray work pants, he came—and, over the next three weeks, when we had some four more of these encounters, I came as well during one of them.

We do not even have a term for the perversion complimentary to fetishism. The myth of the sexual fetish is precisely that it is solitary. Its assumed pathology is the fact it is thought to be non-reciprocal. A major symptom of the general insensitivity of our extant sexual vocabulary is that as soon as fetishism is presumed to move into the realm of reciprocity, the vocabulary and analytical schema of sadomasochism takes it over; and to me this seems wholly to contravene common sense and my own experience.

Mike and I became rather friendlier now—when we were not directly engaged in sexually encountering one another. If we met outside the theater on the street, we said hello and nodded. If we passed in the theater stairwell, we might exchange brief small talk. There were no words at all, however, about what we were doing. It was clear to me that Mike did not want to flaunt his practices before the other patrons, with some of whom he was rather more friendly than he was with me. Among the theater's younger clientele were a number of hustling drag queens and pre-ops: their teasing and joking could be intense. And these were the people who, in the theater, were Mike's conversational friends.

Running shoes, at least the brand I'd bought at that time, do not last as long as they should. Soon it was time to replace them.

I thought of Mike.

By now, though, I'd glimpsed him several times get as involved with other men's running shoes or sneakers as he could from time to time with mine. I felt nothing but empathy and goodwill toward him. But clearly some excited him more than others. The specifics of his preference, however, I hadn't been able to piece together. How, I wondered, do I ask about such a thing? How do I put such a question into language?

Not much later, when I was getting up from my seat in a legitimate 42nd Street movie house where I'd gone to see some genre horror film, I saw Mike—also leaving. We smiled across the crowd and nodded to each other. I decided the best thing to do was to be as open and aboveboard about my curiosity as possible.

"You know," I said, as we joined each other, walking toward the lobby, "I've got to get a new pair of sneakers, one of these days soon. What kind do you think I should get?"

He seemed not to have heard me. So I persisted: "Is there any kind you like particularly—some kind you think are the best?"

Mike stopped, just inside the lobby door. He turned to me, a look blooming on his face that, in memory, seemed a combination of an astonishment and a gratitude near terror. He leaned forward, took my arm, and whispered with an intensity that made me step back: "Blue...! Please...*Blue!*" Then, he rushed away into the street.

I'd expected an answer at the same level of fervor I'd offered my question. But, I confess, that afternoon, with an anxiety that, somehow, did not seem all my own but borrowed, at Modell's Sporting Goods I purchased a pair of blue Adidas.

Two days later, when I wore them to the theater, however, Mike was not there. Nor did I see him on any of my next dozen visits.

After a few months, I realized he had dropped the place from among his regular cruising sites. Three times over the years I glimpsed Mike in his green jacket with the yellow letters, now on a far corner under the marquis at the Port Authority bus terminal, now by the subway kiosk at 72nd Street, now, with his hands in his pockets, hurrying down 45th Street toward Ninth Avenue. But I never saw him in the theater again. I've often wondered if our encounter in the second movie had something to do with his abandonment of the first: I can only hope that, among his friends, he might be telling *his* version of this tale—possibly somewhere this evening—for whatever didactic purposes of his own.

A few years ago, however, when I first wrote about Mike to a straight male friend of mine—a Pennsylvania academic—he wrote me back: "If you can explain the fascination with licking sneakers so that I can understand it, you can probably explain anything to anybody!"

My first thought was to take up his challenge; but, as I considered it, I realized all I could explain, of course, was *my* side of the relationship. I'd found Mike desirable—well before I had known of his predilections. Using some formulation by Lacan—"One desires the desire of the other"—it seems easy enough to understand that, if Mike's desire detoured through a particular focus on my sneakers, it was still *his* desire, and therefore exciting—perhaps not quite as much, for me, as it would have been if it had focused on my hands, my mouth, over all my body, on some aspect of my mind, or on my genitals; but it was exciting nevertheless.

As I thought about it, it occurred to me that, in similar environments, I'd actually observed many hours of fetishistic behavior by any number of men over the years, though most of those had involved work shoes or engineers' boots in specifically S&M contexts—so, therefore, I knew something quite real about that behavior. But, at the same time, I'd spent perhaps less than a single hour talking about that behavior with any or all of the men involved—including Mike.

That meant there was a great deal I *didn't* know.

What could I explain?

What could I not explain?

Even though I responded sexually to Mike, I could no more speak *for* him than I could speak sexually for any of the very few women I had gone to bed with—or, indeed, for any of the many, many men.

The Freudian dimorphism in the psychoanalytic discussion of fetishism is one of the empirical disaster areas in the generally brilliant superstructure of Freudian insights: men can be fetishists but women are kleptomaniacs. And within the last two years I have heard at least one psychoanalytic critic state all but categorically that no one has ever found a female fetishist.

Those of you who have read my autobiography of a few years ago (*The Motion of Light in Water* [1988], New York: A Richard Kosak Book, 1990) may remember that my own fetish is men's hands—especially the hands of men who bite their nails. Nor do I have any problem analyzing my particular perversion *as* a fetish. This critic's pronouncement put me in mind of a gathering of artists and artisans some fifteen years ago in Greenwich Village, that included a lean, good-natured, redhead, who was both a carpenter and a leather craftsman and whose hands were large, work-soiled, and (to me) sexy—and his petite, blonde wife. In the course of an afternoon, where the group was jesting with one another loudly about sex, I heard the redhead's wife declare, "Someday Todd's going to wash his hands, get them completely clean—at which point I'll probably leave him forever!"

To say my ears perked up is to use a wholly inadequate metaphor for my response. At the time, I was still trying to understand my own sexuality in these matters; minutes later I'd contrived to question the young woman as to exactly what she meant. And, while the others joked on at the other side of the table, we spoke in some detail about her own attraction for men's hands soiled from work, and how this attraction has been—and currently was—constituted into the range of her sexual life: we exchanged childhood experiences, jokes, and current observations. Granted that there were idiosyncratic differences between her object and mine, nevertheless by the end of the conversation I simply have to say: if I have a fetish, then so did she.

And unless she was prevaricating, to say it is impossible that she exists simply will not do. Nor can I think that all those leather dykes have merely snitched their jackets, studded belts, wristbands, chains, and engineer's boots.

In other places I have written that the single, empirical example—and that is all the particular orders of narrative I indulge here can give—is the place from which to start further, operationalized investigation. It is not the place to decide one has found a general fact. And I mean it—here, too. Certainly I would like to see such operationalized study begun. And my utopian hope is that in such stories as these such study might begin. That is why I've told so many of the tales I have.

But this suggestion of an egalitarian fetishism brings us to a truism of the field of gay studies that, like any truism, it might be time to review. It is one that again and again, in other discussions, I have felt must stand at the head of any number of talks and articles on matters gay. Let me quote from the last time someone else quoted me on just this point.

Here is Teresa de Lauretis, writing in her introduction to a 1991 issue of a special number of *differences*, devoted to Queer Theory:

> Delany opens his introduction [to *Uranian Worlds*] with the words: "The situation of the lesbian in America is vastly different from the situation of the gay male. A clear acknowledgement of this fact, especially by male homosexuals, is almost the first requirement for any sophisticated discussion of homosexual politics in this country." [De Lauretis goes on:] And, as if he were reading my mind or telepathically sharing the thoughts I put into words in this introduction, he adds: "Gay men and gay women may

well express solidarity with each other. But in the day to day working out of the reality of liberation, the biggest help we can give each other is a clear and active recognition of the extent and nature of the different contexts and a rich and working sympathy for the different priorities these contexts (for want of a better word) engender."

Then de Lauretis goes on to quote my co-introducer, Joanna Russ, in her delineation of precisely what some of those differences were in terms of literary availability.

Paradoxically, it is because I wrote that—and because I still stand by it—that I want to tell another, worrisome tale.

It is a simple one. It happened on a chill, early spring afternoon, during my middle twenties, when I sat on the rim of the fountain in Washington Square with a hefty young woman about my age, who wore glasses, black jeans, a leather jacket, and who went by the name Hank.

We talked—talked from the breeze-laced height of the day till the sky above us deepened to indigo, sharing our sexual histories. We were not talking of my adventures on the docks or in subway johns or about my frustrations at trying to establish a more lasting relationship in such a context; we did not discuss her bar life or the cycle of seemingly endless hurts that were serial monogamy.

Rather we talked about the burgeonings of our sexual awareness, in the family, in school, in the street, and in the times we moved from one to the other, now in our early summer camp experiences, now on our visits to cousins in the country, or with playmates away, at last, from overseeing adults. We talked mostly of happenings that occurred before ages thirteen and fourteen, and of experiences that certainly seemed, for both of us then, directly constitutive of who, sexually, we had become. Both of us, again and again, were astonished at how many experiences we shared, how many of the separate lessons that we'd learned were clearly congruent, and how much of the stuff of the initial awareness of the sexual—from the body out—seemed all but identical for the two of us. But, given the time we had our conversation, no one had yet told us that we were supposed to be all that different. Hank remarked on the similarities. So did I.

For better or for worse, the solidarity I feel with many lesbians is still based on such experiences. What my understanding of that vastly differing context explains for me is why those conversations are rarer for me with women than with men. An understanding of that vastly differing context allows me to translate from women's experiences to mine—when such translation is possible. An

understanding of that vastly differing context explains for me why so frequently no translation takes place at all. But what that context does not do in any way
is validate the notion for me of some transcendental, irreducible sexual difference between men and women, either in terms of sex or gender, straight or gay,
a difference that becomes the ground for any and every social difference one
might want to elaborate from it. Indeed, it is precisely my understanding of the
specific complexity of the context that makes an acceptance of that irreducible
and transcendental difference impossible for me.

Certainly the identification I speak of is always partial, problematic, full of
mistakes and mis-readings.... But, that is my experience with any identification
I feel with *any* other, male, female, gay straight....

Thus even the similarities are finally, to the extent they are living ones, a play
of differences—only specific ones, socially constituted. Not transcendental ones.

Thinking about discussing this with you tonight, I was wondering at the same
time about the inside/outside metaphor that common sense so frequently asks
us to use—but which has come under an intensive critique in recent years.

For, in terms of the progression of my narrative, didactic argument, we are
about to take up the phrases "inside language" and "outside language."

I did not tell Hank all my stories.

Doubtless, she did not tell me all hers.

I told her, for example, none of the stories I've so far told here. And the stories
I did tell—it occurred to me when I was reviewing the incident for inclusion in
this account tonight—were, none of them, included in the autobiography I
wrote twenty years later...though I still remember them very well! Which is to
say, they still remain largely outside language.

Diana Fuss has written, introducing the fine volume she edited, *Inside/Out:
Lesbian Theories, Gay Theories* (New York: Routledge, 1991): "The figure of
'inside/outside' cannot easily or ever finally be dispensed with; it can only be
worked on and worked over—itself turned inside out to expose its critical operations and internal machinery" (1).

Fuss begins the argument I have quoted from the "philosophical opposition
between 'heterosexual' and 'homosexual,' " heterosexuals representing the inside
and homosexuals the outside. But I think there's a finer economy of inside and
outside where her point is just as valid: that is the notion of sexuality itself as
always occurring partly inside language and partly outside it.

I am not speaking of a hypostatized language as an unarticulated totality,
beside which some sex acts occur in an ideal silence apart from the word, while

others are swaddled in a constant, approved, and privileged discourse. I speak rather of language as an articulated and variegated set of discursive fields, many of them interpenetrating, but many of whose distinct levels bare a host of economic relations one to another. Some of those levels are privileged, some are not; some are notably more ephemeral than others. These levels fall into hierarchies of reproducibility, accessibility, and permanence. And some never leave that most ephemeral state—that internal speech of the individual we call unarticulated thought. In that sense, of course, all human activity is inside language. But by the very same set of distinctions, all human activity takes place inside certain orders of language and outside certain others—and that is the force of the metaphor behind what I've said about activities inside language and outside language till now, as it will be behind what I have to say in the discussion to come.

As comfortable as I am calling the tales I tell here "true," these tales are nevertheless quite coded—coded as to their selection, as to their narrative form, as to their referents, their texture, and their structures; and the conventions that code them were more or less sedimented well before the incidents that prompted the accounts took place. Despite their sedimentation, however, these codes have also shifted with history: such tales certainly could not have been told, say, thirty-five years ago at a formal, public, university gathering—inside this particular order of language.

No less coded—and no less true—is this last of my tales. Its coding today may even be the most self-evident, the most obvious.

One bright, November afternoon, as I was passing just across the street from the theater I was telling you about before, a young man in his early twenties, slight and half-a-head shorter than I, came up to me. Pretty clearly Irish American, he was wearing a jean jacket and a broad smile. His hands were in his pockets, and, in the sunny chill, he breathed out white wisps. "Hey, you want to get together with me? I seen you comin' around here a lot. Somebody told me you write science fiction. I like that stuff. I read it all the time. Makin' it with somebody who writes about spaceships, and time machines, and flying saucers and stuff, that'd be pretty cool."

I laughed. "Sorry," I told him. "Not today." And went on about my business.

A few days later I passed him again, and again he approached me: "Hey— when are you an' me going to get together?"

Smiling, I shook my head and walked on.

Days later—the third time I passed him—he called me over to a doorway he was standing in and, when I came, bombarded me in an intense whisper with a detailed and salacious account of what he could do for me. He finished up: "And I ain't expensive either. Man, I'm a street person. I can't afford to charge high prices—isn't that a bitch? I just want to make enough to get high."

"Look," I said. "First of all what's your name?"

Let's say he said it was Billy.

"Billy," I said, shaking his offered hand, "I was about to get something to eat. I'll buy you a sandwich. But that's all."

"Sure," he said. "It's a start. Maybe something'll develop."

"Nothing's going to develop," I told him, "except a sandwich. But come on."

At a hot-plate bar two blocks south on Eighth Avenue, I had a pastrami on rye, while Billy had a roast beef on whole wheat, which he ate with two or three fingers of both hands pushing and working inside his mouth, for seconds at a time, to tear the food apart. No beer; he just wanted a soda. While he drank it, he listed the titles and summarized the plots of the last dozen science fiction novels he'd read. I allowed as how he had good taste. Wiping at his mouth with his napkin now, he apologized: "You know, I used to be a pretty neat eater, would you believe it? But I guess living out here, I'm turning into kind of a pig. It's my teeth. They give me a lot of trouble, and a lot of things I can't really chew. How come you won't give me a tumble?"

"Do you really want to know?"

He sat back in the high, wooden booth seat and countered: "Do you really want to tell me?"

I laughed. "You seem like a smart kid. You're actually pretty good-looking— and you keep yourself clean. I'd never have thought you were living rough."

"I wash in the bathroom at Port Authority every morning." He winked at me. "I do sort of okay out here."

"Billy, the truth is, I just don't find you sexually attractive. And if I'm going to pay for it—even the price of a bottle of crack—it seems to me I should be getting something I'll enjoy."

"You'd enjoy it," Billy said, with a nod of mock smugness. "I'd see to that. But I get your point." Then he narrowed his eyes. "You say I look good; so how'd you know I was a crackhead?"

"How did you know I was a science fiction writer?" I asked. "It's a fairly small world out here."

"*Mmm.*" Billy nodded.

But two weeks later, the next time I ran into him, Billy approached me with:

"I'm hungry. You wanna buy me a sandwich?" Which I did—the second of per-haps a dozen over that winter and into spring. During our meals I got the pieces of a story, tedious in the similarity of its details to any hundred like tales of like young men and young women: relations severed angrily and violently by a Brooklyn family because of his drug involvement; a penally checkered career throughout his late adolescence; his last two years (he was twenty-four) living on the street—most of that time, in Billy's particular case, sleeping in the upper tier of the Port Authority Bus Station's Gate 235, which, because the gate was not in service that year, became the rotational sleeping space of some dozen young people (all but Billy, in those days, black) in an uneasy and often violated truce, both with each other and the Station authorities. Some of those details bespoke a level of organization, however, notably higher than most street drug-gies maintained—especially those on crack. Billy always kept two shirts and a pair of pants in the dry cleaners around on Ninth Avenue, one of which he took out every three or four days. Sometimes I gave Billy science fiction novels to read.

As such friendships will, this one tapered off to where we just called hello to each other on the street when we passed; later, from time to time, we only nod-ded, or raised a hand. Then, one summer's day as I was walking up Eighth Avenue, I saw Billy sitting on the single step in a doorway, plaid sleeves rolled up his forearms, still neat and clean enough so that most people would not guess immediately he was homeless.

As I nodded, he looked up at me, elbows on his knees and one hand holding his other wrist. "Well," he said. "I got it."

That halted me. I searched about for a reasonable response. Billy was not above feigning illness to put the touch on you. For three months, about six months before, he'd had a low-grade ulcer which, while he'd treated it with Mylanta and emergency room prescriptions, he'd not been above working up into something more serious to hustle a few dollars from sympathetic passers-by. But this seemed outside Billy's usual range of fictions. I asked: "Any idea how you picked it up?"

"Oh," he said, "sure. Needles. I'd never do anything sexually that would give it to me." He nodded. "Sharin' needles."

"Well," I said, at a loss to think of an appropriate rejoinder. "You've got to take care of yourself." Then I walked on…while I realized the fact that Billy had *not* asked me for a handout as I moved away was probably the surest confirmation of the truth of what he'd just told me.

I saw Billy a couple of other times—even had another sandwich with him. "I had the pneumonia," was how he put it, at the hot-plate bar; he dug inside his mouth. "They said, at the hospital, if I got it again, that would be it. They also said, since they knew I had it now, if I showed up with pneumonia again, they *wouldn't* take me back. Can they do that? I guess, if you don't got any money, they can do what they want. Right?"

All I could say was that, honestly, I didn't know.

Work had already taken me out of state; the next few times I saw Billy were in my sporadic trips back to the city. October a year ago, when the weather took a final leap into Indian summer warmth, briefly I was in New York and walking up Eighth Avenue. In the same doorway where I occasionally used to find Billy sitting, I noticed a gaunt man, his shoulders near nonexistently thin. His eyes and temples were sunken. The lower part of his face was swollen so that he seemed a sort of anorexic Neanderthal. He wore a baggy blue t-shirt, and his legs came out of a pair of even baggier Bermudas like sticks. He looked up to catch me staring at him—and I thought to look away. But, slowly, he smiled and said: "What's the matter, Chip—don't you recognize me?"

"Billy…?" I said. Then, because I couldn't think of anything else to say, I said, "How're you doing?"

"Pretty bad," he said, matter-of-factly. His voice was decidedly slurred, and I wondered if the swelling in his jaws was the packing of some internal bandage. But I don't think so.

I kept on walking, because for the last year, that's what I did when I saw Billy.

But later that evening, I was in one of the neighborhood gay bars—Cats. I'd come down to talk with a gay friend, Joe, a recent Jesuit novice, who'd left his calling and whom I'd helped get a job in publishing. We'd been catching up on his adventures and mine, when the door opened and three young men came in, Billy among them. He saw us, grinned, came over, draped one matchstick arm around Joe's neck and one arm around mine. "Hey," Billy said, with the same slur of the afternoon, "you guys know each other? Joe's my special friend here." Which Joe confirmed by a grin and a hug.

"Just a second. I'll see you in a minute." And Billy was off to say something to the hustlers he'd come in with.

Again, I had no idea of the protocol for such situations. "Billy's a good kid," I told Joe. "How long have you known him?"

"Oh, about three weeks."

"*Mmm*," I said. Then I said: "You know, of course, he's got AIDS. At least he told me he did, sometime back."

"I kind of…" Joe nodded. "Suspected it. He doesn't say the word. But he talks about it."

That didn't make me feel much better.

But Joe said: "We don't really do anything, anyway. We lie around and hold each other. He says he likes it and it makes him feel good. But that's all."

At which point Billy was back, arms again around our shoulders, bony head thrust between. "Joe says he'll take care of me whenever I get real sick," Billy announced, straight off. "He's a special guy. Like you."

"That's good," I said.

Joe, at any rate, was smiling. Billy reached behind him and pulled a stool up between us. As he sat, his baggy Bermudas rode up his gaunt thighs till his uncircumcised genitals hung loose. Reaching down with one finger he hooked the plaid edge back even more. "It's amazing," he said, and I realized I was getting used to his slur, "most of my johns haven't deserted me. But that's because I always gave 'em a good time, I guess." (Though I had never been his john, looking at him now it was a little hard to believe.) Gazing down, Billy apostrophized himself: "You bought me a lot of dope. Made me some money—some friends. Gave me a good time." Shifting to the side, he pulled his shorts leg down now. "Got me into a lot of trouble, too!" He looked back up, grinning at us with swollen jaw and bony face.

And, for the first time in the years I'd known him, to my distress, I felt sexual excitement rise toward Billy. I had another drink—I bought him and Joe respectively a ginger ale and a beer. I shook hands with them both, wished them well—and went home.

October's weeks of Bermuda-shorts weather are brief.

A month and a half later, when I happened to get Joe on the phone at work, I asked how Billy was. He told me: "A little while after I saw you at the bar, when it started to get cold, Billy showed up sick at my place. I kept him there for a week of *spectacular* diarrhea! Really, the guy was exploding shit—or water, mostly, after a while. Then he said he wanted to leave—I didn't think he could leave. But he went off somewhere. I haven't seen him since."

No one has seen Billy since—for a year now.

You and I know Billy is dead.

Nor is Billy the only one in these tales to die:

Carla was killed in an accident during a rainstorm, when a metal piece fell from a building cornice and struck her down as she was hurrying to bring her lover an umbrella in a Brooklyn subway station. While I rode the subway, I saw the *Daily News* headline across the aisle, "Lawyer Slain in Brooklyn," and only a day later learned that the lawyer was my friend—and it was as stunning, and as horrid, and certainly more tragic and interruptive in the lives of her friends than this intrusion of its awful and arbitrary fact is here.

I spoke at Carla's memorial service. And, whatever I have said of her—here—she was an easy person to praise.

Billy's death?

I called a number of hospitals—so did Joe. As far as we could learn, Billy did not die in any of them, though his name was on record at two: outpatient treatment for a junior ulcer at one and a stay for pneumocistis pneumonia in the other. But unless he went very far afield, he probably *wouldn't* have been admitted. And Billy was bonded to that central city neighborhood—sometimes called the 42nd Street Area, sometimes the theater district, and occasionally the Minnesota Strip—through his very familiarity with it, by his knowledge of the surge and ebb of its drug traffic, because so much of what he knew was how to eke from it the limited life it allowed.

Well, why, in our clean, well-lighted space this evening, do we need this story? Why do we need to add to these others this tale of a moment's fugitive desire *en route* to an untraceable death behind some burned-out building or in an out-of-service bus gate at the Port or beneath a bench in an Eighth Avenue subway station?

It was four years ago I first realized that, among my personal friends and acquaintances, AIDS had become the biggest single killer, beating out cancer, heart disease, and suicide combined. Certainly Billy is not typical of my friends—nor is his death typical at all of theirs.

Why not, then, tell of a cleaner, more uplifting death? Well, I tell it because such deaths are *not* clean and uplifting.

I tell is because the story troubles me—the purpose of all these tales: it troubles me because it is as atypical as it is.

Understand: I recount these stories not as the "strangest" things that have ever happened to me. Purposely I am not going into particulars, here, about the well-dressed sixty-year-old gentleman in the 96th Street men's room who asked for my shit to eat, or the American tourist who picked me up in Athens who could only make love to me if I wore a wristwatch with a metal band, and that band low on the arm, or the young Italian who had me hammer his stretched scrotum to a piece of pine planking with half-a-dozen ten-penny nails.

What I'm trying to remind you is, simply enough, that these are all part of a gay experience—*my* gay experience. I can't claim them as characteristic of some hypostatized universal gay experience involving the range of gay women and gay men, black and white, middle-class and working-class. They are not even characteristic of my own. Perhaps they could occur only in the margins of the experience of one sexually active black-American, urban gay male, in the last decades of the twentieth century. But—in terms of that experience—they are a good deal more informative than Sunday brunches and Judy Garland records, in that they are parts of a sexual experience—with men and with women—which, as a gay male, I would not trade for the world with anyone else's.

You must understand, there are sexual experiences—with both men and women—I would happily give up. As I once told Carla, I have been held down by two men and raped. When I was seven or eight I was sexually abused, very painfully, by a girl a few years older than I at my first summer camp. Both experiences, believe me, I could easily have lived without.

The tales recounted here—as they touch on the sexual, however troublingly—belong to a *range* of sexual occurrences, the vast majority of which have never and can never make their way into language, the range that gives me my particular outlook on human sexuality, an outlook certainly different from many other people's; and those experiences have done more to dissolve any notions I ever held of normal and abnormal than all my readings on gender, perversion, and social construction put together.

But "the gay experience" has always resided largely outside of language—because all sexuality, even all experience, in part resides there. Simple aversion—at whatever social level—is enough to divert our accounts from much of what occurs. But even to seek the averse is to divert our accounts from the characteristic. And because of this economy, in anything that I can recognize as a socially and politically meaningful discussion of sex, the triplicity of aversion, perversion, and diversion cannot, as far as I know, be avoided—here, tonight, anywhere....

To make such a statement about the realm of sexuality is another way of saying that what has been let into language has always been highly coded. That coding represents a kind of police action that, even while it is decried in the arena of politics, is often, among us in the academic area of Gay Studies, unnoticed.

This is why I have tried to bring up these specific and troubling tales, to help cast into the light the smallest fragment of the context of—no, not Gay Studies in general, but simply the context of the talk that I am now in the process of giving. And if, when we take as our object of study, say, some lines by Shakespeare or Whitman to a boy, citing the contestation of other, homophobic scholars, when we examine some profession of love to another woman in a letter by Emily Dickinson or Eleanor Roosevelt or Willa Cather, contested equally by still other homophobic scholars, or the coded narratives of Melville's wide world of navigation, of Oscar Wilde's or Dorothy Strachey's London, of Thomas Mann's circumscribed tourist town of Venice, or Djuna Barnes's wonderfully sophisticated Paris—if we take these tales and assume that we are not dealing with a code that, in every case, excludes a context at least as complex and worrisome as the one I have here gone to such narrative lengths to suggest, then, I maintain, we are betraying our object of study through a misguided sense of our own freedom, by an adoration too uncritical of that wonderfully positive tale we all, perhaps, adore.

What I hope worries you, what I hope troubles your sense of the appropriateness of these tales for the here and now of what, certainly, most of us will experience as a liberating academic occasion, is what suggests that, even with the surge of linguistic freedom that has obtained since '68 and with the movement toward political freedom that has been in motion since the Stonewall riots of '69, what is accepted into language at any level is *always* a highly coded, heavily policed affair. Though strictures relax or tighten at different places and in different periods, the relaxation never means that the policing or coding has somehow been escaped.

The sexual experience is *still* largely outside language—at least as it (language) is constituted at any number of levels.

Ludmilla Jordanova's book *Sexual Visions* (University of Wisconsin, 1989) is a stunningly fine and informed study of gender images in science and medicine over the last three hundred years. It was recommended to me by a number of astute readers. I have since recommended it to a number of others perusing like topics of concern.

In its preface, however, Jordanova takes to task Paula Weidegar's book, *History's Mistress* (Viking Penguin, 1985), which reprints a selection of extracts from an 1885 book by a gynecologist, Ploss, *Woman: a Historical Gynecological and Anthropological Compendium.* Writes Jordanova of Weideger: "Her fictional scenario is supposed to make the point that the thirty-two photographs of breasts in the 1935 English edition are included for prurient reasons. Yet the way she makes the point, her chosen title, and the whole presentation of her book serve to heighten any sense of titillation in readers and buyers."

Jordanova then goes on to advise, most wisely, a careful study of such works and their circumstances in order to understand the object it represented.

Yes, a wise suggestion. But the problem with such a suggestion, however, is that such works—especially in 1935, if not 1885—belonged to a category which tried as carefully and as ruthlessly as possible to exclude the specifically sexual component from all the language around them. Some years ago, I talked to a handful of men, fifteen to thirty years older than I, who recalled using such books as pornography in their youth. What made such works both accessible and pornographic was precisely that the sexual *was* excluded from any overt mention: it is not an absurd assumption to assume that art works, medical works, and legal works occupied such a position all through the nineteenth and the first three-quarters of the twentieth century—especially given that 150 years' proscription on pornography *per se.* But the problematics of dealing with sexual research in periods when much of sexual discourse was all but nonverbal is as much a problem for the historian of heterosexuality as it is for the historian of Gay Studies.

Because both today and in earlier times what of the sexual that has been allowed into language is notably more than what was allowed in during that period of extraordinary official proscription any of us over forty can still remember, we must not assume that "everything" is *ever* articulated; we are still dealing with topics that were always circumscribed by a greater or lesser linguistic coding and a greater or lesser social policing. Because Alexander Kojève and Jerome Carcopino have discussed the double writing of the Emperor Julian and Cicero, and because Robert Martin has traced a like process going on in Melville's tales of the sea, we must not forget that double codes as well as single codes still exclude, still police. They simply do it at two stages for two audiences—even if one of those audiences is gay. And what is excluded by the code, that code exists specifically in *order* to exclude. And because the whole analytical bastion of psychoanalysis lies there to talk about repression both in the areas of the socially articulated and the socially unarticulated, we must not fall into any easy uncritical alignment of the socially excluded with the unconscious and the socially articulated with the conscious. Repression takes place at a wholly other economic order.

It is often hard for those of us who are historians of texts and documents to realize that there are many things that are directly important for understanding hard-edged events of history, that have simply never made it *into* texts or documents—not because of unconscious repression but because a great many people did not want them to be known. And this is particularly true about almost all areas of sex.

Though our academic object as textual explicators must begin with what is articulated in a given text, we must always reserve a margin to deal with what is excluded from articulation, no matter the apparent inclusiveness.

That goes just as much for my tales this evening as it does for Musil's *Young Torless* or Gide's *The Immoralist*. It goes just as much for Hall's *The Well of Loneliness* or Brown's *Ruby Fruit Jungle*. It goes just as much for the text collected by a sociologist from a gay informant, female or male, who is being questioned about the realities of gay history.

In 1987 I published an autobiography a good deal of whose motivation was to retrieve various historical articulations in just this context as I had observed it, between the years 1957 and 1965. The advent of AIDS made, I feel, absolutely imperative an inflated level of sexual honesty that dwarfs the therapeutic exhortations for sexual openness that can be seen as the fallout of a certain industrial progress in methods of birth control coupled with Freud's, if not Reich's, sexual ethics, and enhanced with the political strategy, dating from Stonewall, of "coming out" (a strategy devised specifically to render the sexual blackmailer without power)…a code, a police action if you will, that controls a good deal of what I say here.

It seems to me that when one begins to consider the range of diversities throughout the sexual landscape, then even the absolute unquestioned normalcy of the heterosexual male whose sexual fantasies are almost wholly circumscribed by photographs of…female movie stars! suddenly looks—well, I will not say, "less normal." But I will say that it takes on a mode of sexual and social specificity that marks it in the way every other one of these tales is marked, i.e., as perverse.

Similarly, the heterosexual woman whose fantasies entail a man who is wholly faithful to her, and who, only while he is wholly faithful, does she find sexually attractive, but whom upon showing any sexual interest in another woman—heaven forfend that it be another man—immediately is rendered sexually unacceptable to her; well—like the male above, her sexual condition seems only a particular form of a socially proscribed perversion—one that I could even, for a while, see myself getting behind. Certainly, it would be no more difficult than getting off on someone licking my sneakers. (And it would be, for me, a lot easier than getting off on female movie stars—or most male ones, for that matter.)

But both strike me, as do all the other situations I have described tonight, as socially constituted and perverse. And in this case, for all my sympathy, neither perversion happens to be mine.

Similarly, when one surveys the range of fetishes, at a certain point one begins to see that the sexualizing of a hand, a glove, a foot, a shoe, a breast, a brassiere, a buttock, a pair of panties, a jock strap, a sailor's uniform, a policeman's uniform, a riding crop, a cigar, a swastika, or the genitals themselves—whether the possessor be a man or a woman—all work essentially by the same mechanism. All are generalizable and proscribable. All, if you will, are fetishes.

But even as we recover ourselves—at this moment of general inclusiveness, I hope for at least a few moments I have been able to maneuver some of you this evening into thinking: "Is *this* what Gay Identity is supposed to be? What does all this sneaker licking, drunken undergraduate mischief, and another sob-story of a hapless drug user have to do with *my* sexuality—*my* gay identity?" For certainly raising that question was precisely my intention. I said these tales were to trouble. And the troubling answer I would pose is fundamentally as simple as any of the tales themselves:

Quite possibly not much.

The point to the notion of Gay Identity is that, in terms of a transcendent reality concerned with sexuality *per se* (a universal similarity, a shared necessary condition, a defining aspect, a generalizable and inescapable essence common to all men and women called "gay"), I believe Gay Identity has no more existence than a single, essential, transcendental sexual difference. Which is to say, I think the notion of Gay Identity represents the (happily) only partial congruence of two strategies, which have to do with a patriarchal society in which the dominant sexual ideology is heterosexist.

In terms of heterosexist oppression of gays, Gay Identity represents a strategy for tarring a whole lot of very different people with the same brush: Billy, Mike, my perpetual virgin—at least, that is, if the people with the tar believe in a transcendent difference between male and female. (For those are precisely the people who historically have contrived to keep male homosexuality not talked of and lesbianism trivial.) And if, on the other hand, they simply believe deviance is deviance, then it includes as well, you, me, Carla, and Hank. The tar is there in order to police a whole range of behaviors—not only in terms of the action that is language but also in terms of the language that human actions themselves must generate: that includes the language of these tales tonight.

In terms of gay rights, Gay Identity represents one strategy by which some of the people oppressed by heterosexism may come together, talk, and join forces to fight for the equality that certain egalitarian philosophies claim is due us all. In those terms, what we need these stories for is so that we don't get too surprised when we look at—or start to listen to—the person sitting next to us. That person, after all, might be me, or Hank, or Mike—or anyone else I've spoken of this evening. In those terms, Gay Identity is a strategy I approve of wholly, even if, at a theoretical level, I question the existence of that identity as having anything beyond a provisional or strategic reality. Nor do I seek what Jane Gallop has written of so forcefully as some sort of liberation from identity itself that would lead only to another form of paralysis—"the oceanic passivity of undifferentiation" (*The Daughter's Seduction*, Ithaca: Cornell University Press, 1982, xii). For me, Gay Identity—like the joys of Gay Pride Day, weekends on Fire Island, and the delight of tickets to the opera—is an object of the context, not of the self—which means, like the rest of the context, it requires analysis, understanding, interrogation, even sympathy, but never an easy and uncritical acceptance.

That is to say, its place is precisely in the politically positivist comedy of liberation we began with—but probably nowhere else. But the reason why that partial congruence between the two is finally happy, is because it alone allows one group to speak, however inexactly, with the other. It allows those who have joined together in solidarity to speak to those who have been excluded; and, to me even more important, it allows the excluded to speak back. That very partial congruence is the linguistic element of the conduit through which any change, as it manifests a response by a vigorous and meaningful activism, will transpire.

Again: in a field of heterosexist dominance and homophobic oppression, however much the policing of what is allowed into language has broadened since the late sixties, the bulk of the extraordinarily rich, frightening, and complex sexual landscape has been—and remains—outside of language. Most of it *will* remain there quite some time. It is precisely because I have talked of it as much as I have that I am so hugely aware of how little of it I have actually spoken. But what is not articulated in certain orders of language—written language, say, and of a certain formality—does not mean that it doesn't exist. Nor does it mean that its effects as a pervasive context do not inform other articulations that either do not reflect it directly—or that reflect only a highly coded, heavily policed fraction of it.

From time to time I have been accused—I have always taken it as praise—of trying to put the sex back in homosexuality. Here, not as a matter of nostalgia, but to facilitate an analytical and theoretical precision, I am trying to trouble the notion both of what we aver and what we are averse to, in its perversity and its diversity—or if you will, through occasional appeals to the averse, I am trying to put a bit of the perversity back into perversion.

I hope many of you so inclined will welcome it. And to all of you tonight,

Love, luxury,
justice, and joy.
Thank you.

3

Too Wilde for Comfort

Desire and Ideology in Fin-de-Siècle Latin America

....

Sylvia Molloy

THIS PIECE IS PART OF A LARGER reflection on turn-of-the-century Latin American cultures, most especially on the paranoid construction of a gender and sexual norms, and of gender and sexual difference.[1] It will assume that the definition of norm does not precede but is arrived at, and indeed derives from, the gender and sexual differences that purportedly deviate from it, in the same way that the definition of "health," in psycholegal studies of the period, follows that of disease, and decadence gives birth retrospectively to notions of maturity and fullness. This assumption measures the anxiety informing those constructions and those definitions. By focusing my reflection on Latin America at the turn of the century, that is, at the moment of its complex entrance into modernity, I must take into account two related issues: first, the ideological implications of these constructions in debates on national identity and national, even continental, health; second, the double pressure of continued cultural dependence vis-à-vis Europe and of United States political expansionism, a pressure informing these debates on national identity as, indeed, all forms of Latin American cultural production of the period.

I would like to focus on a particularly revealing cultural encounter in turn-of-the-century Latin America and on the gender unease resulting from it. On the evening of January 7, 1882, the Cuban writer José Martí attended a lecture in New York City. In spite of rival attractions, there was a very large crowd at Chickering Hall, Martí reports in *La Nación* of Buenos Aires, one that struck him both for its size and its elegance. The title of the lecture Martí heard was "The English Renaissance of Art" and the lecturer, of course, was Oscar Wilde. This occasion, which I have chosen to make emblematic for the purpose of my argument, is culturally significant. Martí, arguably the most important Latin American intellectual figure of his time, encounters this other, influential inno-vator, come to the United States, as prophet of a "new imagination," to reveal to his public that "the secret of life is in art."[2] Encounter is too generous a word, of course, since the two men never met and since Wilde was totally unaware of Martí's existence. What interests me here, to begin, is precisely that imbalance which affords Martí a particularly interesting vantage point. Lost in a New York crowd, Martí, the foreign correspondent, gazes upon, better still, spies on Wilde, carefully taking in the man and his words, the better to report his experience to the Spanish American readers of *La Nación*. I quote from his description of the moment he lays eyes on Wilde:

> Look at Oscar Wilde! He does not dress as we all do but in a singular man-ner…. His hair falls over his neck and shoulders, like that of an Elizabethan courtier; it is abundant, carefully parted down the middle. He wears tails, a white silk waistcoat, ample knee breeches, black silk hose and buckled shoes. The shirt collar is cut low, like Byron's, held together by an ample white silk cravat knotted with abandon. A diamond stud shines on the daz-zling shirtfront; an ornate watch-chain hangs from the fob. Beauty in dress is imperative; of this, he is the perfect example. But art demands of all its works temporal unity, and it hurts the eye to see a handsome man wearing a waistcoat from this period, breeches from another, hair like Cromwell's, and a foppish turn-of-the-century watch-chain.[3]

This first, detailed description subtly hints at a dichotomy that will become increasingly evident in Martí's piece. On the one hand, he sees in Wilde a kin-dred soul, one who would teach others (in this case the materialistic North American other despised by Martí) love of beauty and devotion to art. Yet, on the other hand, Martí is clearly disturbed by the *extravagance* he has before his eyes. This costume, this affectation, work against Martí's appreciation, literally becoming an obstacle. Far from dispatching Wilde's unusual appearance after the first description, a fascinated Martí keeps harking back to it in wonder, attempting to excuse it for his readers, for himself. Wilde does not dress, writes Martí, the way *we* all dress. But who is this *we?* The usual first-person plural, so frequent in Martí as a means to separate the Latin American *we* from an antag- onistic North American *they*, gives place here to an atypical, panicked *we*—that of all "normally dressed" men, whatever their national origin—before the "strange," the "childish," the "extravagant."[4] With his long hair, velvet knee- breeches and black silk hose, Wilde "hurts the eye," his costume "adds little to the nobility or slenderness of the human form, and is but an inefficient rejec- tion of vulgar habits of dress"(367). Admiring Wilde's artistic zeal, Martí enthus- es: "What praise does this gallant young man not deserve, *in spite of his long hair and his knee breeches*, for trying to turn the dullish red gleam hanging over the melancholy English into the sun's vibrant rays...!" (367; my emphasis).

Martí, it is true, is not the only one bothered by Wilde's appearance nor, more generally, by his attitude. The Cincinnati *Commercial*, finding Wilde too deli- cate, dared him to soil his hands: "If Mr. Wilde will leave the lilies and daffodils and come west to Cincinnati, we will undertake to show him how to deprive thirty hogs of their intestines in one minute."[5] The choice of words betrays a transparently anxious *machismo*: Wilde's difference is not only mocked, it is per- ceived as a menace. To his credit, Martí does not ridicule Wilde nor does he show his anxiety in such uncompromisingly anal terms. He is willing to hear him out, even applauds his message; yet Wilde's physical person is another mes- sage offered up for decoding, a corporeal inscription of fin-de-siècle aestheticism with an obviously homoerotic subtext which, as such, puzzles Martí.

The notion of temporal unity, which Martí, rather surprisingly, uses against Wilde ("but art demands temporal unity in all its works"), deserves some com- mentary here. For within Martí's system, lack of temporal unity is usually a positive, if violent, creative force: witness his defense of anachronism and het- erogeneity as constitutive of the new American man in "*Nuestra América*."[6] It is not really heterogeneity, then, that is at stake in Martí's critique of Wilde's cos- tume. Martí evaluates the mixture of disparate elements positively when he, Martí, as a founding voice, can give that mixture a name—the new American man—and thus provide ideological unity for the fragments. Instead, the mixture that is Wilde defies Martí's nomenclature: Wilde is the unspeakable, with no place within Martí's founding fiction. Martí then needs to fall back on classic criteria of temporal harmony, at odds with his habitual ideology of art, in order to critique Wilde's unresolvable, unsettling difference.

Eighteen years later, on December 8, 1900, another Latin American, Rubén Darío, writes about Oscar Wilde. I must go into the particulars of this piece since they allow me to measure significant changes in what, rather loosely, might be termed a Latin American perception of Wilde. Darío writes his piece in Paris, eight days after Wilde's death. Entitled "The Purifications of Pity," it begins in the following manner:

> Tolstoi tells a story about a dead dog, found lying in the street. Passers-by stop and each comments on the remains of the poor animal. One says that it had the mange, and so it was fitting that it die;[7] another supposes that it may have been rabid, and therefore it was just and useful to club it to death; another says that it is disgusting and smells; another, that it reeks; yet another that this thing is hideous and foul and should be taken soon to the dump. Before the swollen, rank carcass, a voice suddenly cried: "Its teeth are whiter than the finest pearls." People thought: "This must be Jesus of Nazareth and no other, since only he could find something to praise in that fetid carcass." Indeed, that was the voice of supreme Pity.[8]

That is the first paragraph of Darío's piece. The one immediately following it begins:

> A man has just died, a great and true poet, who in the last years of his life, suddenly cut short, suffered pain and affront, and who, faced with misery, decided to leave this world. (468)

These two paragraphs, containing Darío's strategy in its entirety, set the sanctimonious tone of the piece. One does not have to look very deep into the pseudo-parable to read an ultimately judgmental subtext, barely masked by bleeding-heart sentimentality. Wilde, like the dead dog, is confined to the role of a particularly disgusting victim, foul to the senses and hazardous to health. Men are repulsed by him and only Christ in his "supreme pity"—a pity that, in its very perfection, is implicitly inaccessible to most mortals—is capable of redeeming him. If Darío's piece invites the reader to heed Christ's words, it also, in an ambiguous maneuver that informs the whole of this article, indicates that the goal may well be unattainable given the superhuman effort it presupposes.

Throughout the piece, Darío stigmatizes Wilde in the name of "the purification of pity." Not only is the choice of adjectives eloquent—*unfortunate, infamous, wretched, ill-fated*—but the summary of Wilde's life reveals a very anxious agenda. Wilde's life is a cautionary tale: "the confusion between the nobility of art and capricious display, in spite of his immense talent, in spite of all the advantages of his good fortune, brought him down very low, to shame, to prison, to poverty, even to death" (470). If Darío, in principle, endorses Wilde's break with bourgeois convention—this was, after all, one of the tenets of the *modernista* movement he contributed to found—it is the particular modality of this break, and the way in which it is publicized, that Darío finds fault with. Yes, Wilde is a victim of society; but first and foremost, Darío tells us, he is a victim of himself. He is (note the order of the terms) "a victim of his own eccentricity and of honorable England"(471). Once again, it is Wilde's *visibility*, a thousand times greater now than when Martí wrote his piece, that is at stake. It is this "capricious parade" that Darío frowns upon, chiding Wilde for not understanding that: "times change, that ancient Greece is not modern day Britain, that psychopathies are treated in clinics, that deformities and monstrous things must flee from light, must hide from the sun"(471).

If Darío's corrective reading of Wilde's life dooms him to the clinic or the closet, Darío's reading of Wilde's death is even more telling. For when he describes Wilde as "a man…who decided to leave this world," he means this quite literally. Surprisingly misinformed (he writes, after all, in Paris, barely a week after Wilde's death), he states:

> The perfumed cigarette he held in his lips on lecture nights foreshadowed the strychnine in his mouth as, in the last desperation, this *arbiter elegantiarum* died like a dog. Like a dog he died. Like a dead dog his wretched body lay in his lonely room. In truth, his poems and his stories are worth the finest pearls. (471–472)

This recreation is, needless to say, apocryphal: Wilde did not commit suicide nor was he alone when he died. But the sleazy suicide of the pathetic queer is a fiction of homophobic discourse that Darío must resort to in order to settle accounts with Wilde's only too visible body. The *arbiter elegantiarum*, he with the long hair, the velvet, the green carnation, the perfumed cigarette, is now a dead dog, his intolerable physical presence no longer an obstacle or a threat. Only with that body gone—that body literally incarnating perversity, that site of "deformities and monstrous things"—can Wilde's writing be appreciated, can the disembodied "pearls" of his art live on.

Wilde, writes Darío, "played at being a ghost and ended up being one"(471).

Bearing in mind that Spanish has but one word for ghost and phantasm—*fantasma*—one may submit the phrase to an additional twist and say that Wilde ended up being the disturbing phantasmatic construct of many, certainly haunting Martí and Darío. Yet I will go one step further and propose that this anxiety may be, and indeed should be, contextualized in a larger cultural framework. In other words, I want to argue that Darío and Martí are voicing a collective anxiety, one with which their Latin American readers will identify, the ideological import of which I shall now try to clarify.

There is the commonly held belief that late nineteenth-century Latin American literature imported fin-de-siècle decadence wholesale and, in so doing, naturalized it into a typically Hispanic expression. While not denying the process of translation and *bricolage* that is at the base of all Latin American literature, indeed at the base of all postcolonial cultural configurations, I want to call attention to the paradoxical nature of that translation as put into practice at the turn of the century in Latin America. Why would new countries make decadence—a term implying enervation, aboulia, and, above all, in accordance with pseudomedical diagnoses of the time, disease—the starting point for a new aesthetics, for *modernismo*, which one could argue is the first self-consciously *literary* reflection in Latin America?

Octavio Paz claims that what turn-of-the-century Latin American writers found in European decadence was less the ominous "dusk of nations" prophetized by Max Nordau in *Degeneration* than a rhetoric that allowed Latin America to attain modernity: "*modernistas* did not want to be French, they wanted to be modern.... For Rubén Darío and his friends, modernity and cosmopolitism were synonymous."[9] Paradoxically then, the appropriation of European decadence by Latin America was less a sign of degeneration than an occasion for regeneration: not the end of a period but an entrance into modernity, the formulation of a strong culture and of a new historical subject. Yet the process of translation of decadence is, one can't but help notice, patchy and uneven. I would like to reflect on this unevenness, ask what it is that Latin American cultures *can* borrow for self-constitutive purposes, what it is that they cannot, and why this may be so. In other words, my reading will attempt to identify some of the gaps, overreadings, and deviations from the text of European decadence (or from what Latin America perceives as being the text of European decadence) in order to grasp the ideological significance of those critical differences. Latin America read European literature voraciously, cannibalistically: to quote Paz once more, "its mythology was that of Gustave Moreau; its secret paradises, those of Huysmans' *A rebours*, its infernos, those of Poe and Baudelaire"(20). But at the same time Latin America read and incorporated, with equal voracity, texts that signified another form of modernity, texts belonging to a scientific or pseudo-scientific corpus that, while providing a base for incipient psychiatric research, denounced the very decadence *modernismo* emulated in literature. Thus, due mainly to the influence of Nordau and Lombroso, the emergence of what one might term the double discourse of *modernismo*, one in which decadence appears *at the same time* as progressive and regressive, as regenerating and degenerating, as good and as insalubrious. Nowhere of course is that doubleness made so apparent as in discourse relating to the body sexual.

If Latin American *modernismo* espouses decadence's celebration of the body as locus of desire and pleasure on the one hand, and, on the other, recognizes it as site of the perverse, the latter recognition is more nominal than real—and then strictly observant of heterosexual mores. If sensuality, sexual role-playing, erotic voyeurism abound in these texts, there is hardly a true adhesion to the transgressive nature of the works of high decadence, to the reflection on morals resulting from that transgression, or to the reformulation of sexualities that such a reflection would propose. Texts are read more for their titillating effects than for their subversive import: Latin Americans admire Huysmans; they do not, or cannot, rewrite him. Moreover, they tend to distance themselves from transgression when they perceive it, even denounce it in the very terms used by decadence's staunchest critics, anxious not to be caught deviating from a tacit code of decorum. Rubén Darío, while admiring Rachilde's *Monsieur Vénus*, calls its author "a red flower of sexual aberrations," adding that this is "a book that only priests, doctors and psychologists should read."[10] The same doubleness, the same attraction mixed with prudishness (the soft-porn effects of which are obvious) is to be noted when Darío speaks of Lautréamont: "It would not be prudent for young minds to converse at any length with this spectral man, not even for the sake of literary curiosity or the pleasure of trying new nourishment. There is a judicious saying in the Kabbala: 'One must not play at being a ghost for one ends up being one.' If there is a dangerous writer in this respect it is the count of Lautréamont.... If I were to take my muse near the place where this madman is caged, howling at the wind, I would cover her ears."[11] The reader will have recognized, in passing, the transgressive ghost-playing attributed to Wilde.

It may be argued that these essays by Darío (and, to a lesser extent, those by Martí) were above all circumstantial pieces, the product of hasty journalism and not of critical reflection; that Darío, especially, may have been trying to court a public of middle-class readers not exactly initiated in, much less approving of, some of the attitudes towards the physical and, more precisely, the sexual, that the authors he discusses rendered explicit. I concede that this is so, and the fact, in a way, adds to my argument. For it matters little what these authors "really" thought on the matter, it matters more to note that this doubleness that had them introducing decadence to a Latin American public even as, to save themselves, they criticized it, was a necessary attitude given the context in which this literature was read.

Let me give some idea of that context by focussing on a little-known text, *Buenos Aires, La ribera y los prostíbulos en 1880* [*Buenos Aires, the River Bank and the Bordellos in 1880*], written in the early 1900s by an Argentine assistant chief of police, Adolfo Batiz.[12] The book, significantly subtitled "A Contribution to Social Studies," reflects the same doubleness I have pointed out in literature, that is, on the one hand, attraction for and tolerance of "natural" sexuality, on the other, rejection of the perverse. Batiz begins his purportedly "scientific" study, with a dream he has in Italy—in Rome to be precise; the choice of geography is not inconsequential—a dream which takes him to Dante's tomb. Dante comes to life, greets him, and they have a little chat. "I mentioned to him that, as in the past, there was lust all around us, and now, lust and pederasty.... I shall write on this, I told him. Sharing my opinions, he [Dante] encouraged me to do so.... After a loving farewell, I started to walk away dejectedly when, from the door, I heard Dante, raising his voice so that I might hear him, say to me very earnestly: 'Take courage....'"[13]

What follows in Batiz's book, after a first chapter proposing the medical and legal surveillance of prostitution, is not a sociological study at all but a curious *flânerie* around Buenos Aires that is not without charm. Actually, bordellos are described rather benignly. It is another section of the city, the *Paseo de Julio*, that meets with Batiz's condemnation for "it was the refuge of passive pederasts who gathered round the statue of Mazzini, the revolutionary hero of Italian freedom" (25). Batiz describes heterosexual prostitution with a tolerant eye, even resorts to the sensuous *modernista* vocabulary of the time to describe women. The main scourge, Batiz claims, is the "*granujería cosmopolita*," the cosmopolitan scum that exploits prostitution and takes it to extremes. Amongst those extremes, of course, we find the substance of his dream conversation with Dante, lust and pederasty:

> Prostitution has taken on alarming proportions, it has grown beyond what is normal and logical, we are on the verge of Roman decadence. This is not an exaggeration after hearing about the scandals in Germany concerning Prince Eulenburg, after hearing about the trial of the two generals. For it is publicly known that there exists in Rome, Corso Umberto I, an agency in charge of finding models for passive pederasts, there is a shameless international traffic in these models, the same as with women's flesh, there is no romance. (79)[14]

This house on Corso Umberto I so fires the imagination of the good chief of police that he will come back to it again and again, as Martí went back to Wilde's costume:

> We must insist on this house in Rome, the one supplying passive pederasts with models, about which much has been written in the press.... This proves that homosexual degeneration, as well as the practice of prostitution in women, and degeneration in general, have achieved truly exceptional proportions, only comparable to those of the decadent Roman empire. (86)

When prostitution and pederasty are set side by side, the excesses of the former pale in comparison with the latter, and are excused in the name of heterosexual nature and needs. "Every man has the right to hide his weaknesses from the world (except pederasts) and I don't know to what extent one should call weaknesses certain whims [*caprichos*] imposed by nature" (100). The police, adds Batiz, can do little to punish "the new scandalmongers in Argentine society," those who (once again!) "come to Rome looking for models, like the prince of the German scandals came to the house on Corso Umberto I" (83). It should be remembered that these scandals in the Kaiser's entourage erupted precisely at the time when Argentina was restructuring its army according to the Prussian model, a fact that surely contributed to the anxiety of the good chief of police.

I am interested here not only in the anxiety awakened by genital homosexuality—not the least merit of Batiz's book is to document the existence of a thriving gay community in Buenos Aires[15]—but by the notorious slippage of the term *pederast*, the ease with which it is either metaphorized or fused with other threatening types. Pederasts (always, in Batiz's book, "passive pederasts") become synonymous with rather "active" unsavory characters: pimps, burglars, informers. Most importantly, pederasts (and by extension, pimps, informers, etc.) are invariably linked to the non-national. Homosexuality exists in Argentina, Batiz tells us, but in reality, *le mal vient de plus loin*, from Italy, from that house on Corso Umberto I exporting decadent Roman models to Buenos Aires.

The use of the word *model* is of course of capital interest here, since it inscribes this sexual transaction in a colonial context even as it critiques it. Who are, after all these models, *what exactly do they do*? Taking the term literally, one could assume that these are models on which the "passive pederasts" fashion themselves, European "originals" for Latin American "copies." Yet this is surely not quite so, given that the subject of Batiz's book is the denunciation of prostitution grown "beyond what is normal and logical." Suggesting a commerce more intimate than mere emulation, *model* means rather a sexual provider, "imported" to Argentina for the satisfaction of "passive pederasts," by the same "cosmopolitan scum" trafficking in female prostitutes. This being the case, the term becomes much more "active" (and more threatening) than it at first would seem. But why, precisely, use *model*? Could the term refer to the popular nineteenth-century "model artists," posing in *tableaux vivants* of doubtless erotic charge[16] or would it be a euphemism? Although the meaning of the term is obscure, what matters is the way it functions within its sociocultural context and the eerie effect produced by such a contextualization. For let us not forget that *model* is a key notion in the poetics of imitation adopted by turn-of-the-century Latin America with the purpose of creating new cultural forms; or, as Darío would have it, "*Qui pourrais-je imiter pour être original?*" So that Batiz's reprehensible scenario— the "passive pederast" seeking the Roman "model" for sexual and/or aesthetic gratification—parodies a pattern of dependency and incorporation that is not censurable but on the contrary acceptable, even desirable, when applied to texts and not bodies. In Batiz's use of the term *model*, which felicitously brings together for the reader the dominant literary attitude of the day with its perverted bodily counterpart, could one not then read *something else*, something that *cannot be told* within the hegemonic discourses of the period, that is, that new constructions of literature also imply new constructions of sexuality and gender, new remappings of bodies?

For Batiz, however, such a conflation of *models* would have been unthinkable: good came from abroad, to be imitated, in the form of "high" literary models; evil too came from abroad, to contaminate, in the form of despicable models bringing bad "low" habits. The latter perception was, of course, not new and, in countries like Argentina, where the make-up of the population was rapidly changing due to an overwhelmingly male immigration, it became an urgent issue. Darío and Martí's preoccupation with Wilde finds its parallel in the technical discourses of the budding nation states, discourses wielded throughout Latin America at the turn of the century by psychiatrists, sociologists, legal scholars and, yes, police inspectors attempting to define, classify, analyze "foreign" sexual deviance as one of the diseases brought on by immigration.[17] The paranoid taxonomy resulting from these discourses made rejection, if not persecution, natural and therefore inevitable, like the rejection of Oscar Wilde's dog-like carcass by ordinary men. Doomed to the closet of non-nationality, the alien was then constructed as a diseased, perverse, and ultimately threatening other. As the discourse of the Spanish conquest had feminized the native American other,[18] as the discourse of metropolitan Spain had feminized its Creole subjects,[19] so the hegemonic discourse of nineteenth-century nationalism perverts, and in particular evirates, the male immigrant. He is asssigned a sort of performative effeminacy that, according to the danger he is felt to pose, can go from the simply grotesque to the socially and morally threatening.[20]

Neither Darío nor Martí, nor for that matter other writers of the period, openly mention homosexuality (or, to use the more term of the day, pederasty) in their chronicles. If they allude to it, they do so obliquely and, above all, defensively. Martí, writing on Whitman, denounces "those imbeciles who, in the love of a friend for a friend, celebrated in 'Calamus' with the most ardent images of which the human language is capable, believe they find, like dirty-minded schoolboys, the vile desire of Vergil for Cebes, of Horace for Gyges and Lyciscus." He then hastens to correct (as, one should not forget, did Whitman himself)[21] such intimations: the Whitman *he* proposes, "trembles, contracts, swells, disseminates, goes mad with pride and satisfied virility."[22] Martí's defensive bonding with Whitman, achieved in the name of hypervirility, brings with it the necessary devaluation of the feminine. Thus Whitman, in Martí's priapic rendering, is "like a ravenous hero smacking his bloodthirsty lips as he describes the various parts of the female body"(137). With comparable scorn, Darío dismisses references to Verlaine's homosexuality as "a nebulous legend that has provided fodder for cads,"[23] and, when reviewing Lepelletier's pious biography of the French poet, states that "the famous Rimbaud question" is proven beyond all doubt to be false: whatever allusions to it that may be found in Verlaine's poetry are "mere aspects of simulation."[24]

Now what calls attention in both Martí and Darío is not that the issue of homosexuality is avoided but, precisely, that it *is* brought up; that it appears, indeed, unavoidable. Furthermore, once it is out, it must be energetically denied, attributed to calumny. With regards to its cultural mentors, Latin American *modernismo* not only subjects texts to a creative process of cultural translation, it also translates lives (at least some lives) into an acceptable cultural script, feels it must erase marks of a deviance by which not only the mentors but they themselves fear to be judged. Possibly the most strikingly homosocial movement in Latin American literature (although the so-called boom of the 1960s comes in a close second) this tightly bonded literary *brotherhood*, to use the Pre-Raphaelite term so dear to Rubén Darío himself, is most anxious not to be found guilty by association and most anxious to be "read well." Even years later, this anxiety will be visited upon *modernismo*'s critics. Twice, in comparing Darío to Verlaine, Octavio Paz feels the need to tell us that Darío's poetry was virile, while Carlos Fuentes, when speaking of Rodó's *Ariel*, praises it for its "huskier moments."[25]

The slippage between homophobia and xenophobia, the systematic perversion of a frightening "outside" carried out with a zeal that only indicates, as is obvious, how "inside" that "outside" really is, consolidates, by contrast, the notion of national, even continental, heterosexual health; a notion elaborated, discussed and perfected in, foreseeably, all-male atheneums, often (although not always) grouped around a senior mentor. I shall venture one step further, by contextualizing this notion of health not just in terms of a body social but of a body politic, and shall briefly consider one of the prophilactic projects to preserve national health designed by precisely one of those mentors, the Uruguayan José Enrique Rodó.

A pedagogue (I use the word advisedly) who might be best described as a cross between Arnold and Renan, Rodó drew early attention to himself as a *maître à penser* with an 1899 article on the poetry of Rubén Darío. The piece functioned both as a diagnosis and as a cautionary tale, beginning, memorably, with a statement that totally disempowered the by then famously acclaimed Nicaraguan poet: "Undoubtedly, Rubén Darío is not the poet of America."[26] Without going into the detail of the piece, wrought as minutely as any fin-de-siècle bibelot, I want to chart the principal points of Rodó's exemplary critique, for I see in this piece signs of that very doubleness I mentioned earlier. On the one hand, this is a cautiously sympathetic reading, in which Rodó literally takes on Darío's voice, in an act of poetic ventriloquism; as he writes, he carefully recreates Darío's poems, re-producing Darío's sensuality (and often adding to it) in the sole interest, as he rather improbably claims, of serious literary criticism. Yet, on the other hand, there is a permanent curbing of Rodó's passionate ventriloquism, a disquiet that filters into Rodó's appreciation of Darío, a sense that in this poetry there is something wrong and, more precisely, that there is something wrong for Latin America. There is something sickly, artificial, morbid, and excessively soft in Darío's poetry, Rodó tells us even as he delights in the very softness he denounces. There is no heroic passion, no strong tragic gestures, no sincerity in this poetry of *pose* but, in their stead, "morbid and indolent obliqueness, idealized serenity, pensive languor, all that allows this actor's tunic to drape his sinuous body in the most graceful folds" (172). And Rodó goes on to add:

> When, in our austere language, has voluptuousness fashioned, from poetry, darts such as these for its quiver? For voluptuousness is at the very soul of these verses: they stretch out, they purr, like sensuous cats they sink into voluptuous softness. Inviting verses, tempting and delicate verses, verses capable of making a Spartan legion swoon…. If there were an imminent war, I would forbid them… (179)

Although the orthodoxy of Darío's sexuality does not come under suspicion here, that of his poetry definitely does. It should be remembered that Martí, in his programmatic introduction to Pérez Bonalde's "*Poema del Niágara*," had already passed a similar judgment on "unmanly" poetry in general, with identical intimations of homoeroticism:

> Men would resemble females, weak females, if, crowned with garlands of roses, in the embrace of Alexander or Cebes, they chose to drink the honeyed Falernian that seasoned Horace's banquets. Pagan lyrical poetry is out of style bacause of its sensuality.[27]

Although Martí's statement antedates Darío's *Prosas profanas* it could be applied to him retroactively since, just like Rodó's piece, it resorts to classical homophobic markers to indicate weakness. The swooning Spartan legion, Alexander's embrace, the wine and the roses bring up the "wrong" kind of Hellenism, the one that should be proscribed—the one we should censor within ourselves.

Rodó performs a voyeuristic reading of Darío not unlike the one that Martí had performed of Wilde; not unlike the one Batiz had performed of the "Sodom of the River Plate"; not unlike, finally, the one Darío himself had performed of Wilde's death. Rodó, the teacher of Latin American civic virtue—of whom one disciple wondered why he locked himself up in his bedroom to read Plato's dia-logues[28]—Rodó is as fascinated by the languor of Darío's poetry as Martí was fascinated by Wilde's hair and Batiz by the mythic Roman agency providing pas-sive pederasts with their models. But Rodó inscribes his attraction for and fear of the morbid, his preoccupation with virility and eviration, in a political context. Through Darío, he reads the threat not merely as coming from without (from Victorian England, from the Roman agency, from the boatfuls of Southern European immigrants) but as a possibility within, immensely more dangerous. For it is in Darío and not in a foreigner, in a Latin American himself, that Rodó senses (and is both seduced and frightened by) the languor, the softness, the unhealthiness, the lack of heroic fibre, the feminization, the possible homo-eroticism. At a time of continental panic, when Latin America fears loss of its precarious identity through penetration by the United States—an alien impos-sible to pathologize or evirate, however softly he may speak: he carries, as we all know, a Big Stick—at a time, indeed, of "imminent war," both physical and ide-ological, sensuous Darío cannot, shouldn't be, according to Rodó, "*el poeta de América.*" Thus the need for Rodó's *Ariel*, the influential essay he dedicated one year later to "the youth of America," and, for generations, the most popular pro-posal for a Latin American identity. A holistic program for a healthy continent, it seductively posited self-improvement through renewed contact with Latin America's "strong" European forebears, Greece and early Christianity. A blend of evangelical *caritas* and Renanian Hellenism, whose sentimentalized virility (and attendant panic) would successfully glue together a community of male intel-lectuals for years to come, *Ariel* was the pedagogue's lesson. It proposed a "cure" for the *mollitia* of European decadence, it provided a safeguard from the mus-cular utilitarianism of the United States. In a word, it instructed the intelligentsia in ways of being good (male) Latin Americans together.

It is not surprising that Darío, after Rodó's critique of his poetry and the didactic *Ariel* that followed, took a deliberately new approach, posited himself as a poet of "human energy" and to a point rejected, in *Cantos de vida y esperanza,* his previous aesthetics. Nor is it surprising that a formulation of moral and political correctness as compelling as that of *Ariel,* where homosexual panic was gratifyingly replaced (in reality, compounded) by male bonding *pro patria,* was to mark not only latter-day *modernismo* but the literature that followed it. Nor is it surprising, finally, that José Ingenieros, one of the founders of forensic psy-chiatry in Argentina, found it necessary to invent a category, that of *simulators,* to distinguish "real" perversions from simulated perversions (the latter, a category into which he placed all Latin Americans writers who might seem suspect), in an attempt to provide Latin American culture with a clean bill of health.[29] One of the results of turn-of-the-century homosexual panic has been the near-total suppression of the male body from Latin American literature: the sentimentalized virility preached by Rodó is above all a *cosa mentale*, an abstraction never accompanied (as were similar national movements elsewhere)[30] by the rediscovery and aesthetization of the body. And, as the body is hidden, so have all sexual and erotic manifestations deviating from "healthy," patriarchal, heterosexual norms successfully remained in the closet of literary representation and, especially, in the closet of literary criticism. One of the tasks that awaits the critic is to look, with the same intensity with which Martí scrutinized Wilde, the same curiosity with which Batiz looked at Buenos Aires, the same sympathy with which Rodó recognized Darío, and hopefully without the anxiety present in all three, at the textual production of Latin America since the turn of the century in order to figure out the forms taken by silence, the oblique figurations to which it has resorted to speak the unspeakable.

NOTES

1. Although I use the term "Latin America," my remarks refer principally to Hispanic coutries and should not be expanded to the literature and culture of Brazil. This restriction is due chiefly to the fact that the construction of gender and sexual difference in Brazil develops along distinct lines and deserves to be considered separately. For an introduction to the latter, see Joâo S. Trevisan, *Perverts in Paradise*, trans. Martin Foremen (London: GMP Publications, 1986).
2. H. Montgomery Hyde, *Oscar Wilde* (New York: Farrar, Straus & Giroux, 1975), 54.
3. José Martí, "Oscar Wilde," in *Obras completas*, XV (Havana: Editorial nacional de Cuba, 1964), 362. Further quotations will refer to this text. All translations are mine unless otherwise stated.
4. I use the term *panic* as understood by Eve Kosofsky Sedgwick in *Between Men: English Literature and Male Homosexual Desire* (New York: Columbia University Press, 1985) and *Epistemology of the Closet* (Berkeley-Los Angeles: University of California Press, 1990). I take this opportunity to state the extent of my debt to her work.
5. Hyde, 55.
6. "We were [*somos*] military epaulettes and magistrates' robes, in countries that came into being with sandals on their feet and headbands on their foreheads. The true genius would have been to combine, with the love of the heart and the boldness of

founders, the headband and the robe." (José Martí, *Nuestra América* [Caracas: Biblioteca Ayacucho, 1977], 30). Martí's fetishization of dress (we are our clothing) is remarkable throughout his work and deserves further study. For a perceptive analysis of Martí's political articulation of the heterogeneous, see Julio Ramos, *Desencuentros de la modernidad en América Latina: Literatura y política en el siglo XIX* (Mexico: Fondo de cultura económica, 1989), 229–243, especially 232–3.

7. The Spanish uses the colloquial *reventar*, literally "to burst," metaphorically "to croak." Darío proves to be uncannily accurate. Wilde's body, minutes after his death, did indeed burst: "He had scarcely breathed his last breath when the body exploded with fluids from the ear, nose, mouth, and other orifices. The debris was appalling." (Richard Ellman, *Oscar Wilde* [New York: Knopf, 1988], 584).

8. Rubén Darío, "Purificaciones de la piedad," in *Obras completas* III (Madrid: Afrodisio Aguado, 1950), 468. Further references to this article appear directly in the text.

9. Octavio Paz, "El caracol y la sirena," in *Cuadrivio* (Mexico: Joaquín Mortiz, 1965), 19.

10. Rubén Darío, "Rachilde," *Obras completas* II, 367.

11. Rubén Darío, "El conde de Lautréamont," *Obras completas* II, 436.

12. I owe the discovery of this text to Jorge Salessi, whose work on the construction of homosexuality in turn-of-the-century Argentina has inspired much of my thinking in these pages.

13. Adolfo Batiz (subcomisario), *Buenos Aires, la ribera y los prostíbulos en 1880. Contribución a los estudios sociales (libro rojo)* (Buenos Aires: Ediciones Aga-Taura, n.d.), 13.

14. The reference to Phillip Eulenberg and to the homosexual scandals that were uncovered in Wilhelm II's entourage (some of them implicating the Kaiser himself) allows us to date Batiz's book precisely. The Krupp scandal broke in 1902, the Eulenberg scandal in 1906, so Batiz's book was written after that. These dates reveal an interesting aspect of Batiz's strategy: since his book purportedly deals with the Buenos Aires in 1880, it is clear that he is projecting these scandals—and the house on Corso Umberto I—onto the past. For information on the scandals themselves, see Isabel V. Hull, *The Entourage of Kaiser Wilhelm II, 1888-1918* (Cambridge: Cambridge University Press, 1982), 57–145.

15. Batiz does not speak of lesbians and little documentation is available on the subject. An article such as Víctor Mercante's "Fetiquismo y uranismo femenino en los internados educativos" ["Fetishism and Female Uranism in Boarding-Schools"], in *Archivos de Criminología y Ciencias Afines* (1903), 22–30, calling educators' attention to this "morbid state" in the schools of Buenos Aires shows that it was at least a subject of concern for the medicolegal establishment.

16. See Michael Moon, *Disseminating Whitman* (Cambridge and London: Harvard University Press, 1991), 70.

17. Jorge Salessi, "Medics, Crooks and Tango Queens" (forthcoming).

18. Margarita Zamora, "Abreast of Columbus: Gender and Discovery," in *Cultural*

Critique, 17 (1990–91): 127–151.

19. José Piedra, "The New World Made Me Do It," (forthcoming).

20. This weakening through homosexualization is particularly virulent in cases when the alien occupies, or is perceived as occupying, an "unnatural" position of power. Witness the following description of Jewish money lenders, "notably averse to women," by a leading Argentine psychiatrist of the time:

> Their habit of keeping an eye on their debtors, of hovering around the building to which they hold mortgages, of cunningly following men they perceive to be most in need, asking after the state of their souls, gives them the air of mysterious lovers…. Their seduction techniques finally betray their true moral nature, enrolling them in the ageless depravity of inversion. (José María Ramos Mejía, *Los simuladores de talento* [1904; rpt. Buenos Aires: Tor, 1955], 166–167).

The same Ramos Mejía, when discussing the bad taste of relatively harmless Italian immigrants (*guarangos*), mocks them by calling them "cultural inverts":

> [T]hey resemble sexual inverts in that they manifest their dubious energy in a capricious manifestation of appetites. They [Italian *guarangos*] need very bright colors and very shrill music, as erotomaniacs need intense bodily odors; they like things combined in bizarre and tasteless ways, as inverts like twisted attitudes and scabrous procedures to satisfy the special idiosyncrasies [*sic*] of their sensibility. (José María Ramos Mejía, *Las multitudes argentinas* [1899; rpt. Buenos Aires: Talleres Gráficos Argentinos L.J. Rosso, 1934], 257).

21. Sedgwick, *Between Men*, 203.

22. José Martí, "El poeta Walt Whitman," in *En los Estados Unidos, Obras completas*, V. 13 (Havana: Editorial Nacional de Cuba, 1964), 137.

23. Rubén Darío, "Verlaine, in *Los raros, Obras completas* II, 298.

24. "La vida de Verlaine", in *Obras completas* II, 718.

25. Octavio Paz, 31 and 39. Carlos Fuentes, Prologue to José Enrique Rodó, *Ariel.* Trans. by Margaret Sayers Peden. Foreword by James W. Symington. (Austin: University of Texas Press, 1988), 17.

26. José Enrique Rodó, *Rubén Darío. Su personalidad literaria. Su última obra*, in *Obras completas* (Madrid: Aguilar, 1967) 169–192.

27. José Martí, "El poema del Niágara," in *Nuestra América*, 303.

28. Víctor Pérez Petit, *Rodó. Su vida, su obra* (Montevideo: Imprenta Latina, 1918), 45.

29. "D'Annunzio (an Italian who has suffered psychological contamination from the French) has simulated approval of incest and homosexuality. It is fitting to consider such 'refinements' of the sexual instinct as simulations. It is clear…that he did not copulate with his sisters or with other men…. In truth, Nordau has seriously erred when interpreting as signs of degeneration mere simulated acts, simple products of imposture mixed with aestheticism.

   "Among Latin Americans, we know of some subtle minds, attracted to similar intellectual delusions. It would be indiscreet to name them in these pages." (José Ingenieros, "Psicología de los simuladores," *Archivos de Psiquiatría, Criminología y Ciencias Afines*, II (1903): 477).

In Ingenieros' classification, Latin American writers are always *simulators*, never "really" degenerate: "[A] young decadent [Argentine] writer, influenced by French humbugs, felt obliged to simulate the refinements and vices the latter themselves simulated, thinking them authentic. He pretended to be a passive pederast [later versions say *maricón*, that is, faggot—so much for Ingenieros' scientific pretense], pretended to be addicted to haschish, to morfine, to alcohol.... This was all a product of his childish imagination, the result of the impostures of those aesthetes and supermen whose works he read avidly to shape his life, trying to adjust his actions and his ideas to the 'manual of the perfect decadent' " (486).

How the young writer pretended to be a "passive pederast" is left to our imagination in Ingenieros' text. What is clear, instead, is the role of the diagnostician who, in declaring homosexuality a writer's fiction effectively robs it not only of its threat but of its physical and cultural reality.

30. See George L. Mosse, *Nationalism and Sexuality. Middle-Class Morality and Sexual Norms in Modern Europe* (1985; rpt. Madison and London: University of Wisconsin Press, 1988), especially chapter 3.

4

AIDS and the Politics of Queer Diaspora

Simon Watney

NINETEEN-NINETY-THREE HAS been an exceptionally grim year in relation to HIV/AIDS.[1] The prospect of effective, available anti-HIV drugs seems more elusive than ever, whilst the scale of suffering and death continues to worsen, as many of those infected in the late seventies and early eighties become symptomatically ill. It is a moment of intensely painful contradictions, as for example the Lesbian and Gay Studies movement rapidly gains academic respectability, while all the resources of cities as large and sophisticated as New York and Paris cannot sustain a reliable weekly or even monthly lesbian and gay press. Much of the energy which accompanied the emergence of activist organizations such as Queer Nation in the U.S. and Outrage in the U.K. have run out of steam, while the AIDS activist movement continues to flounder.[2] The inability of the organizers of the 1993 Washington March to articulate the epidemic political-ly in relation to other lesbian and gay issues is symptomatic of a deeper failure to understand AIDS as a national tragedy which strikes to the very heart of gay culture. This is in itself evidence of the long term fall-out of the epidemic, as many of the ablest have already died. It also reflects the vast scale of personal devastation, death, and loss throughout our communities, across every division of class, race, age, and region.

In this article I want to consider some of the international implications of current lesbian and gay political tactics, focusing in particular on the relations between Europe and the United States, where I have had most direct experience for many years. It is initially prompted by an article and a letter, both published in the gay press, which suggest much about the great difficulties we face. Writing in a July 1993 edition of the American fortnightly *The Advocate*, columnist Lance Loud quoted scriptwriter John Singleton on the subject of "the AIDS problem in the black community, where the disease continues to claim a rising number of victims, most of them intravenous drug users."[3] Such casual statements are typical of a country in which not even gay journalists appear to understand the actual local epidemiology of HIV/AIDS. Looking at the most recent quarterly *Surveillance Report* from the U.S. Department of Health and Human Services it is transparently clear that the great majority of AIDS cases amongst black, Hispanic, Asian, and Native American men in the United States have resulted *not* from injecting drug use, but from sex with other men.[4] There is surely a terrible irony here, in so far as a torrent of antiracist rhetoric within the wider field of lesbian and gay politics has conspicuously failed to identify the single most devastating example of racism as it directly affects American gay and bisexual men. Indeed, I am only aware of a single article in the American gay press on this topic.[5] The figures on which policies should be based are not difficult to obtain. While the U.S. AIDS activist movement has properly and honorably insisted on articulating the collective interest of everyone infected by HIV, this has in effect lead to a paradoxical neglect of those who remain at demonstrably greatest risk, namely gay and bisexual men. For example, at the Eighth International AIDS Conference in Amsterdam in 1992, ACT UP (Los Angeles) distributed a detailed flyer on the subject of "The Marginalization of AIDS Afflicted Communities of Color in the U.S." Although there were sections on prevention and education, treatment, research, funding, prisons, and women's issues, there was not one word so much as acknowledging the mere existence of gay and bisexual men of color. This is frankly extraordinary, given that gay and bisexual men constitute by far the largest number of cases amongst communities of color in the United States.

The question of the reporting of statistics in the U.S. also has wider ramifications, since as far as I am aware, the United States is the only country in the developed world which does not routinely publish the most recent HIV statistics alongside cumulative totals, but only AIDS figures. It should be appreciated that AIDS statistics speak of transmission events which took place on average some ten years ago. They are helpful in planning care and services, but tell us nothing about the directions in which the epidemic is moving, and may be changing directions. We can only plan and implement effective education if we understand such constantly shifting patterns of infection. Yet there is little or no debate on this vital matter in the United States. The situation is only comprehensible from the outside in relation to the emphasis all along in the U.S. on AIDS itself, largely to the exclusion of HIV-related issues in the U.S. lesbian and gay communities.

In cities as vastly different as San Francisco, London, and Amsterdam, only five percent or less of available resources have gone for HIV/AIDS education amongst gay and bisexual men, in spite of the fact that we continue to make up eighty percent or more of the death rate from AIDS in all three cities.[6] The professional de-gaying of AIDS service organizations around the world has had disastrous consequences, especially in the field of education and prevention, which almost invariably tends to play second fiddle to other services in such organizations. Indeed, only rarely is education properly understood as a service in the first place, let alone as an entitlement. Almost without exception, national HIV education campaigns financed by governments around the world have neglected the needs of those at greatest risk, and concentrated on those at least risk. Thus the aim of preventing a heterosexual epidemic has in most countries almost entirely eclipsed the task of fighting the actual HIV epidemics which continue to grow. At the same time the U.S. AIDS activist movement was long since effectively hijacked by other political interest groups, and has become a platform for any number of different issues, losing its effectiveness precisely because it lost the sense of clearly defined, achievable aims and objectives. Thus American AIDS activism now all too frequently provides an unhelpful model in other countries where oppositional politics may be played out in their proper place, within oppositional political parties, rather than under the umbrella of the fight against HIV/AIDS.

Aiming at the chimerical goal of risk *elimination*, much HIV education in the U.S. has ignored earlier and demonstrably effective campaigns which were based upon the achievable goal of risk *reduction*.[7] This has much to do with specifically American perceptions of risk, a word which in American English has large-ly lost its sense of relative probability, and has become more or less synonymous with the concept of danger.[8] In a period of intense environmental anxiety, the notion of risk in the U.S. has become oversimplified, unlike in Europe, where risk is till thought of as fluctuating and variable, relative to other contingent fac-tors. Thus in the U.S. purely theoretical risks are frequently regarded as if they were on the same level as scientifically verifiable dangers. Thus much U.S. HIV education tends to greatly exaggerate the actual risks of HIV transmission, as is immediately apparent from advice concerning oral sex, which is all but univer-sally regarded as a form of Safer Sex in other countries, according to the criteria of risk reduction. Sadly, America's international power and prestige guarantee that U.S. models of HIV prevention may cause great harm, and wholly unnec-essary anxiety, outside the United States, by making Safer Sex seem a largely impossible goal. There is furthermore another more hidden irony here. As younger American men and women increasingly socialize together as never before under the rubric of queerness, exaggerated and wholly unscientific claims concerning the theoretical possibility of woman-to-woman transmission may have a feedback effect on younger men, at genuinely high risk of infection. This is not of course to question the need for effective HIV education for lesbians. It is only to question the ways in which the assumed commensurability between lesbians and gay men at the political level is frequently projected across the field of HIV/AIDS. Lesbians may be at risk from HIV via unprotected sexual inter-course with men, or from sharing needles. But there is frankly no scientific commensurability between lesbians and gay men in relation to the risk of HIV transmission. Moreover, the United States AIDS establishment is strongly resis-tant to the mere idea that America might learn anything from overseas colleagues. For example, I shall never forget the experience of a weighty and doubtless well-intended introduction a few years ago at a national U.S. lesbian and gay health conference, when an assembled audience of overseas delegates were cheerfully informed that the speaker and her colleagues were there to pre-vent us "from reinventing the wheel." Behind this statement lies the familiar American inability to recognize the great variations in international experience, as well as the consequences of working in countries whose HIV and AIDS epi-demiology varies greatly from the United States situation. There can be no danger of "reinventing the wheel" for the simple reason that the epidemic is not the same in any two countries. Such patronizing and essentially xenophobic comments are unfortunately hardly rare in the U.S. AIDS arena. Hence it is hardly surprising that there is emerging a widespread grassroots resistance to what is often perceived, however unfairly, as the imperial global ambitions of the U.S. lesbian and gay movement, in both its goals and method.

A recent letter published in the U.K. lesbian and gay weekly *Pink Paper* expressed this type of resentment very clearly, in relation to the ongoing U.S. debate about gays and the military, which has inevitably flushed through the global network of syndicated stories appearing in different national presses and on radio and TV around the world. The writer regretted that

> This wholly peripheral issue is taking up so much of our time and energy that could be much better spent on other more important issues (such as) the age of consent, homelessness, anti-gay violence and getting adequate care for those with HIV/AIDS.[9]

He also strongly criticized

> the way the gay establishment here, especially activist groups and the press, see the British gay community as some sort of ultra-loyalist, unswerving colonial outpost of gay America in much the same way as Margaret Thatcher saw Britain as being an outpost of Reaganite America.[10]

This may be simply the old, tired voice of unreflecting European leftist anti-Americanism, but it also reflects a growing international acknowledgement of the importance of national specificities in lesbian and gay issues around the world, issues which may differ as greatly as overall political systems from those that prevail in the United States.

The sheer size and confidence of the U.S. lesbian and gay movement make it likely to lead many international debates, not least within the academy. There is thus a special and important challenge to establish international dialogue and information channels, rather than retreating back into pre-1989 Cold War postures. It is moreover always salutary to remember that every nation has its own distinct queer history, both in relation to the affirmation of homosexual desire, and the obstacles to such "movements of affirmation."[11]

At this point it may prove helpful to attempt a little clarification on the distinction between the terms "gay" and "queer." In Britain, gay identity has been founded since the early 1970s on the assumption that lesbians and gay men share certain identifiable patterns of oppression, from specific institutions, including the churches, psychiatry, the National Health Service, political parties, and so on. Gay identity is thus distinctly different from the older "homosexual" identity, founded on notions of a fundamental individualism, and assumed to derive directly from homosexual desire. In British English, the word "queer" has a powerfully ambiguous meaning, sometimes a term of affection, cheerfully accepted as an identity by some throughout this century, violently contested and refused by others as an insult. Elsewhere within Anglophone culture the situation is different again, as in Australia, where the word "queer" never has had popular associations with homosexuality, and simply means "funny," in the sense of being amusing rather than inferior. In the U.K., the emergent queer identity has stood in conscious opposition to what are perceived by many to be the shortcomings of gay and lesbian identity politics, and culture.[12]

As new post-lesbian and post-gay identities emerge and variously flourish throughout the developed world, there is a greater need than ever to be able to articulate American to non-American queer national histories, and queer national cultures. The nomenclature "gay" has inevitable connotations of Americanness outside the U.S., even on the part of those born long after the Stonewall Riot. It is therefore important to recognize that the new rhetoric of queerness may obliterate national differences as easily as it may illuminate them. At the same time it remains important to be able to confidently challenge the fundamental naivete of the position taken by the letter writer in the *Pink Paper.* For while our political and social aims and tactics may vary greatly around the world, the epidemic remains always simultaneously local, national, and international. The world of biomedical research is by its very nature international, as is the work of multi-national pharmaceutical companies who ultimately control the production and distribution of potential treatment drugs. Given the nature of our global economy, and the global network of communications in the mass media *about* us, it is clear that our analyses must be international if they are fully to comprehend local and national circumstances. This point is only underscored by the close international connections between homophobic political parties of both the left and the right, travel restrictions, religious organizations, insurance companies, and so on. Hence the immediate significance of ongoing debates about nationalism and national identities, in relation to both queer politics and the future course of the epidemics in our midst.

There is also an equally pressing reason for international experience of the epidemic from a lesbian and gay, or queer perspective, since it is becoming increasingly apparent that the few institutions which theorize and respond to HIV/AIDS on global terms do so in ways which are increasingly neglectful of the needs of gay and bisexual men, who make up the great majority of cases throughout much of the undeveloped world. For example, the United Nations is planning to unify the AIDS work it undertakes in its various departmental specialist areas, including UNICEF and UNESCO and the World Health Organization, and to relocate them under one roof. Ever since the 1991 Seventh International AIDS Conference in Florence it has also been obvious that the World Health Organization has decided to prioritize the needs of the developing world to the virtual exclusion of the situation in the developed world. Furthermore, such huge bureaucratic agencies are invariably homophobic in their wider world view. To summarize, there is simply no organization or institution on earth which is currently able to assess and respond to the needs of gay and bisexual men on an international scale, from the Untied Nations to the European Community, and far beyond. At a time when the very notion of "the global epidemic" has come to refer exclusively to the epidemics resulting and potentially resulting from heterosexual transmission, who is to speak for men having sex with one another in Eastern Europe, let alone in southern Africa or in southeast Asia? Hence the great timeliness of recent queer debates about the diasporic nature of our culture, if not of our explicit political goals.

NATURE AND DIASPORAS

The metaphor of diaspora is seductively convenient to contemporary queer politics. Unlike the tendency of seventies and eighties lesbian and gay theory to develop overly monolithic notions of identity and cultural politics, the concept of diaspora is suggestive of diversification, of scattering, fracturing, separate developments, and also, perhaps, of a certain glamor. It also suggests something of a sense of collective interest, however difficult this may be to pin down. It implies a complex divided constituency, with varying degrees of power and powerlessness. The concept of diaspora has been developed in recent years in especially important ways by the black British sociologist, Stuart Hall, in a series of exemplary analyses of Caribbean cultures and identities. In much of this work, Hall contrasts an older black political model which emphasizes an essential "oneness" of worldwide black cultures, to more recent debates which have questioned this notion of a single, originating cultural past, which might yet be restored. Thus he writes with admirable sensitivity and insight of the many ways in which black culture frequently offers

a way of imposing an imaginary coherence on the experience of dispersal and fragmentation, which is the history of all enforced diasporas. They do this by representing or "figuring" Africa as the mother of these different civilizations.[13]

There are evidently close parallels here in the recent history of lesbian and gay culture and politics to the type of "imaginary reunification" described by Hall. For example, it is laudable and understandable that lesbian and gay politics have sought political unity between women and men as perhaps its highest internal goal. Yet it has been less than helpful that the relations between lesbians and gay men have so frequently been simply assumed to be exactly commensurate and continuous. There have been comparatively few serious attempts to articulate the constantly shifting ideological frame which sometimes casts us together as targets of new legislation, or affects us separately as women or as men. We cannot however assume a given or "natural" alliance between lesbians and gay men for the simple reason that we are not in any case dealing with stable, coherent constituencies of women and men in the first place. On the contrary, there are profound divisions among lesbians and among gay men on any issue one might care to name, from the vexed topic of gays and lesbians in the military, to "pornography" or drug use. Hence the immediate significance of the term "queer" in the nineties, with its accompanying sense of diversity, and its cheerful embrace of the perverse.

Yet the concept of diaspora also introduces new problems of its own onto the terrain of queer culture and queer politics, not least because homosexuality is fortunately only very rarely a reason for forced expulsion from one's country of origin, though it should not be forgotten how many lesbians and gay men are indeed only too directly affected by forcible repatriation *to* their countries of origin as a result of their homosexuality. However, it is not so much external exile that we experience, but more often a form of internal exile, more strictly akin to legal and cultural quarantine, or to the state of "inner emigration" described in different circumstances by Hannah Arendt.[14] The actual Jewish diaspora may attract anti-Semitism because, as Zygmunt Bauman points out, Jews may be regarded as "foreigners inside" the nation, thus producing projective anxiety and hostility on the part of those who seek to define and defend narrowly rigid boundaries of language, custom, culture, and so on. For diasporas always imply a blurring of such boundaries, a porousness of social categories, and a tragic awareness of involuntary migrations.

Wherever the nation is popularly envisaged as if it were a closed family unit, homosexuality may also be perceived as similarly threatening, a refusal of homogeneity and sameness understood as indispensable aspects of properly "loyal" national identity. Sometimes, as in France, a seemingly democratic concept of national citizenship may be equally obliterative of national sexual differences, together with questions of race and gender. The question remains whether we can effectively articulate a productive sense of international commonality structured from the shared basis of homosexual desire, which is not at the same time itself obliterative of the great diversity of sexual identities through which homosexual desire is acted upon and lived by different people in different historical periods, and in different societies. For while we are all national subjects, our sexuality intersects in often unpredictable ways with our contingent national identities. One powerful strand of lesbian and gay politics has long sought to remove such anomalies, by recourse to civil rights legislation. Yet such politics, especially in the United States, frequently leads directly to a homogenizing, minoritist vision, which also demonstrates a marked tendency to greatly exaggerate the actual number of self-conscious, "out" lesbians and gay men in any country. Such a political vision is likely to gravitate towards such vague ideas as the supposed "right" to marry, and so on. These are indeed weighty and painful issues for lesbians and gay male Christians, but they are theological issues, to be decided within individual churches and congregations, and hardly compatible with the wider demands of queer politics, not least in relation to the institution of marriage, and the social and economic status of women.

Yet the sense of a queer diaspora remains stubbornly attractive, if only because it is likely to accord so well to our direct experience of overseas travel, as well as of queer culture and its constitutive role in our personal lives. Few heterosexuals can imagine the sense of relief and safety which a gay man or lesbian finds in a gay bar or a dyke bar in a strange city in a foreign country. Even if one cannot speak the local language, we feel a sense of identification. Besides, we generally like meeting one another, learning about what is happening to people "like us" from other parts of the world. At the level of the unconscious this is also, always, a site of powerful sexual fantasy—the core of all travel literature. Yet the question remains, in what sense "like" us? The worsening gravity of the international AIDS crisis requires that we consider such questions, since with the single exception of Australia, there is no political system on earth that has responded to our needs in this terrible emergency, precisely because we are so rarely recognized in political terms as a legitimate social constituency, or as deserving national subjects, by the state or other institutions which define "the national interest." This is not entirely surprising, given that it remains far from clear on what basis current lesbian and gay political "leaders" claim to "represent" their constituency, or how that constituency itself might best be conceptualized, beyond exhausted and inadequate notions of lesbian and gay "community."

Hence the many anxieties around the world about contemporary American minoritist lesbian and gay politics, and their dependence on categories and concepts such as "hate speech," and the widespread use of addiction models to supposedly explain immensely complex personal and social phenomena ranging from drug use to HIV transmission. For example, the bulk of U.S. prevention research is firmly committed in advance of any actual findings to the belief that unsafe sex is closely linked in a direct one-to-one causal manner to either alcohol consumption or drug addiction. A vast pathologizing literature has been amassed on this topic in the U.S. writings on HIV education. Yet I think it is fair to say that most non-American HIV/AIDS educators find this literature, and its effects in actual policies, far more harmful than helpful. As Peter Wetherburn explains:

> Large sums of money were suddenly released...by the United States government for research into HIV and AIDS. A proportion of this money went to fund social and behavioral research which soon emerged from being a low-status Cinderella of the high-powered American academy, to be "where it was all at"—reputations to be made, careers advanced and accolades expected.... They assumed that unsafe sex can be explained by isolating the personality traits of the individuals who engage in these activities...reminiscent of the search for the "homosexual personality" in the early part of this century. It is underpinned by the spurious notion that since [gay men] are on the whole well-informed about HIV transmission and are logical and rational and concerned for their own well-being, then those who engage in unsafe sex must be illogical, irrational, or unconcerned with their survival. Hence people who have "unsafe sex" must suffer from some defect of the intellect (denial, depression, low-self-efficacy, poor sexual communication skills, sexual compulsiveness, etc.) or be under the influence of external factors (usually drugs or alcohol), any of which can render them helpless to their baser instincts. This agenda implicitly privileges the clinician: it is aimed at providing the medical and ancillary professions with the means to identify the individuals who are being irresponsible.[15]

I cite this article at length for two reasons. First, it eloquently embodies a series of common beliefs throughout northern Europe and Australia, based on good qualitative and quantitative research, which at the same time are regarded as sheer heresy in the United States. Second, the article appeared in one of the many lesbian and gay publications which proliferate in the U.K., and not in some obscure academic journal. Yet just across the English Channel in France there is no such gay press in which a politically active gay academic might publish such work in order to reach a wider, community-based audience. This, together with the virtual absence of a French equivalent to Anglophone gay identity, is not unconnected to the tragic fact that France has the worst HIV epidemic in Europe, with a vastly disproportionate impact among French "homosexuals."

Another symptom of "imaginary reunification" may be found in the widespread U.S. political dependence on a new form of heavily biologized, neo-eugenic gay politics, typified by the national Human Rights Campaign Fund's promotion of the notion that lesbian and gay identity is hardwired to genetic determinants. This is not to question the role genetics plays in all areas of human behavior, but it does raise the important issue of why the U.S. gay movement should so casually adopt a position which threatens to collapse all aspects of human sexual diversity together as if they were of purely biological origin. This effectively pushes the clock back some seventy years to early twentieth century German arguments that if "we" are different "by nature" then it is biologically pointless to persecute "us." Such attempts to ground "tolerance" in a biologistic notion of object choice which in turn supposedly explains everything about our lives and feelings is perhaps not unrelated to the wider influence of crude behaviorism within American academic and popular thought.

Such misguided political campaigns return us to the vexed issue of the relations between gay and lesbian political organizations, and those they claim to represent. Indeed, it is only too apparent in many countries, including the U.K., that some twenty years of puritanical leftist and feminist lesbian and gay politics have achieved less for most self-defining lesbians, gay men, and queers than has resulted from changes and expansion within the commercial scene, including the dramatic expansion of social facilities, cable TV, the gay and lesbian press, and so on. And such differences in ordinary, everyday quality of gay and lesbian life issues have always had the most powerful diasporic impact on our lives, as we campaign for greater freedoms on the basis of what is available to other people in other countries. Besides, the sense of international unity felt most strongly by gay men around the world these days is surely forged in relation to our direct experience of protracted illness, suffering, loss, and mourning, together with the cultural solidarity we obtain from what has always been a diasporic queer culture. Neither in the U.S. nor in Europe has the gay political leadership responded adequately to AIDS. It is as if the epidemic were to them merely an embarrassment, something which cannot be permitted to derail the triumphalist vision of a squeaky-clean, network-TV-worthy, *VanityFair*-respectable, and unquestionably patriotic new lesbian and gay citizenship. Indeed, little can have had more direct effect on the explosive emergence of the new queer identity in all its national variants, than the inability of a lesbian and gay politics grounded in the seventies, to respond to the changed realities of the eighties and nineties. This is sadly apparent, for example, in the stunning inanity of political analysis on display in the recent "Queer Nation" special edition of *The Nation*.[16] It is on the High Ground of representative political claims that new would-be power formations are emerging, much more similar in many ways to the various homophile lobbying groups of the forties and fifties than to the descendants of gay liberation, which as far as many people, including such influential figures as Clinton's advisor David B. Mixner, are concerned, might never have happened.

In other words, what we are witnessing is the beginning of the process whereby political formations working on the terrain of homosexuality will emerge, and either flourish or disappear, to be replaced by new, more adequate approximations to people's experience. Within Anglophone societies it seems likely that the terms lesbian and gay will retain their previous political purchase, since their goals are also yet to be achieved. But "underneath" gay identity, as it were, we are likely to find a proliferation of innovative ways of living homosexual desire in the world. And these will, by definition, be largely invisible from the perspective of the older lesbian and gay identities, and the institutions they created. Moreover, local responses to the injustices surrounding most aspects of the epidemic are already bringing into being new, articulate groupings of men in countries such as India and the Philippines, where homosexual acts were not related to notions of identity before the epidemic. This will lead to still further diasporic diversity. For example, it is clear that there is no single answer to such questions as how one thinks of oneself if one is Indian, British, and gay. One man will identify as a black man, another as a gay Asian, while a third may reject the validity of the category of gay altogether. There can be no easy resolution to such issues, nor is resolution required. On the contrary, it is the conflict between a gay political imperative to think of its constituency as unified and homogeneous, and the actual constantly changing complexity of gay culture as it is lived, that stimulates most of our greatest challenges today.

In conclusion, a properly diasporic analysis of the epidemic from a queer perspective must, at the very least, be able to account for differences of needs and strategies in countries with different types of epidemic. For example, the needs of gay and bisexual men who made up sixty-two percent of newly diagnosed U.K. cases of HIV infection in 1992, are quite different from those of other gay and bisexual men elsewhere in the European Community, where they may constitute a minority of new cases in different epidemiological settings. Both types of situations will be largely determined by local varieties of homophobia, but these may vary in their affects and degrees. All are likely to be equally harmful for our health. We need far, far more rigorous thinking. The potential damage to the fundamental principle of sexual choice posed by the new genetic determinist strand of gay politics is still more dangerous than the anti-activist rhetoric which opposed the emergence of ACT UP in the late eighties.[17] The entire vocabulary of "positive images," "sexual addiction," and so on, speaks from a set of beliefs about sexuality that are positively dangerous in an epidemic since they obscure the central fact that avoiding HIV has nothing to do with what is so laughably described as "the gay lifestyle," but depends upon socially learned skills, and a shared morality, which might well be best understood as a form of ethical sexual etiquette. This is how homosexual desire is lived by men in the nineties. It is also vitally important that in our headlong rush for normality and "equal rights" we do not neglect or offend our queer cultural divinities—the great iconic, transcultural figures of a queer culture that is increasing diasporic, including to name but a few—Divine, John Waters, Derek Jarman, Pasolini, Virginia Woolf, Elizabeth Bishop, Sylvia Townshed Warner, Morrissey, Frank O'Hara, k.d. lang, and on and on. We have our own queer canon, and it is nothing if not diasporic. Indeed, this is one of its profoundest characteristics.

CONCLUSION

In many developed countries we are currently witnessing a widening divergence between the old gay liberation, leftist lesbian and gay intelligentsia, and the generation who has "come out" since the epidemic began. This is not least perhaps because so many of the ablest men of that generation have already died long before their time, indeed, ironically, just when their wisdom is most needed. It seems to me that of all the many great achievements of the American lesbian and gay movement since the sixties, the work of treatment activists in the AIDS crisis has been the most remarkable, politically, ethically, intellectually, and most important of all, in terms of practical, direct consequences—better health and longer lives for people living with HIV.

It is inexpressibly sad to visit the great cities of the United States for European gay men of my generation, who learned so much from the great confidence and vitality of the American gay scene in the seventies. We marvel at the scale of courage, both public and private. And since our epidemics are running approximately four or five years behind those in the U.S., we can also see what lies ahead for our local gay cultures, as our HIV epidemics slowly and inexorably turn into AIDS epidemics. Everywhere I travel in my work I find increasing levels of stress and emotional exhaustion, expressed as symptoms of many kinds, from the flourishing of conspiracy theories and open hostility to the very concept of scientific method, to the proliferation of lesbian and gay New Ageism. Yet what has lesbian and gay politics to say on these issues? Not a lot. Certainly the astonishing achievements of organizations such as New York's Treatment Action Group (TAG) are rarely seen as even a part of the wider intellectual world of Lesbian and Gay Studies.[18]

In these volatile and painful circumstances, it seems to me that the emergent discipline of Lesbian and Gay Studies has arrived at just the right time, in order to be prepared and able to contest HIV/AIDS issues as they arise within the academy. This will range from internal HIV/AIDS education, to an assessment of how different disciplines function in relation to the management of the epidemic. The universities may now be further than ever from seats of government, but nonetheless vital areas of policy are implemented on the basis of research which only academics are qualified to design and undertake. This is not of course to say that all queer academics should immediately put down their tools and do nothing but work in relation to the epidemic. It is however to imply that gay male academics do indeed have at least some moral responsibility to try to find out how their specialist discipline may be involved in HIV/AIDS issues. Thus the queer teaching of literature would be incomplete if it did not posses some reflexive awareness of the role of AIDS fictions in our culture. Although we will never begin to do justice to the realities of HIV/AIDS if our work is only concerned with the public domain, at the same time, social and physical scientists also have responsibilities, especially since their disciplines have been so polluted by bad, homophobic research, which has only very rarely ever been criticized in the United States.[19]

There is a cruel and ironic paradox in the emergence of a confident, articulate Lesbian and Gay Studies movement, which is enthusiastically "re-gaying" the academy, while at the same time throughout the developed world with all too few exceptions AIDS service organizations continue to "de-gay" the epidemic in a process quite distinct from governmental "de-gaying."[20] At the same time, it would seem that the U.S. Lesbian and Gay Studies movement, which is of course the flagship of parallel maneuvers in other countries, has retreated in recent years from intellectual involvement with HIV/AIDS issues. In this respect the 1988 Yale Lesbian and Gay Studies conference marked a high-point of academic attention, for by the time of the 1991 Rutgers conference only one out of eighty panels dealt specifically with the epidemic. It is difficult not to regard this situation as further evidence of the complex displacements and projections at work throughout the wider queer nation, of which the academy is but one relatively small territory.

The academy matters however because it remains one of the primary institutional/discursive sites where "truth" is defined and negotiated and questioned, with unpredictable consequences for the rest of society. The great challenge here is to be able to articulate our social and cultural goals in relation to the multifaceted nature of the epidemic. Out there in the Queer Nation a great change is taking place, and far beyond, throughout the international queer diaspora. This change has no single coherent form, but is everywhere involved with the great principle of equality in law, and an angry refusal of the violence and injustice which is sadly still so widely experienced in relation to homosexuality. On the one hand we witness the fully-fledged emergence of an immensely sophisticated fetish culture, organized around physical pleasures which are inseparable from HIV/AIDS awareness, while on the other we also find an explosion of involvement in 12-step programs, and psychotherapeutic programs, many of which are extremeley conservative in their depiction of homosexuality, and sex in general, widely regarded as primarily a dangerous, addictive activity. In other words, the epidemic has already generated complex, conflicting cultural responses at the level of personal lived identities, which may be either puritanical, or libertarian, and sometimes both. At the same time the contingent commercial scene of clubs, bars and so on has been dramatically expanding in many parts of the world, from the smaller cities of the U.S., to London, and Melbourne and Vancouver.

In these circumstances we should note that growing conflict between the broad tradition of social construction theory in the academy, and its widespread rejection among nonacademics, including many leading figures in the U.S. lesbian and gay politics movements. This conflict revolves above all around rival notions of *choice*. On the one hand we speak confidently within the field of lesbian and gay studies about "homosexual object choice" understood to be involuntary and unconscious, and relatively fixed, though potentially mobile in the lives of individuals. It should be noted that this mobility is usually considered only from the direction of "coming out" as lesbian or gay after previously exclusive heterosexuality, rather than in the opposite direction from homosexuality to bisexuality or heterosexuality. At the same time it is insisted with equal fervor by many others, that sexual object choice or "orientation," is entirely voluntary, and conscious. This position is ironically shared by both moralistic homophobes, aiming to prevent the "promotion" of homosexuality, and by some libertarians and feminists. Yet another, and far more extensive constituency holds that we have no "choice" about our sexuality, and that identity is hardwired to biology. This position in turn is shared both by crude genetic determinists, and those who simply feel convinced they were "born this way."

Yet in many respects these oppositions are more apparent than real. For the assertion that homosexuality is grounded in infantile desiring fantasy (like all other forms of sexual object choice), it is hardly incompatible with either the empirical observation that people may "come out" at different ages, for many different reasons, or the strongly held sense of personal difference in childhood described by most "out" lesbians and gay men. What does remain problematic is the enthusiastic retention of the idea that sexual object choice is *infinitely* mobile and fluid, rather than its expression, both in the lives of individuals and sexual collectivities. This is a major stumbling block to the kind of intellectual politics which are so urgently needed in response to the epidemic. The question remains why this particular fantasy of absolute sexual mobility is so devoutly upheld within some sections of the queer academy.

HIV has in many respects served to reconstitute homosexuality and identities founded upon homosexual desire. This reconstitution involves many overlapping elements, from attitudes towards sex, towards illness and death, mourning, and so on. It informs the totality of our social and psychic lives in ways that we hardly begin to understand. After all, there have never been people quite like "us" before, at least in relation to our necessarily simultaneous focus of love, sex, and death. Never before has it been so urgently necessary to mobilize concrete policies founded upon notions of commonality and solidarity, yet never before has the very notion of lesbian and gay *political* identity been less fashionable in the academy, where it is so frequently "deconstructed" as if it were merely a vulgar "essentialist" error. Such a position stems from the widespread belief that gay and lesbian identities are no more than a response to some primary level of regulation. This is to ignore the fact that as the marginal yet extensive field of queer historiography demonstrates, women and men have also, always, responded positively to their own homosexuality, and developed identities which should not be regarded as merely reactive and basically passive byproducts of power, understood to be universally homophobic. This is simply ahistorical. It also colludes dangerously with precisely the type of widespread academic "de-gaying" which until recently has tended to deny or obscure the very existence of earlier historical social formations and groups based on the shared experience both of desire *and* its regulation. Always the challenge is to be able to articulate together the two currents at work in the process of forging identities, the one deriving from complex shared feelings and pleasures, the other from shared discrimination and induced shame. What is not going to change is the central presence of HIV in our midst, and the conflicting tides of fatalism and hope to which it gives rise.

If the new queer academic intelligentsia is unable or unwilling to even try to grapple with the fundamental issues raised by the epidemic, other formations will doubtlessly challenge its authority. With fifty percent of gay men already infected in several U.S. cities, the social and psychological consequences of the epidemic in our communities must be faced. The immediate future looks very grim indeed. If Lesbian and Gay Studies has nothing to say on the details of social policy, care, services, and clinical medicine, as well as HIV education, then it can hardly expect the wholehearted loyalty it presumably seeks from its primary constituency, including the not inconsiderable number of "independent scholars" who have traditionally constituted the bedrock of lesbian and gay intellectual life, far away from the academy which has traditionally denied the validity of their studies. It would indeed be a tragic irony if the vanguard of Lesbian and Gay Studies were to follow suit.

NOTES

1. See Derek Link, "The Collapse of Early Intervention at the Ninth International AIDS Conference," *Treatment Issues* Vol. 7, no. 6 (New York, July 1993); and Edward King, "Experts gloomy at drugs' limited benefits," *AIDS Treatment Update* Issue 8/9 (London, June/July 1993).

2. See Edward King, "The end of the American dream," *The Pink Paper*, London, 9 July 1993, 12; and Simon Watney, "Read My Lips: AIDS Art & Activism," in Nicola White, ed. *Read My Lips: New York AIDS Polemic*, (Tramway: Glasgow, 1992).

3. Lance Loud, "AIDS in the Hood," *The Advocate*, Los Angeles, 27 July 1993, 77.

4. *HIV/AIDS Surveillance Report*, vol. 5, no. 2 (July 1993) Atlanta, Georgia: U.S. Department of Health and Human Services.

5. Sara Simmons, "Death by Genocide," *NYQ*, 22 December, 1991, 28.

6. Information from the Ninth International AIDS Conference, Berlin 1993. For the UK see Edward King, et al., *HIV Prevention for Gay Men: A Survey of Initiative in the UK*, (July 1992) London: National AIDS Manual Ltd.

7. See Simon Watney, "Emergent Sexual Identities and HIV/AIDS" in Peter Aggleton et al., eds. *AIDS: Facing the Second Decade* (London: Falmer Press, 1993), 13–19.

8. See Mary Douglas and Aaron Wildavasky, *Risk and Culture*, (Berkeley: University of California Press, 1982).

9. John Burke, "British gay establishment in colonial outpost of U.S.," *The Pink Paper*, London, 6 August 1993, 8.

10. ibid.

11. See Jeffrey Weeks, *Sexuality*, (London: Tavistock Press, 1986).

12. See Keith Alcorn, "Queer and Now," *Gay Times*, London (May 1992), 20–24.

13. See Stuart Hall, "Cultural Identity and Diaspora," in Jonathan Rutherford, ed. *Identity: Community, Culture, Difference* (London: Lawrence and Wishart, 1990), 224. See also, Stuart Hall, "New Ethnicities," in *Black Film British Cinema*, Erica Carter, ed. (London: ICA Documents No. 7, 1988), 27–31.

14. Hannah Arendt, "On Humanity in Dark Times: Thoughts on Lessing," *Men in Dark Times*, (San Diego: Harcourt Brace Jovanovich, 1968) 22.

15. Peter Wetherburn, "Alcohol and Unsafe Sex," *Rouge* 11 (London 1992), 12–14.

16. *The Nation*, 5 July 1993.

17. See Simon Watney, "The Possibilities of Permutation," in James Miller ed. *Fluid Exchanges: Artists and Critics in the AIDS Crisis*, (Toronto: University of Toronto Press, 1992), 329–369.

18. See Keith Alcorn, "We Don't Have Time," *Gay Times*, (London, June 1993), 38-41.

19. See the debate on this subject in *AIDS* 7, 279–300. See also *Sex, Gay Men and AIDS*, ed. Peter Davis, et al. (London: The Falmer Press, 1993); Edward King, *Safety in Numbers: Safer Sex and Gay Men*, (London: Cassell), 1993.

20. See Cindy Patton, *Inventing AIDS*, (New York: Routledge, 1990), chapter five; also Edward King, *Safety In Numbers: Safer Sex and Gay Men*, (London: Cassell, 1993, Routledge, USA, 1994).

How Do You Wear Your Body?

Bodybuilding and the Sublimity of Drag

....

Marcia Ian

Without all doubt, the torments which we may be made to suffer,
are much greater in their effect on the body and mind, than any
pleasures which the most learned voluptuary could suggest.
—Edmund Burke, "Of The Sublime"[1]

I just summon power within my soul / It has given me life, beyond
life / I take blame for my murderous problem / my signature
—Pantera, "Message in Blood"[2]

ACCORDING TO PSYCHOANALYSIS,
sexuality "develops," specifically, from the indiscriminate polymorphousness
of infantile libido, through an increasing awareness of gender difference and
its ramifications to (ta-da!) purposeful desire for someone of the "opposite"
gender. This theory assumes, among other things, that there is an entity called
"gender" that a person can and should acquire. Indeed, acquiring it is precisely what is meant by psychosexual "development": one develops by moving up
the sexual food chain, as it were, from the omniverous instinctual sexuality of
the ungendered infantile organism to the more discriminating sexual taste of
the civilized person defined (refined, confined) by gender. Having assumed
that there is such a thing as gender, psychoanalytic theory also assumes that
there is such a thing as "opposite" gender (or maybe it assumes these in the
reverse order)[3], and that what "opposite" means is self-evident, just as it is
supposed to be discernible when two people are the "same." But these two

assumptions which constitute the psychoanalytic narrative of sexuality—which constitute sexuality as narrative—seem less cogent every time I go to the gym, which is virtually every day. In a way, but only in a way, all bodybuilders' bodies, male or female, are masculine, and the activity of bodybuilding a masculinizing praxis, given the conventional association of physical strength and lean muscularity with maleness. Certainly much of what goes on in and around the gym, including the socializing that occurs during training sessions, the training rituals themselves, and the performance and judging of bodybuilding and weightlifting competitions, seems intended to shore up and maintain, if not exaggerate or even exalt, conventional gender roles.[4]

At the same time, however, what goes on in the gym is not about gender, but about something less cultural, perhaps, but more social, somatic, and spiritual, insofar as these may be synonymous—insofar as the "soul" may be defined as the totality of the body's experience, and "spirituality" as the testing of the body's limits (as opposed to its limitations). Bodybuilding is about the body's self-loathing, its horror at its own repulsive beauty, and is therefore sublime. It fulfills the wish to objectify the already unfamiliar body, to make it even more unrecognizable, to transgress or explode its limits, to metamorphose, to expose the deep materiality of its interior. To "build" more muscle, one must tear the extant muscle fibers; for the bodybuilder, getting "ripped" or "shredded," as the clearly defined and striated muscularity of the competition-ready physique is conventionally described, is not just a metaphor. It is something one does to oneself, but it is not just physical. As in an orgy, according to Georges Bataille, "the total personality is involved, reeling blindly towards annihilation, and this is the decisive moment of religious feeling."[5]

Bodybuilding enacts something psychoanalysis can only categorize, and devalue, as regressive, as representing a psychosexual phase "prior to" or more primitive than gender consciousness but which, if one doesn't buy the psychoanalytic narrative of development, or accept that sexuality *is* a narrative, one must explain in some other way. In our eagerness to discredit reigning gender ideologies, we sometimes give them all the credit in the world, as if gender were causal, the key to all mythologies, as if the vagaries and subtleties of gender, its histories and subtexts, its measly antitheses, could explain everything, all our pain and bafflement at being human, at being, at once and involuntarily, isolate individuals and social selves. Psychoanalysis has always equated socialization with gender-ization, and in general both feminist theory and gender studies have followed suit. Yet the two hardly explain or exhaust each other, or account fully for what seems to me to be the fact that most of us are obliged to live riven at moments by heart-rending desire and stupefied at others by desire's failure to materialize.

The notion of a before and after—specifically, the before and after *gender* that constitutes the plot of the sexual narrative—falsifies by pseudohistoricizing and rationalizing what remains, so long as we draw breath, the painfully polymorphous desirous disorder of our everyday lives, and wills to the psychological past the incompleteness we wish we could outgrow. Time may not be reversible, and we may not be able or willing to ever go "home" again, but we do not outgrow unreasonable wishes. About this much at least Freud was right. Yet psychoanalysis tells us that the masochistic fervor of everyday life, the wish to invade or be invaded by the other, to transgress out of love or hate what divides us from each other and from our own lives, is necessarily regressive. Psychoanalysis tells us that such wishes are perversions, turnings back to psychosexual prehistory, to a Jurassic Era ruled not by T. Rex but by P. Mom, the phallic mother, rapacious queen of indifferent gender. But one could argue that in psychoanalysis there is no history, only the uncanny oscillation of "before" and "after," really of two different Edenic befores and postlapsarian afters: before and after birth, and before and after the realization of gender difference. According to psychoanalysis the psyche is constituted in response to these two traumatic losses: one, the loss of union with mother, the breast, or whatever nurturant person or object first represents undifferentiated being (a plenitude experienced to perfection only *in utero*, and thus always already lost); and two, the loss of (the illusion of) an intact self or body-image represented by the onset of castration anxiety and the realization of sexual difference (a plenitude intermittently recuperable by narcissistic satisfaction, mood alteration, or "perverse" acts like fetishism.) *Because psychoanalysis confuses and conflates these two traumas— because it can't distinguish between (the loss of) mother/baby love and the (desire for) sex— it diagnoses the rejection of teleological heterosexuality as regression and polymorphousness as perversion. As an institution psychoanalysis is founded on this conflation between the desire for mother and the desire for sex; in a sense this is all that psychoanalysis is.* To make matters worse, all it offers to stave off this double loss is the ideal of gender complementarity—whatever that means—and the paradise regained of desire sublimated into domesticity.

Sometimes when I'm in the gym I glance over at some Neanderthal-looking bruiser as he stands there glaring at the loaded barbell he is about to wrest from the grip of gravity—or, if he has just pushed or pulled the thing from here to there, stands there blinking the sweat out of his eyes and waiting for his heart rate to slow so he can do it again—and I think to myself: "This must be the guy for whom the endearment 'you big lug' was invented." And then I think: "Hey, wait a minute. That's what *I* look like to other people. Relative to most women, I am that guy. I'm a female Neanderthal." Which is why, no doubt, I am so fond of that big lug. I don't feel essentially "other" from him, differently shaped genitalia and superior literary skills notwithstanding. I feel we're siblings, or comrades, or colleagues, or littermates. But, as far as I can tell from ten years of serious weightlifting, the male Neanderthal doesn't feel that way about me. I may identify with (and desire) him, but he (I think) doesn't identify with (or desire) me. It seems to me that, while he is included in my universe, I am not included in his.[6] To him I am an aberrant female, but not a woman: a Neanderthal wannabe.

To make matters more confusing, the same usually holds true when I encounter (all too rarely) another female Neanderthal: the circuitries of identificaton and desire do not flow unimpeded here either. My guess is that this has to do with what is a shared but usually inadmissible conviction that, whatever gender we are perceived to represent, it is not the one(s) we think we enact. We're not sure, when we look at each other, whether we are looking into a mirror at our own outrageous femaleness or at the very demon dedicated to its annihilation. Perhaps serious lifters of whatever gender just have so much testosterone, adrenalin, and whatnot surging through their veins that they look at other lifters of whatever gender with a sense of aggressive desire which they (I) experience as desire, mistrust, and threat all at once. I'm aware in addition of the incomprehension, the amusement and repulsion, that many non-Neanderthals feel about the bodybuilder whose physique emulates an anatomical transparancy. One afternoon about eight years ago, while training at a gym in Charlottesville, Virginia, I was sweating and straining, happily, which is to say miserably, doing heavy dumbbell curls for biceps, when a prospective new gym member, an excessively (suspiciously?) feminine young woman of the sort I generally referred to as a "cupcake," strolled by in the company of one of the gym staff. I felt her look at me for a moment, then heard her say to her guide in a hoarse whisper: "I *don't* want to look like that." As if by just joining the gym she would uncontrollably and automatically turn into the "that" I had become.

Perhaps this cupcake had looked too credulously at those proverbial "before" and "after" photos used to promote bodybuilding products, like those of Charles Atlas, Jack LaLanne, Joe Weider. In the gym the only "befores" and "afters" that count are before and after a training session, before and after each lift, each set, each rep: before, dread, excitement, fear; after, exhilaration, as if one has pressed from inside upon the envelope of one's own skin and torn it just enough to let in a little light, let out a little darkness. What is the meaning or purpose of the act that turns one, in the popular image, from the "before" into the "after"—or, as bodybuilding must be understood from the psychoanalytic point of view, from the "after" back into the "before?" What is this "that" which the feminine person did not wish to become, perhaps because she rightly sensed the extent to which bodybuilding is a kind of revenge against her (my, anyone's) sex? How do I account for the dismay I feel when I realize that I go to the gym to create a monster; or the paradoxical relief and joy I feel when momentarily I become that polymorphously sexed and gendered thing?

One day three years ago, in the middle of a workout at the Apollon Gym then in Highland Park, New Jersey, I paused to chat with a pleasant young man with orange hair and red sweat clothes. We were speaking about a woman who had been training there for about a year, and who already possessed an admirable "V": that is, the double V-shape most desirable for the bodybuilder, who, ideally, should have wide shoulders and back (preferably, so wide he or she cannot fit through the door) tapering like a V down to a punctiform waist, from which the thighs are supposed to flare outward to form the legs of another, upside down V. The bodybuilder's physique, in other words, should resemble an hourglass made of rock-hard muscle, with blood running through it instead of sand, a form which combines and exaggerates aspects of both conventionally feminine and conventionally masculine bodies, although the mostly male heterosexual, mostly homophobic and homosocial bodybuilders don't admit this except inadvertently when they mock each other as "wusses," "fags," or "pussies."

The orange-haired man looked me over curiously and, when he couldn't make out my physique through the oversized sweatclothes I was wearing, he asked, "How do you wear *your* body?" "Wear?" I asked. "Yeah," he said, "you know—hard, ripped, bulky—what?"[7] As I thought about his question, my body seemed to peel away from my mind like a suit of clothes from my skin, and I experienced a Cartesian separation of my consciousness from my body such as I had not felt since the experience of "natural" childbirth. In a flash the notion of "wearing" one's body seemed to cut in two the very unity of mind and flesh which bodybuilders go to the gym to forge, partly in order to deny the extent to which the masculinity they flaunt is not a natural attribute they're born with but a style they must work hard to create, a body that plays a role, a body masquerading as itself, as a hyperbolically sexed "look." This willed monism, this unification of will with form is itself a masquerade of sorts; and while Cartesian dualism may still be an unfashionable subject position to try on even for a minute, it seems logical nevertheless that a dualist, agonistic relation of mind or wit to body is required in order to masquerade at all. The very idea of a masquerade, in other words, posits a dualism of self and role, wearer and wear-ee, subject and subject position. This is obviously not news; queer theory is willing to make use of lots of duos and dualisms with which un-queer theory remains uncomfortable, such as the idea, say, of a woman "trapped inside"—"wearing" might be more apt here—a man's body, to take one example, or a woman trapped inside a woman's, to take another.

Such identities, with their seemingly incongruent if not antithetical "insides" and "outsides," raise the question of essences. Although we often do not think of it this way, identity is implicitly a dualism; it connotes unity, but only insofar as two or more things resemble or replicate each other. An identity is an equation or equivalence, a sameness or continuity, of one thing or state of that thing with another.[8] In the case of the "self" or subject, identity may be understood as the virtual unity of essence and appearance, whether one wants to define those terms ontologically, phenomenologically or, as Diana Fuss might say, strategically;[9] or as the virtual unity of multiple, concatenating, but ultimately somehow cohering, identifications and subject positions. We approach each other with what Wyndham Lewis has called "gauche ritual of self" while "the fetish within…would still cling to these forms."[10] "Spirituality" may just represent the wish to give up those rituals, those forms and fetishes of self to pursue instead a para-doxically "personal" experience of the mere virtual-ness of this unity by cultivating simultaneously two points of view, that of the body from the point of view of what seems not to be the body but rather its repertory of relations, and that of everything not the body from the point of view of the imprisoned flesh. In short, one may experience oneself as an essence (or self or subject) wearing a body as a kind of drag as one cruises life, cruises the living.

Since at least the 1960s various kinds of radical critique have sought to under-mine the humanist rationalism of Western patriarchal discourse by exposing the racist gynophobic heterosexism upon which it is founded. Such critiques have often proceeded by trying to unbind what Hélène Cixous called the tight "double braid" of binary "hierarchical oppositions"—mind/body, art/nature, nature/mind, culture/nature, and man/woman, etc.—that has led "us through literature, philosophy, criticism, and centuries of representation and reflection."[11] Disentangling this braid, we try to accept ourselves as individuals, rather than as incomplete halves of mythical couples, to appreciate each other as versions of the different, as much as versions of the same, to theorize subjects as actors in particular cultural contexts, rather than as embodiments of those metaphysical or essentialized categories we take to be "constructed" by these binary oppositions. At the same time, however, the identity politics of queer theory permit us, even require us, both to take seriously and experiment with ways of thinking and being which more conventional radical theory is ready to consign to its epistemological closet. All of which is to say that, having spent centuries conceiving of ourselves *ab ovo*, as it were, as defined by dualist categories like "identity" and "subject," it seems unreasonable to expect all binarism to disappear just because we have begun to tell ourselves we had better theorize our way out of it.

Bodybuilding in a sense enacts the same theoretical ambivalence; it both depends on and tries to minimize or camouflage the Cartesian dualism which has historically structured our relation to our "own," owned bodies, the sense that we are subjectivities surreally wearing our bodies, that our bodies conform to and play variations on types and styles just as our clothes, our hairdos, our gestures do. We can see that this is true, that our bodies have styles which themselves have histories, especially women's bodies: we see this when we look at the bodies of female fashion models in magazines; we can see, for example, that from year to year the body type, body size, skin color, and curvaceousness of the so-called "ideal" female figure changes. We can read statistics which report an "increasing discrepancy between [the] ideal and actual weights" of women, based on comparisons researchers have made between the weights of women offered to the American public to exemplify feminine beauty (like beauty contestants and winners of the Miss America Pageant and models in dieting articles in popular women's magazines), and the corresponding actuarial norms for comparable women in the general population.[12] And we know men's body types also change over time when we compare the iconic physiques of "desirable" male models, celebrities, and action heroes from different years or decades. Even so, the fashion trends in male bodies have varied less drastically than those of female bodies, and therefore represent even more compulsively, and certainly more rigidly the conspicuously and reassuringly gendered body.

Perhaps no one more enthusiastically represents the conspicuously and conventionally masculine body than the male bodybuilder, who strives to embody all the clichés of masculinism from the sublime to the barbarous—from Praxiteles to Hercules—not a far cry, really. Competitive female bodybuilders do the same—that is, they also strive to embody in their own disciplined flesh all the clichés of masculinism from the barbarous to the sublime. Female body-builders do this not because they want to be men, but because, like men, they want to eradicate from themselves their sentimentalized "femininity," and its historical equivalent, immanent passivity. The past decade in women's body-building has in fact witnessed a dramatic change in the style of body physique female athletes are wearing. Those who have watched the movie *Pumping Iron II: The Women* (1985) about the 1983 "Miss Olympia" (now called the "Ms. Olympia"), America's most prestigious bodybuilding competition for women, know that female competitors used to be judged explicitly, unlike the men, not only on the basis of their muscle density, definition, overall symmetry and pro-portionality, and the style, skill, and fluidity of their posing, but also for the extent to which they represented the ideal image of their gender type. Women were judged, given numerical scores, for a quality called "femininity" which sur-reptitiously but effectively limited all the other qualities.

On the last page of the November 1990 issue of *Muscle and Fitness*, Bill Dobbins reminded us of this controversy "regarding the muscles-versus-femi-ninity question in bodybuilding for women" which greeted the appearance in that 1983 contest of Bev Francis, former professional dancer and world-cham-pion powerlifter, who lost the title that year, despite the clear superiority of her physique, because she was judged "unfeminine." Dobbins doesn't criticize the 1983 decision but he does point out that Bev's winning the World Pro title four years later was a milestone in the sport. That was the day, Dobbins writes: when "the controversy [about femininity] ended" and the principle " 'may the best bodybuilder win' became the rule of the day, rather than 'we can't let the sport go in this direction' " toward the "manlike" woman Bev Francis; the day "when the judges clearly opted for the aesthetics of bodybuilding over other and often irrelevant standards of female beauty." Even more significant, if one cares about these matters, is the fact that in his article in the same issue on the leg-training regimen of Lenda Murray, the current Ms. Olympia, Dobbins, clearly awestruck by Murray's physique, can't help pointing out that, given her tiny waist, her "exaggerated V-shape" and "shockingly wide, well-developed lats," the dramat-ic sweep of her thighs as curved "as a pair of parentheses" with hamstrings to match, Murray resembles no less an athlete than Sergio Oliva, Mr. Olympia 1967-69 and Arnold Schwarzenegger's "legendary adversary." In the past this could have been meant only as an insult to a woman, though it would have been high praise for a man. As praise for a female bodybuilder it was an astonishing first.

The champion female bodybuilder, then, is catching up with the male in terms of how much shaped, hard muscle mass she displays to the judges. And while in a way she is sporting a suit made of ungendered muscle, at the same time she is both transforming the female body she used to wear into a manly one, and altering the fit of the female body. The bodybuilder's "project" of eradicating femininity, however, goes beyond the herculean effort to appear herculean for men and women alike. When bodybuilders plan, a year in advance, to "peak" for a contest, they time their cycles of bulking up and trimming down so that on the day of the contest they will display as much tumescent muscle as possible: the skin must be well-tanned and oiled, the physique rock-hard, showing striations and bulging veins from the calf muscles to the trapezius. The whole idea in other words may be to look as much like a giant erection as possible. Perhaps the bodybuilder is not trying to be a man, but a penis. S/he is a Penis Wannabe. I was struck by this fact in 1985 when I looked at myself admiringly in the mirror at the Iron Works gym in Charlottesville, noted the taut, moist, flushed flesh of my chest and shoulders, with its tracework of throbbing veins, and announced happily: "I look like a penis." To which my friend Jennifer (who owned a small Schnauzer whose teeth she periodically brushed with Crest tartar control gel and who therefore clearly could not understand my point of view) said, "Yeah. Right." In his book about his brief career as a bodybuilder, Sam Fussell, academic brat turned author, relates that when he walked offstage after performing his posing routine at a competition, his friend Vinnie welcomed him thus: "Oh, Sam...You looked like a human fucking penis!"

Why might this be, and what does it mean? Does it merely represent the wish, in a patriarchal phallocratic culture, to become the quintessential phallocrat? In other words, does it represent a wish to regress, or progress? Is there a history, a poetics, of the wish to be "a human fucking penis?" The answer to this last question is of course yes, in psychoanalysis, for which reason I wish to talk here about the poetics of fantasy according to psychoanalytic theory, where the phallus, as we know, figures prominently. Besides, for all its problems, psychoanalytic theory is still the only discourse which takes the constitutive effects of fantasy to be its object of study. Psychoanalysis is itself the discursive institution of a particular fantasy—the fantasy of the phallus as the ruling trope, the shape flesh would have if it had a shape, the phallus as *le sujet supposé savoir*—

a fantasy which remains culturally, historically, politically real. As André Green sums it up,

> It is psychoanalysis which gives to the child, woman born, a significance bearing on his entire development: namely, that he is a substitute for the penis of which the mother is deprived, and that he can only achieve his status as subject by situating himself at the point where he is missing from the mother on whom [from whom?] he depends. This substitute is the locution and link of exchange between the mother and the father who, possessing the penis, still cannot create it (since he has it).[13]

According to psychoanalysis, the significance of the "child, woman born," in other words, of every single one of us ever to have lived, is thus twofold. The subject is, first, a human dildo designed to serve as the symbolic substitute for the penis of which the mother is deprived, to be "situat[ed]...at the point where he is missing from the mother on whom he depends"; and, second, as what Green calls "the locution and link of exchange," or what Lacan calls the "logical copula," between the two parental bodies.

In all of psychoanalytic theory these remain the two basic conceptions of the subject position of the subject of fantasy—that is, of the subject who is having a fantasy (because in effect he is a fantasy). One of these is highly determined and the other relatively protean. The first conception of the subject of fantasy, the relatively determined one which corresponds to Green's first formulation of the child as mother's dildo, is of someone who needs to see confirmed the presence or absence of the phallus. This, in other words, is the subject as fetishist, for whom the undecidability of this binary opposition is eroticized. I say that this subject is relatively determined because she really only oscillates between two dialectical alternatives. The second conception of the subject, that which is relatively protean, even social, "assumes" the phallus as the link, not so much between the subject and the other, as among the subject and two or more others, or even just among those others to the exclusion of the subject as such. This subject in theory can perform an impressive psychosexual repertory, able to go in and out of a variety of orifices, organs, worlds, and subject positions. This is the subject of the primal scene, the subject as human fucking penis. Both theories of the subject reflect the masculinist heterosexist narcissism typical of psychoanalysis insofar as "the child" they posit is assumed to be the male child, the basic sexual act, heterosexual genital intercourse, and the fundamental fear that of castration. But a closer look at these theories reveals, I think, that both can be interpreted as screens, as anchors for the more frightening fluidity of the subject Henry James attests to when he laments that "really, universally, relations stop nowhere." The psychoanalytic theorist, just like the artist James has in mind, or just like anybody else, can only "draw, by a geometry of [her] own, the circle within which they shall happily *appear* to do so."[14] To show what I mean I would like to articulate briefly in just a little more detail both of these models of the subject of fantasy. First: the subject as fetishist.

In 1968 Robert C. Bak wrote an article called "The Phallic Woman: The Ubiquitous Fantasy in Perversions," a piece intended to argue against what he took to be an unfortunate new trend in psychoanalysis: namely, too much research into the so-called pre-genital, pre-oedipal (read "maternal") phase and its relation to autonomous ego functions. This was a mistake, he felt, because, as he claimed, following Freud as he thought, all perversion is basically fetishism since the mother's castration is the principal trauma which organizes psychic life. Fetishism is, he argues, "the basic perversion" because, in all perversions "the main [subject] position...[is] the reinvestment of the fantasy of the phallic woman" (16–17).[15] "In all perversions the dramatized or ritualized denial of castration is acted out through the regressive revival of the maternal or female phallus" (16). What Freud called in his notorious essay on "Fetishism" (1927) the simultaneous "denial and asseveration" of the existence of the maternal phallus thus constitute the sole alternatives of the bipolar fetishistic subject.[16]

And yet while Bak invokes the fetishist as proof of the primacy of the oedipal, he defines the oedipal in relation to an obviously regressive, historically "prior" wish for the phallic mother. In 1924 Otto Rank had already explained this fundamental contradiction—this psychoanalytic *méconnaissance*—by arguing that castration anxiety is really a screen for the true origin of all anxiety, namely the universally traumatic experience of birth. As far as he was concerned "the child's every anxiety consists of the anxiety at birth" while "the child's every pleasure aims at the re-establishing of the intrauterine primal pleasure."[17] Rank thought that it was the female, not the male, genitals which worry us, and that castration anxiety was a substitute formation in which the phallus served as "a [displaced] 'symbol' for the umbilical cord"; "thus the importance of castration is based...on the primal castration at birth, that is, on the separation of the child from the mother."

Even the so-called primal scene—which Freud defined as primal because, consisting as it does of the copulation of the subject's own parents, it simulates and reenacts the biological and symbolical constitution of the subject—even the so-called primal scene can be easily reconceived as a primal screen for pre-oedipal scenes. Freud tells us that the Wolf-Man, whose analysis inspired Freud to "invent" the notion of the primal scene, fantasized about being back inside his mother's womb in order to imagine incestuous intercourse with both his mother, whose genitals he had thus imaginatively entered, and his father, whose penis he could imaginatively receive while inside his mother (102 SE, XVII).[18] The Wolf-Man's wish for intercourse with his father and his mother come together, Freud claims, in eroticized fantasies of his own anal rebirth. Freud had already suggested here, in other words, that the options for the subject in fantasy were not exhausted by the phallic to-be or not-to-be. As Melanie Klein would argue about ten years after Freud, the series of organic personae which the subject could imaginatively assume include at least that of the penis, the nipple, the child, the womb, the father and, as Richard Rorty might say, *what not*.

My point is not, however, to say that the uterine-maternal is more "primal" than the phallic-paternal; I see no need to essentialize, primalize, or prioritize here, particularly in light of my wish to question the psychoanalytic drive to narrativize sexuality. Both scenarios represent ambivalent visions of incorporation either by or of the other, of either deliquescence into a hungry host of indistinguishable others, or concretization out of their erotic conjugations: orgasmic realizations all of the liminality of one's own embodied character, and dependent all on the primal dualism of what Lacan called the vegetative "dehiscence" or splitting of the subject into fragments each of which regards the other with aggressive fictionalizing intent. In their 1968 article on "Fantasy and the Origins of Sexuality," Jean Laplanche and J.-B. Pontalis point out that sexual fantasy in general is "characterized by the absence of subjectivization," that is, the author of the fantasy tends not to be aware of herself as such. Rather than seeming to watch her fantasy like a spectator at a stage play, "the subject is present in the scene [not experienced as separate from it]: the child, for instance, is one character amongst many in the fantasy 'a child is beaten.' Freud insisted on this visualization," Laplanche and Pontalis write, "of the subject on the same level as the other protagonists." Furthermore, precisely where the subject "will be immediately located" in a fantasy cannot be predicted; she can be almost anywhere" (13–14). In the relatively unconstructed narrative world of fantasy, in other words, it is the subject who comes and goes, not the object, i.e., the subject herself, and not the mother, who comes and goes in the *fort/da* game which according to psychoanalysis structures the subject's relation to reality. Anxiety about our own "subject constancy"—not about *object* constancy—insecurity about the perdurability of the bodies within which we discover ourselves to be temporally and temporarily located, is thus, I would argue, our primary worry, and for good reason, since we know we are mortal and that's about all we know. The subject of fetishism, like the subject of the primal scene, eroticizes the idea of her own nonexistence, as if practicing for its realization. It is the subject which is at stake in fantasy, rather than the objects in which the subject likes to see herself reflected. Psychoanalytic scenarios which cast us as lifelong worriers about the phallic to-be or not-to-be, the phallic to-have or not-to-have, are in a way beside the point, which is at the same time precisely their point, and why we like them. Insofar as we try to identify ourselves as identical to our bodies, and insofar as our cultural narratives about the power and autonomy of the body figure that body as phallic, we will probably continue to see ourselves—paradoxically even at those private moments when we think we are most alone with ourselves—as entwined with and as various others in fantasmatic conjugations from which we at the same time publicly defend ourselves and them.

That desire is fundamentally labile, imaginative, and insatiable strikes many as the most radical and liberating insight psychoanalysis had to offer. That, on the other hand, psychoanalytic theory has betrayed or shied away from that insight as often as it has championed it has disappointed and angered at least as many. Queer theory has responded with particular poignancy to that betrayal, especially when it manifests itself as heterosexism. My wish to get behind or around or beyond the whole question of gender—to have done with it, or at least for a while—grows out of the sense that to continue to focus on it is to promulgate its factitious appeal. It also grows out of the sense that gender theory, which is presumably about the social lives of sexed bodies, has little to say about the strange experience of having a body, while psychoanalysis, which is presumably about the desiring subject, can't distinguish between the wish to re-enter the womb and the desire for sex. A Freudian might interpret the wish to be a "human fucking penis" as the desire to re-enter the mother, any mother; I once consulted a family therapist who thought that, for a mother, I had an unhealthy desire to be "ambiguous." But the philosophical bodybuilder might rather interpret this wish as the desire to abolish any separation between mind and body, wearer and wear-ee, and become one with the tightest fitting bodysuit imaginable, a suit made of veins and translucent skin that looks like the inside worn on the outside.

The bodybuilder's will-to-monism strives to annihilate the dualism of the Cartesian drag she nevertheless enacts. In bodybuilding the material and the ideal are violently at war with each other even as they struggle toward each other. This oscillation between the monistic body-as-aggressor and the dualistic body-as-performer comprises the ritual of bodybuilding as much as the routines of muscle-shredding and muscle-building that are its "objective correlatives." Another way to describe these two bodies might be to borrow the distinction Slavoj Žižek makes in his reading of Hitchcock's film, *The Trouble with Harry*," between what he calls the "natural" body and the "sublime" body.[19] In his analysis of Harry, "the corpse that wouldn't die," Žižek elaborates "the Sadian notion of a radical, absolute crime that liberates Nature's creative force," implying the logical reality of two deaths: "natural death, which is a part of the natural cycle of generation and corruption, of Nature's continual transformation, and absolute death, i.e., the destruction, the eradication of the cycle itself, which then liberates Nature from its own laws and opens the way for the creation of new forms of life ex nihilo" (100–01). Because the victim in "the Sadian fantasy," in *Juliette*, for example,

> is, in a certain sense, indestructible, she can be endlessly tortured and can suffer it, she can endure any torment and still retain her beauty—as though, above and beyond her natural body, a part of the cycle of generation and corruption, and thus above and beyond her natural death, she possessed another body, a body composed of some other substance, one excepted from the vital cycle—a sublime body (101).

Žižek also applies this logic to "various products of 'mass culture,' " Tom and Jerry cartoons, for example, and video games, in which the figure representing the player can overcome obstacles and earn "one or several supplementary lives." "The whole logic of such games is therefore based on the difference between the two deaths: between the death in which I lose one of my lives and the ultimate death in which I lose the game itself" (101).

The bodybuilder in effect comprises as one "subject" this sadomasochistic couple: the natural body and the sublime body. Daily they struggle for dominance. In the gym on a daily basis, rep after rep, set after set, the natural body ritually shreds the sublime body, its sentimentality, its tenderness, its pretense to beauty, its claims to transcendence. Typical of the exhortations (often to be found emblazoned on gym-inspired sportswear) lifters growl or grunt to each other by way of encouragement are: "No mercy!," or "Come on, burn 'em, burn 'em," or just "Get another one! I said, another one!" "No pain, no gain" is certainly the best known such imperative, though I haven't heard anyone say this for about eight years. But lifters lash each other this way in order to add support to the chorus of imprecation and demand already sounding in each one's own head. In competition, however, or while flexing before the mirror, or even when just glimpsing the reflected image of the "that," the sublime body perversely re-emerges, as though "she possessed another body, a body composed of some other substance, one excepted from the vital cycle—a sublime body." I would like to give one further example of this "couple," though here it is divided into two characters rather than unified, namely, Jame Gumb and Hannibal Lecter, the two serial killers (played by Ted Levine and Anthony Hopkins) in Jonathan Demme's film, *The Silence of the Lambs* (1991).

Jame Gumb, aka "Buffalo Bill," is trying to fashion for himself a "natural body" that he mistakenly thinks is sublime. He suffers, as Judith Halberstam has written, from "a kind of literal skin dis-ease."[20] Unlike Dr. Lecter who, by the end of the movie "is dressed to kill," Buffalo Bill "kills to dress": he captures big women, starves them to loosen their skin, kills them, flays them, and makes piecework of their skin, sewing pieces of skin together to fashion what Halberstam calls "his beautiful gender suit" (48). His pathology, as Lecter explains, is that he "hates his own identity" and is thus obsessed with "transformation." Like Halberstam, I "agree with Hannibal Lecter's pronouncement that Buffalo Bill is not reducible to 'homosexual,' or 'transsexual.' He is indeed a man at odds with gender identity or sexual identity and his self-presentation is a confused mosaic of signifiers.... He is a man imitating gender, exaggerating gender and finally attempting to shed his gender in favor of a new skin. Buffalo Bill is prey to the most virulent conditioning heterosexist culture has to offer. He believes that anatomy is destiny." (41)

Halberstam argues, however, that the corpses Bill uses "have been degendered": they are "postgender, skinned and fleshed...reified, turned at last into a fiction of the body," while in turn "gender is always posthuman, always a sewing job which stitches identity into a body bag" (42, 51). Although this argument tries to rescue the film from the barrage of gender debates it provoked by making an end-run around them, to me it is unsatisfying for two reasons. The first is the specious logic of the gender narrative itself with its "pre" and its "post." The second is that, if one did apply this psychoanalytic paradigm to Buffalo Bill, one would have to characterize him as "pre-" gender and (or) "pre-" human. When agent Clarice Starling (played by Jodie Foster) asks Dr. Lecter whether Buffalo Bill is gay, Lecter answers (cuttingly) no, that "his pathology is a thousand times more savage." Bill's pathology, in other words, represents a stage of development more primitive or primordial than homosexuality would connote. Bill "hates his identity" and therefore has not yet even made it to gender. He is too busy trying just to become a person in a body, to fashion an identity, an equivalence, between his sense of his inside and his sense of his outside, whatever that might mean.

The irony is that, although the mystique of the death's head moths he uses to link himself symbolically to his victims would seem to represent the gothic sublimity of his mania and the exaltation of his metamorphosis, the moths signify more precisely the lowly niche he occupies as a lifeform in the psychological ecosystem. At the end of the harrowing scene in which Starling shoots Bill to death, he lies on his back oozing thick dark blood, extremities in spasm, with even his goggles twitching, resembling less a dying man than an insect. Buffalo Bill does not possess a "sublime body"; he wants to get into the cycle of generation and corruption, not to eradicate it. He must attain a "natural" body "first" though because, paradoxically, it is only from the perspective of the natural that one can glimpse the sublime. What is the sublime if not mortality's intoxication with the smell of its own corruption? Bill, a grown man, is so far from his goal that, from where he stands, entry into the cycle of generation and corruption seems as distant as the gates of heaven. The problem is that to get into the cycle one must be able to simulate the natural, and for this one needs to be wearing skin, to be dressed in/as a body.

Hannibal "The Cannibal" Lecter, on the other hand, represents the sublime body precisely because he at the same time completely embodies the "natural." He is appetite personified, appetite unfettered by morals (though not by manners) yet mastered and choreographed by an intellect so keen that it too functions as a kind of appetite. There is yet another way in which Lecter represents the natural which elsewhere I have elaborated in more detail in order, as I do here, to critique psychoanalytic theory's equation, on the one hand, of the pre-oedipal, the oral, the pre-symbolic, and the perverse, with the maternal and, on the other hand, of the oedipal, the phallic, the symbolic and the "mature," with the paternal (as if mothers are babbling idiots).[21] Lecter functions in the movie not only as the embodiment of amoral, aestheticized, oral pleasure, but also as the "good father" who gives fledgling agent Starling "a chance for what [she] love[s] most…advancement" in her chosen profession, by teaching her how to read the law of desire.

Starling ignores the warning of Jack Crawford, Chief of Behavioral Sciences, who sends her to interview the Cannibal, that under no circumstances should she allow Lecter "inside her head" by giving him personal information. By the end of her first visit to Dr. Lecter, who is incarcerated in the bowels of the Baltimore State Hospital for the Criminally Insane, Starling has agreed to feed him such information in exchange for clues as to the identity and whereabouts of Buffalo Bill. Clarice inevitably agrees to this exchange because, long before she ever saw Dr. Lecter, she had already succumbed to what Luce Irigaray calls "the seduction function of law" by emulating her father the town marshal whom she adored, and enrolling in the FBI academy.[22] Clarice is the phallic daughter of the phallic father.

But because in the film it is Dr. Lecter and not her father who embodies the seduction function of law, and not as primarily a social role but rather as a discerning appetite for organ meats combined with an epistemophilic intelligence, I have dubbed Lecter the "Oral Father" to counterbalance the image of the "Phallic Mother" who thus far has ruled alone in the nether world of perverse sexual fantasy. As the archetypal object of desire and every psyche's supposed "wet dream," the Phallic Mother has symbolized for psychoanalysis the sole stereotype of infantile desire and the "real" referent of every adult's regressive impulse. The oral father rectifies this situation. Hannibal Lecter is a caricature of phallocracy as baroquely and clandestinely primitive, a voracious, only intermittently muzzled mouth, as much pre-oedipal as oedipal.[23] Or, rather Lecter demonstrates the simultaneity, in a highly evolved, specialized, cultivated, refined "adult," of the absolutely pre-oedipal with the absolutely oedipal. Lecter is no doubt an avatar of Chronos who, after all, did beget the human race by eating his children.

Furthermore, Dr. Lecter is *magister ludi*, master of the cycle of generation and corruption, which he plays as a kind of game. Just by talking to him, Lecter compels "Multiple Miggs," the prisoner in the next cell who offends Lecter when he spatters Starling with semen, to swallow his own tongue and die. It is Lecter who choreographs the game of exchange with Clarice, deciding when each exchange begins and ends, what she will give, what he will take. In effect he confers extra lives on her each time she meets the challenge he sets her, when he could clearly take her life at any time.

He reasserts his presence in her mind, and his power over her life, when he phones her just after the ceremony certifying her as FBI and just after Crawford flatters her with the words, "Your father would've been proud." Lecter can see right through Clarice to her "inner child," he can smell her pubescent sexuality, and he can respect her adult ambition without needing to be told about these states although hearing about them from her lips is a keen pleasure that makes his eyes roll back in his head with delight. Digestion is his private mystery—for which he makes no apologies, no accommodations.

If sublimity be the effect of this essentially interior material mystery, the mystery of the material, it is a spectacle that cannot be witnessed but only inferred. We (in academe) tend to speak confidently of the material as if we knew what that meant, whereas we seem equally confident that we do not know or do not believe in anything other than the material. And yet we speak (and write) all the time about meaning, and "cultural construction," as if these were material in the same way as bodies—or as if bodies were semiotic in the same way as they. If either of these is the case, then, I would argue, we are engaged implicitly in a mystical enterprise, materialist ideologies, ethics, and politics notwithstanding, traveling so comfortably we barely know we are moving, by way of intellectual "sublimation" from the material to the ethereal. It is our skin that represents both the limits of our body and of our understanding: Is what we know inside or outside us? Is the "soul," is the "body," inside our outside? Where does the person end and the "world" begin? If we cannot answer these questions, how can we really know our "pre" from our "post"? I ask these old questions anew, in part, as Judith Butler has suggested in a different but related context, to help "promote an alternative *Imaginary* to a hegemonic Imaginary," although I am not certain how there could be "an" imaginary, let alone "an alternative" one.[24] Bodybuilding to my mind is one practice, at least, that makes it possible to disavow, for at least a couple of hours a day, any rigid demarcation between the "hegemonic" and the "alternative," or for that matter between the "imaginary" and the "symbolic," the "imaginary" and the "real," the "natural" and the "constructed," the mature and the yet-to-be-born, the sexual and the not. For now, I don't know of any other way to wear my body.

NOTES

1. Edmund Burke, *A Philosophical Inquiry into the Origin of Our Ideas of the Sublime and Beautiful*, excerpted in *Critical Theory Since Plato*, ed. Hazard Adams (New York: Harcourt Brace Jovanovich, 1971), 310.
2. Pantera, *Vulgar Display of Power*, Atlantic Recording Corporation, 1992.
3. Critiquing the narrative logic of gender and showing how the "pre" is a retroactive construction from the point of view of the "post" has been central to the work of

Diana Fuss, Judith Butler, and Slavoj Žižek. See Fuss, *Essentially Speaking: Feminism, Nature, and Difference* (New York: Routledge, 1989), and "Freud's Fallen Women: Identification, Desire, and 'A Case of Homosexuality in a Woman,'" in *Yale Journal of Criticism* vol. 6, no.1 (1993); Butler, in *Gender Trouble: Feminism and the Subversion of Identity* (New York: Routledge, 1990); and Žižek, passim.

4. I've spoken and written about this elsewhere. See "From Abject to Object: Women's Bodybuilding" in *Post-Modern Culture* vol. 1, no. 3 (May 1991) and, "Individuality and The Semiotics of Gender: Or, Why I want to See a Woman's Superbowl" in *PHOEBE: An Interdisciplinary Journal of Feminist Scholarship, Theory and Aesthetics* (Spring 1990): 23–37.

5. Georges Bataille, *Death and Sensuality: A Study of Eroticism and the Taboo* (New York: Walker and Company, 1962), 113.

6. The occasional exception has presented itself, such as the (huge) corrections officer who one day turned to me where I rested on the decline sit-up bench and said with real nonchalance, "One of these days I'm gonna knock you on the floor and fuck your brains out." This was just his way of saying hello.

7. He no longer recalls having asked me this question, but it's true nevertheless.

8. For this reason, individuality is not the same thing as identity. This point is clarified in Richard Goldwater's unpublished manuscript, "Toward a Maieutic Psychiatry."

9. See Fuss, *Essentially Speaking*.

10. Wyndham Lewis, *Tarr* (Santa Rosa, CA: Black Sparrow Press, 1990), 22.

11. Hélène Cixous, *The Newly Born Woman* (Minneapolis: University of Minnesota Press, 1986), 63–4.

12. Llana Attie and J. Brooks-Gunn, "Women, Weight, and Stress: Whose Ideal? At What Cost?" in *Wellesley College Realia* vol. 77, no. 6 (May 1988).

13. André Green, "Logic of Lacan's object (a) and Freudian Theory: Consequences and Questions," in *Introduction to Interpreting Lacan*, ed. Joseph H. Smith and William Kerrigan (New Haven, CT: Yale University Press, 1983), 166.

14. Henry James, preface to *Roderick Hudson* in *The Art of the Novel*, ed Richard P. Blackmur (New York: Charles Scribner's Sons, 1934), 5.

15. Robert C. Bak, "The Phallic Woman: The Ubiquitous Fantasy in Perversions" in *The Psychoanalytic Study of the Child* 23 (1968): 15–36.

16. Sigmund Freud, "Fetishism," in *The Standard Edition of the Complete Psychological Works of Sigmund Freud* (London: Hogarth Press, 1953), vol. 21, 147–58.

17. Otto Rank, *The Trauma of Birth*, trans. unnamed (1929, authorized facsimile, Ann Arbor, MI: Xerox University Microfilms, 1976), 20.

18. Sigmund Freud, "From the History of an Infantile Neurosis," in *Standard Edition*, vol. 17, 102.

19. Slavoj Žižek, "Hitchcock," trans. Richard Miller, in *October* 38 (Fall 1986): 99–111.

20. Judith Halberstam, "Skinflick: Posthuman Gender in Jonathan Demme's *The Silence of the Lambs*," in *Camera Obscura* 27 (9 September 1992): 35–52, 38.

21. This "elsewhere" is a paper, "Wearing the Fetish on the Other Foot: Hannibal Lecter as the Oral Father," presented at the Semiotic Society of America Conference in Chicago, 31 October 1992. This paper also forms the basis of work in progress.
22. Luce Irigaray, *Speculum of the Other Woman*, trans. Gillian C. Gill (Ithaca, NY: Cornell University Press, 1985), 38.
23. The movie viewer has the sense, however, that Lecter only permits himself to be muzzled because he is angling to get what he wants in the end; or rather, because we know Lecter has secreted Chilton's sharp ballpoint pen, and we can see that he is, while muzzled, planning revenge upon Chilton which we are confident will succeed, Lecter abnegates any sense that he is trapped or at the mercy of his keepers.
24. Judith Butler, "The Lesbian Phallus and the Morphological Imaginary," *Differences: A Journal of Feminist Cultural Studies: The Phallus Issue* 4 (Spring 1992): 133–171, 164.

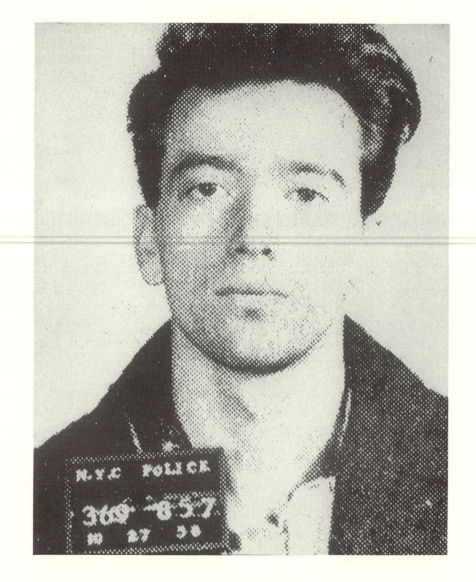

6

Warhol's Clones

Richard Meyer

There is a close relationship between flowers and convicts. The fragility and delicacy of the former are of the same nature as the brutal insensitivity of the latter. My sexual excitement is the oscillation from the one to the other. Should I have to portray a convict—or a criminal—I shall so bedeck him in flowers that, as he disappears beneath them, he will himself become a flower, a gigantic and new one.[1]

PART I: MOST WANTED MEN

In 1964, Andy Warhol was one of five artists invited by Philip Johnson to decorate the facade of the New York Pavilion at the World's Fair. Warhol contributed *Thirteen Most Wanted Men* (figure 1), a silkscreen series of mug shots appropriated from FBI files of the late 1950s. Shortly after the work's installation, Robert Moses, President of the World's Fair, ruled that it could not stand. Less than two weeks before the grand opening of the exposition to the public, Warhol was ordered to remove or replace his mural. In response, he covered over *Thirteen Most Wanted Men* with aluminum housepaint, effectively muting it under a monochrome of silver (figure 2).[2]

The Fair's decision to censor was subsequently attributed to concerns that the mural would offend Italian American visitors to the Fair in that most of the outlaws pictured were, at least according to Philip Johnson, known "mafiosi."[3] An

Figure 1

alternative justification held that Warhol's use of outdated mug shots meant that some of the thirteen felons had already been apprehended, tried, and in a few cases, exonerated of criminal charges. These ex-offenders, so the reasoning went, might now sue the Fair on grounds of libel.[4]

Figure 2

The art historian Benjamin H.D. Buchloh has recently dismissed these defenses as a mere "pretext of legalistic difficulty" and suggested that the Fair's censorship was in fact triggered by the mural's subversive critique of state power.[5] Certainly, *Thirteen Most Wanted Men* tapped into codes of deviance and discipline which the organizers of the World's Fair intended precisely to avoid. According to its publicity literature, the Fair was "dedicated to man's achievements on a shrinking globe in an expanding universe, his inventions, discoveries, art, skills and aspirations,"[6] as well as to providing "wholesome entertainment."[7] In monumentalizing the mug shots of thirteen (male) felons, Warhol willfully transgressed the representational regime of Flushing Meadow, thereby rendering his very contribution to the Fair a form of "outlaw" art.[8] In one sense, however, *Thirteen Most Wanted Men* answered the mandate of the World's Fair even while undercutting it: the mural portrayed individuals at the pinnacle of their chosen careers and showcased a vivid (if entirely deviant) form of American achievement. As Sidra Stich points out, the most wanted men represented "a perverse fulfillment of the American dream"[9] and thus, for Warhol, a perversely appropriate subject matter for a state-sponsored mural at an international exposition.

In endowing the image of the felon with a grandeur he typically reserved for Marlon Brando or Marilyn Monroe, Warhol not only indicted the mission of the World's Fair, he inflected his larger project on the representation of fame. The felons were low-level stars, after all, their images mass-reproduced across the nation, in post offices and police stations rather than films and fan magazines. And, as Warhol himself would observe, the alignment of criminal and movie star was one already current in the larger culture:

> Nowadays if you're a crook you're still considered up there. You can write books, go on TV, give interviews—you're a big celebrity and nobody even looks down on you because you're a crook. You're still really up there. This is because more than anything people just want stars.[10]

The felon's celebrity status is further suggested by the visual similarities which link *Thirteen Most Wanted Men* to the Warhol's portraits of movie stars. The mural's gridded composition of "close-up, deadpan, presentational"[11] portraits strongly recalls such silkscreens as *Marilyn Monroe* of 1962 (figure 3). Beyond their formal affinities, *Marilyn Monroe* and *Thirteen Most Wanted Men* share the use of outdated, even nostalgic, source photographs. The Marilyn series, initiated shortly after the star's suicide in 1962, was based on a movie still (from the film *Niagara*) nearly a decade old.[12] Similarly passé, the mug shots in the *Thirteen Most Wanted Men* feature number boards bearing dates as early as 1942 and criminals whose clothing (sport jackets, crisp shirts, and ties) conforms to a classic fifties image of American masculinity. At an exposition devoted to technological achievement and visionary displays (e.g., General Motors' Futurama exhibit featured "a trip to the moon"[13]), Warhol chose to look backward by recovering decade-old images of male criminality. This retrospective strategy permitted Warhol to pose the following question to his audience: "*If the outlaws pictured here are no longer being pursued by the FBI, by whom are these men most wanted now?*"

Figure 3

One answer, of course, is by Warhol himself. Although the subversive status of the World's Fair mural has been noted in the scholarly literature on Warhol's early work, what has been largely ignored is the strongest aspect of that subversiveness: the circuitry set up between the image of the outlaw and Warhol's outlawed desire for that image...and for these men.[14] To put it another way, *Thirteen Most Wanted Men* crosswires the codes of criminality, looking, and homoerotic desire. The gritty appeal of the mug shots and the pleasures of repetition embedded within the mural's composition (the format of the grid, the deployment of men inside it, the exchange of gazes passing among those men) figure the force of Warhol's homoerotic vision. In addition, the title of the mural—initially known as *Thirteen Most Wanted Men* but often referred to, more simply, as the *Most Wanted Men*[15]—turns on a double entendre: it is not only that these men are wanted by the FBI, but that the very act of "wanting men" constitutes a form of criminality if the wanter is also male, if, say, the wanter is Warhol.

Before delving further into the strategies through which Warhol ties gay desire to criminality in *Thirteen Most Wanted Men*, we might consider the iconography of the mug shot on its own terms. In *The Burden of Representation*, John Tagg describes the visual codes shared by criminal and clinical photography in the late nineteenth century, codes still operative in the mug shots of *Thirteen Most Wanted Men*:

> [T]he body isolated, the narrow space, the subjection to an unreturnable gaze, the scrutiny of gestures, faces and features, the clarity of illumination and sharpness of focus, the names and number boards. These are traces of power, repeated countless times, whenever the photographer prepared an exposure, in police cell, prison, consultation room, asylum.[16]

Warhol's gesture of magnifying miniature mug shots to mural size emphasizes, even spectacularizes, these traces of power. But in elevating a compulsory image of identification to the heroic status of a public mural, Warhol transforms the relation between viewer and depicted outlaw. In their original format (figure 4), the FBI posters situate the viewer in a position of visual and symbolic dominance: we see the criminal's tiny photograph (measuring just 1" x 1 1/2") and read his list of offenses as part of a larger societal effort to identify, apprehend, and discipline him. Warhol's architecturally scaled portraits—each panel measures approximately 4' x 4'—command a quite different kind of visual attention, one which has little to do with identifying criminals or assisting the FBI.

Where the FBI posters would have been displayed in binders or clipboards such that the viewer flipped from one to the next, encountering each criminal individually, the World's Fair mural organizes the mug shots into a complex circuit of visual exchange. *Thirteen Most Wanted Men* constitutes a collective relay of looks which pass not only between the outlaws and the viewer but among the outlaws themselves. Notice that the left-hand image in the FBI poster is a profile

Figure 4

mug shot which, in effect, "looks at" the full-face photograph to its right. *Thirteen Most Wanted Men* revised this format both by separating pendant images of the same criminal, as in the second row of the mural, and reversing the order of profile and frontal mug shots, as in the third. Warhol thus enables the felons to gaze not merely in at themselves (as they do in the original hand-bills) but out at the space beyond the frame and, more importantly, at the faces of one another (figure 5). *Thirteen Most Wanted Men* thus stages the act of male cruising as an image of criminality.

By dispensing with the text of of the FBI posters, Warhol simultaneously abstracts the criminals from the specific history of their crimes and enhances the visual appeal of their mug shots. The men become associated not with particular transgressions (felonious assault and bail-jumping in the case of Louis Joseph Musto) but with the deviant, defiant status of the outlaw as such. Stripped of their names, arrest records, and vital statistics, the most wanted men *become* the very codes of criminal photography: the deadpan gaze, the subjection to profile and frontal poses, the number boards, etc. By "perverting" these codes from their intended function of criminal detection, the mural thwarts the law

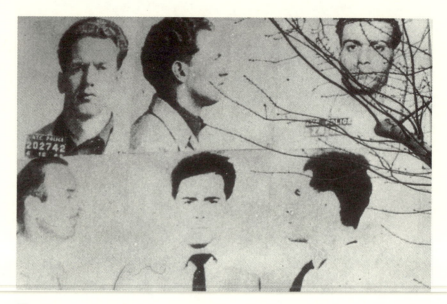

Figure 5

even as it replays its visual conventions. *Thirteen Most Wanted Men* constructs from police photography a counter-model of visual power (and pleasure) in which one kind of outlaw is watched—and wanted—by another. Beyond its direct critique of State power, the mural suggests that societal prohibition imbues gay desire with all the rough-trade allure of a grainy mug shot.

For Warhol, same-sex desire does not simply precede, or react to, the prohibitions of the law (whether compulsory heterosexuality or the criminal code); rather, it is locked in a productive embrace with them. What Judith Butler writes of Foucault's work on sexuality applies equally well to Warhol's *Most Wanted Men*.

> [It] refutes the postulation of a subversive or emancipatory sexuality which could be free of the law…sexuality that emerges within the matrix of power relations is not a simple replication or copy of the law itself, a uniform repetition of a masculinist economy of identity. The productions [of sexuality] swerve from their original purposes and inadvertently mobilize possibilities of "subjects" that do not merely exceed the bounds of cultural intelligibility, but effectively expand the boundaries of what is, in fact, culturally intelligible.[17]

The portraits of *Thirteen Most Wanted Men*, while "culturally intelligible" as criminal mug shots, simultaneously "swerve from their original purposes" to mobilize other interpretive possibilities, including (but not limited to) an out-lawed imagery of same-sex desire and collective male cruising.

Several months after completing *Thirteen Most Wanted Men*, Warhol shot a silent, sixteen-millimeter film entitled *Thirteen Most Beautiful Boys* (figure 6), a film which extends and renders explicit the implied homoeroticism of the World's Fair Mural. The "boys" in the film—Gerard Malanga, Freddie Herko, Dennis Deegan, and Bruce Rudo, among others—have no cause to appear before the camera except as objects of desire, as "beautiful" in Warhol's eyes. Where the mug shots in the *Most Wanted Men* are appropriated from a prior cultural source and diverted from an original use in dominant culture, the footage of the "boys" plainly signifies sex appeal. In short, where *Thirteen Most Wanted Men* encodes same-sex desire in the register of a connotation, *Thirteen Most Beautiful Boys* simply speaks it.

Warhol's encoding of gay content in *Thirteen Most Wanted Men* is evident as well in his decision, when threatened with censorship, to muffle the mural under

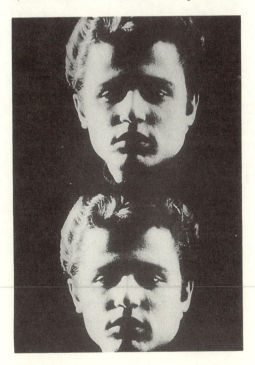

Figure 6

a monochrome of silver paint (figure 2) rather than replace or remove it altogether. As Buchloh puts it, the empty silver field "speaks of having been silenced"; it signifies the compulsory closeting of outlaw(ed) imagery.[18] Indeed, to judge from its subsequent fate, the monochrome mural spoke all too clearly of its own silencing. Several weeks after the work was painted over, Fair organizers further shrouded it in an immense black cloak (figure 7). It was as though the most wanted men still haunted the scene of representation after their evacuation from it, dismaying Fair officials even when muted under a field of minimalist abstraction. The mural, a work explicitly concerned with mechanisms of surveillance and social control, was thus twice covered over, doubly closeted at the 1964 World's Fair.

Figure 7

When Warhol first learned of the Fair's intention to censor his mural, he proposed that twenty-five identical portraits of Fair President Robert Moses (figure 8) be placed over the mug shots of the *Most Wanted Men*, a suggestion that was

Figure 8

predictably, if to my mind regrettably, rejected.[19] Warhol's proposal suggests that the very image of the censor should stand in for that which has been censored by him. Consider what is pointedly sacrificed in the shift from felon to World's Fair official. The markings of discipline and defiance inscribed on the mug shots of the *Most Wanted Men* (figure 9) are replaced by the grinning self-satisfaction of the executive, by the leisure and luxury of an enfranchised man who is not compelled to answer the demand of the camera directly but can instead smile broadly, even buffoonishly, while orienting his gaze elsewhere. Warhol parodies the official power of the Fair President by replicating a vacuous snapshot of him, as though to suggest that while Robert Moses may have the means to censor Warholian desire, he clearly lacks the appeal necessary to serve as its object.

Later in 1964, Warhol would repeat this critique of mainstream masculinity in a portrait, this one commissioned, of yet another company man. Here, Warhol takes a corporate photograph of Watson Powell, the CEO of the American Republic Insurance Company in Des Moines, Iowa, duplicates it thirty-two

Figure 9

times on a rectangular grid, and saturates it in flat tonalities of tan, cream, and beige (figure 10). In addition to the portrait's official title *The American Man—Watson Powell*, Warhol nominated it "Mr. Nobody"[20] thereby making plain his attitude toward corporate masculinity in early 60s America. If the outlaws were among Warhol's most wanted men, then Watson Powell and Robert Moses surely ranked among his least.

Warhol's disavowal of enfranchised masculinity is further dramatized by the comparison of his "organization men" (Powell, Moses) to such contemporaneous portraits of female stars and socialites as *Ethel Scull Thirty-six Times* (figure 11). Where the exact replication of Watson Powell's image and its strict containment within the family of beige banalizes an already vacant portrait of corporate identity, the diversity of color and stance in Scull's portrait emphasizes the range of her theatrical femininity, the ways in which, with just a minimum of props, she can project a seemingly infinite number of affects: high glamour, hilarity, hairdo check. The pleasures of repetition in Scull's portrait

Figure 10

have to do with the way in which recurrence plays off against difference, the way in which each image both mimics and differentiates itself from a chain of adjacent shots, as in a filmic sequence of an object in motion.

For *Ethel Scull Thirty-six Times*, Warhol employed several representational strategies which would reappear in *Thirteen Most Wanted Men* of the following year. In both works, Warhol generates visual power by matching a "low" photographic technique (the photobooth snapshot, the mug shot) with a "higher" genre of painting (the patron portrait, the mural for an international exposition). In addition, each portrait forces the depicted subject out of his or her "appropriate" social space and into venues where they are hilariously unexpected: the socialite in Times Square, the felon at the World's Fair. Finally, both silkscreens employ a grid format which enforces a strict geometry while avoiding any pattern of predictable repetition. Where the visual differences in *Ethel Scull Thirty-six Times* are derived from contrasts of color and pose, those in *Thirteen Most Wanted Men* stem from the multiplicity of subjects, the frequent separation of companion portraits, and the occasional use of a candid photograph in lieu of a mug shot (as in the upper left-hand corner). Warhol further undoes the logic of the mug shot grid by leaving a gap on the mural's lower right corner, as though anticipating future inscriptions onto his list of *Most Wanted Men*.

Visual pleasure in Warhol's silkscreens—and I take *Ethel Scull* and *Most Wanted Men* to be exemplary here—attaches to a model of duplication that

Figure 11

can accommodate difference, whether generated through idiosyncrasies of silkscreen registration, variegations of color, or the unpredictability of compositional format. When such differences are avoided or outright suppressed, as in the portrait of *Watson Powell*, their absence becomes a critique of the depicted subject, implying that his image does not merit the complexities of Warholian repetition.

Warhol most clearly draws out the relation between visual repetition and homoerotic desire in his work on the male movie star. In *Double Elvis* of 1963 (figure 12), for example, Warhol duplicates a publicity still from the 1960 Western *Flaming Star* in which several phallic surrogates (gun, knife, holster, shadow) mark Presley's body. This doubling, beyond simply reinforcing the phallicism of the source image, activates the erotic possibility of man-on-man contact. The pressure points of *Double Elvis*, its moments of maximum charge and ambiguity, are those places at which the two bodies overlap or touch: the cross of upper thighs and the join of outstretched arms. Warhol's alignment of these overlaps gradually permits the left-hand Elvis to pull away from his right-hand partner until the former emerges in a two-fisted gesture of gunslinging. As the left-hand figure becomes a fully engaged outlaw shooting this double-barrelled load, his right-hand companion is consigned to a background station of passivity and pictorial fade-out, to the secondary status of shadow or after-image. What at first seems a precise duplication of Presley's image thus resolves into a relation between slightly but significantly differentiated male bodies, a relation in which several erotic hierarchies are put into play: top and bottom, extension and recession, activity and passivity, dominance and submission.

Figure 12

Of the early pop paintings, Roland Barthes has written, "[l]ook how Warhol proceeds with his repetition…he repeats the image so as to suggest that the object trembles before the lens or the gaze, and if it trembles, one might say, it is because it seeks itself."²¹ When a movie still of Elvis Presley seeks itself through Warholian repetition, it discovers a homoeroticism which its original Hollywood context could not acknowledge. In *Double Elvis*, Warhol recovers the intrinsic queer appeal of a mass-cultural representation which would otherwise disavow the presence of its (admiring) gay male audience.²²

Figure 13

For his first exhibition of the Elvis silkscreens in 1963, Warhol presented the paintings in a "wraparound installation" at the Ferus Gallery in Los Angeles (figure 13). What might it have meant for a queer (or as Warhol would say, a "swish"²³) artist to generate a battalion of Elvis surrogates who fan out across the gallery walls in promiscuous repetition? Where *Double Elvis* activates a fantasy of man-on-man contact, the wraparound installation multiplies the possibilities of homoerotic imitation, figuring not just an Elvis couple but a serial, seemingly unlimited, progression of Presley clones. In considering this proliferation of Elvises, we might consult the following scenario of mass desire from *The Philosophy of Andy Warhol, From A to B and Back Again*:

> So today if you see a person who looks like your teenage fantasy walking down the street, it's probably not your fantasy but someone who had the

same fantasy as you and decided instead of getting it or being it, to look like it, and so he went and bought that look you both like. So forget it.
Just think of all the James Deans and what it means.[24]

One does not possess or become James Dean (or Elvis Presley) but purchases his look and, in doing so, begins to attract other impersonators as well. A loosely organized subculture is generated through the collective fashioning of the self upon an ideal image of (in this case same-sex) desire, through the mirroring of parallel fantasies played out upon the surface of the body. Notice, however, the peculiar syntax of the passage, the way in which the impersonal pronoun quickly slides out of specific reference. By the time we get to that "so forget it," the reader cannot be certain whether "it" refers to the fantasy of James Dean, the James Dean impersonator, the "real" James Dean, or the idea of possessing (or becoming) any one of these. The very difficulty of determining pronominal reference underscores the ambiguity of Warhol's advice to the reader and, more broadly, of his celebrity cloning. Whatever its specific antecedent, "so forget it" would seem to warn against confusing the fantasy on the street with the authentic object of desire, the "real" James Dean. But, in the context of Warhol's larger project, that "so forget it" might also be taken as a directive to abandon the search for an originary fantasy-object and to take pleasure in superficial imitations, obvious mimicries, self-conscious simulations. In the Ferus Gallery installation, as in so much of his work on the movie star, Warhol savored these pleasures to spectacular effect.

PART TWO: PLEASURES OF REPETITION

> [G]ay criticism needs to develop a theory of typing or copying that wipes the tarnish off clones.
> —Wayne Koestenbaum[25]

I have argued above that the pleasures of repetition in *Thirteen Most Wanted Men*, *Double Elvis*, and the Ferus Gallery installation mark out a space of (Warhol's) gay male desire. In the remainder of this paper, I will suggest an affinity between Warholian repetition of the early 1960s and the look and logic of the so-called "clone" of late 1970s gay culture. Within gay vernacular, the term "clone" described, and to some extent still describes, a hyper-masculine, highly codified mode of self-presentation which appropriate the roles (cowboys, cops, construction workers) and attributes (mustaches, muscular bodies, laconic speech) of mythic American masculinity. The notion of the gay "clone" carried with it a derogatory connotation of a masculinity synthesized by non-natural means, as in a laboratory (or a Nautilus club).[26]

The first published use of the term within a gay context has been attributed to a *San Francisco Sentinel* review of an all-night gay disco event, entitled *Stars*, which was held on an outdoor pier in the spring of 1978.[27] The review, written by Edward Guthmann, criticized the men attending *Stars* for "a new kind of mindless, wanton consumerism, the purchase of a mass image" and warned against the moment when "we all turn into Castro Clones…buying the right Levis and tee-shirts, wearing the right bronzer, attending the right disco, sporting the right haircut."[28] The article concluded with an earnest call for gay men to resist the clone lifestyle and recover their "respect for individuality."[29]

Like Warhol fifteen years earlier, the gay clone was attacked for his devotion to consumerism and his frankly imitative style. Where Warhol openly declared his admiration for the machine ("The reason I'm painting this way is that I want to be a machine, and I feel that whatever I do and do machinelike is what I want to do."[30]) the clone fashioned his appearance upon depersonalized, endlessly reproducible images of ideal masculinity. The scandal of both Warhol's work and the clone's style of self-presentation was that each prized the surface of desirable sameness over the depths of humanist subjectivity, each valued "wanton consumerism" above expressive "individuality."

Yet if Warhol's duplications admit nuances of difference while subverting the authority of originary models, so too does the clone revise dominant masculinity even as he seems to embody its very image. Rather than presenting his butch act as an essential identity, the clone acknowledges the preparations of his manly performance, the homosexual labor of selecting the "right bronzer," the "right tee-shirt," and the "right haircut." The gay clone pictured in a 1982 *Drummer* magazine (figure 14), for example, fully expects us to recognize (and admire) the care he has devoted to clipping that mustache, perfecting those pecs, and configuring those denim tears to best effect. Far from merely duplicating the markers of classic masculinity, he re-stages them for gay use and more precisely, for gay sex.

In an essay from 1980 entitled "The Political Vocabulary of Homosexuality," Edmund White argues that

In the past, feminization, at least to a small and symbolic degree, seemed a

Figure 14

necessary initiation into gay life. We all thought we had to be nelly...in order to be truly gay. Today, almost the opposite seems to be true. In any crowd it is the homosexual men who are wearing beards, checked lumber-jack shirts, work boots, t-shirts, and whose bodies are conspicuously built up. Ironically, at a time when many young heterosexual men are exploring their androgyny by...stripping away their masculine stoicism and tough-ness, young gays are busy arraying themselves in these castoffs and becom-ing cowboys, truckers, telephone linemen, football players.[31]

With White, I interpret clone style as a historically specific response to the relent-less feminization of the gay male body prior to the 70s. What I would add to White's account is the way that the clone, for all his seeming simulation of a het-erosexual ideal, insisted on a visible distance and difference from that ideal. The gay clone did not "become" a trucker or telephone lineman but fashions his appearance—his body and attire—upon a fantasy image of these working class bodies. The point of the clone's performance was not to pass as a "real" trucker but to claim for himself this (and other) hotly appealing images of masculinity historically denied to openly gay men.

A 1982 essay in the *Advocate* entitled "Will The Real Clone Please Stand Up" argues for clone style as an avowed masquerade operating along the axes of both sexual orientation and class identity: "We know the lumberjack cautiously eye-ing the construction worker is really an accountant cruising a junior executive and that the cowboy and Marine who saunter down the street hand in hand are respectively computer programmer and college student. We know it's drag."[32] The clone's performance of butch as a kind of self-conscious dress-up, even a form of drag, distinguishes his brand of machismo from its more earnest and tyrannical straight counterpart. We need only to recall that most celebrated example of the clone aesthetic, the Village People (figure 15), to confirm that gay masculinism of the late 70s was frequently in dialogue with its own decon-struction. As Judith Butler has pointed out

> The parodic replication and resignification of heterosexual constructs with-in non-heterosexual frames not only brings into relief the utterly constructed status of the so-called original, but it shows that heterosexu-ality only constitutes itself as the original through a convincing act of repetition. The more that "act" is expropriated, the more the heterosexual claim to originality is exposed as illusory.[33]

Even as the gay clone mimed heterosexual masculinity, he helped to reveal that "so-called original" as "illusory" and contingent, as its own brand of (humor-less) performance.

Figure 15

Like the Village People, Warhol's *Elvis I* (figure 16) demonstrates that the relation between swaggering outlaws and flamboyant divas (between clone and camp styles) is not always an oppositional one but sometimes a subtle shift in costume or context. Warhol applies garish colors to Presley's otherwise manly outfit such that his cowboy shirt becomes a scarlet blouse, his jeans lavender hotpants, his lips lusciously painted pink, his face pancake white. The publicity still's intended identification of Elvis as a gunslinger has been shifted into the royal register of the drag queen. Here, Presley fulfills the promise of his movie's title and indeed emerges as a *Flaming Star.* The aesthetic of Warhol's early pop art, like the culture of the gay clone, could accommodate both masculinism and flamboyance, both pumping and primping.

Figure 16

While the gay clone marked his difference from heterosexual sources through camp and other gender theatrics, his most impressive achievement in terms of an expressly gay identity was the model of sexual adventure he pioneered and perfected. The dream of the clone was that gay sex would be constituted collectively rather than monogamously, serially rather than singularly. For him, erotic exchange entailed not the quest for a primary partner (for a spouse or "significant other") but the sexual traffic of an expansive network of men who signified their availability through a set of easily recognizable codes and costumes (e.g., handkerchiefs stuffed in back pockets and color-keyed to signal favorite sexual practices). With the efficiency of Warhol's factory, the clone streamlined the workings of the sexual marketplace so as to maximize the supply of potential partners and pleasures.

When participating in that marketplace, the clone presented himself as a confident subject who recognized his own desirability because the erotic image he circulated was also the one for which he searched. As Wayne Dynes puts it, "One made oneself over as a clone in order to attract other clones, and success in cruis-

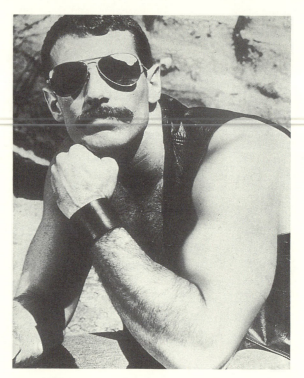

Figure 17

ing meant possessing someone similar to oneself."[34] No longer did gay subculture consider the seduction of straight-identified men (or "trade") as the ultimate sexual triumph.[35] Edmund White wrote in 1980, "Today ...homosexuals have become those very men they once envied and admired from afar."[36] Or, as Warhol might put it, "Just think of all the James Deans [and cops and construction workers and leathermen and daddies] and what it means."

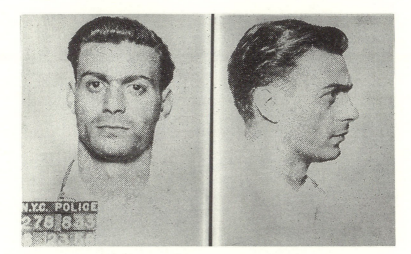

Figure 18

Although the clone successfully created a self-image of gay manliness, he was frequently criticized for his contemptuous attitude toward those gay men who did not (or could not) achieve equivalent desirability. According to Dynes, "in public gathering places, especially bars, gay clones were frequently observed 'giving attitude,' that is, assuming a scornful and haughty demeanor, and offering only laconic and surly replies when addressed."[37] In presenting himself as aware but unwelcoming of the camera's attention, the clone pictured in the 1978 *Son of Drummer* (figure 17), might also be said to be "giving attitude." Such a stance—half defiance, half haughty confidence in one's own desirability—is characteristic not only of the gay clone but of almost all of Warhol's images of desirable men from the early 1960s including, of course, his *Most Wanted Men* of 1964 (figure 18).

Part of the pathos of Warhol's career is that, for all the erotically charged images of men the artist produced, he was rarely able to find his own image appealing or to imagine that others would.[38] In a Duane Michals portrait from 1958 (figure 19), for example, Warhol retreats from representation, covering his face as though unworthy of the camera's attention. It is almost as if desirable masculinity has itself displaced Warhol from the visual field, demanding that he remain off-frame, wanting but not *wanted*. It is on this count that Warhol and the gay clone, for all the pleasures of homoerotic repetition they share, are most distinct from each other: the clone was able, as Warhol was not, to see himself as the object, as the very image of other men's desires.

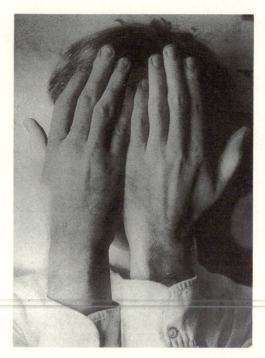

Figure 19

There is, however, at least one image in which Warhol projected himself as desirable and even gave a little attitude. A silkscreen self-portrait dating from the same year as *Thirteen Most Wanted Men* loosely mimics the format of a mug shot (figure 20). In it, Warhol assumes the gaze and bearing of the outlaw: unsmiling and defiant, he lifts his chin and looks down, somewhat sneeringly, at a viewer who must thus look up to him. In the 1964 *Self-Portrait*, the artist duplicates his image as the object of his own desiring gaze. By so doing, Warhol uncharacteristically becomes one of Warhol's clones.

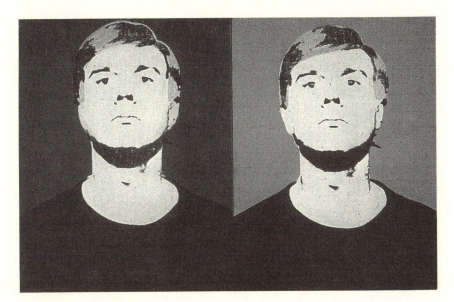

Figure 20

NOTES

A version of this essay was presented to a reading group on gay men and mass culture of which I was a member in 1992–93. But for the interest and response of the other members (Lee Edelman, David Halperin, Philip Brian Harper, Joseph Litvak, D.A. Miller, and Paul Morrison), the paper could not have been completed. I am equally indebted to Whitney Davis and Douglas Melton for support and suggestions regarding earlier drafts of this essay.

1. Jean Genet, *The Thief's Journal*, translated by Bernard Frechtman (New York: Grove Press, 1964), 9.
2. The story of Warhol's World's Fair mural and its subsequent censorship are rehearsed in much of the literature on the artist's early work. See, for example, Rainer Crone, *Andy Warhol* (New York: Praeger, 1970), 30; Benjamin H.D. Buchloh, "Andy Warhol's One-Dimensional Art: 1955-1966" in *Andy Warhol: A Retrospective* (New York: Museum of Modern Art, 1989), 54; Sidra Stich, "The American Dream/The American Dilemma" in *Made in U.S.A.: An Americanization in Modern Art, The 50s & 60s* (Berkeley: University Art Museum, 1987), 176–77; David Bourdon, *Warhol* (New York: Harry Abrams, 1989), 181–82; Victor Bockris, Warhol (London: Frederick Muller, 1989, 197–98.
3. Cited in Rainer Crone, *Andy Warhol* (New York: Praeger, 1970), 30.
4. Crone, 30. See also Patrick Smith (interview with Gerard Malanga) *Andy Warhol's Art and Films* (Ann Arbor, Michigan: U.M.I. Research Press, 1986), 399.
5. Benjamin H.D. Buchloh, "Andy Warhol's One-Dimensional Art: 1955–1966" in

Andy Warhol: A Retrospective (New York: Museum of Modern Art, 1989), 54.

6. New York World's Fair 1964–1965, 1; 15 (January 1916); 2; cited in Robert Miller, "Something for Everyone: Robert Moses and the World's Fair," in *Remembering the Future: The New York World's Fair from 1939 to 1964* (New York: Queens Museum, 1989), 57.

7. Miller, 57.

8. Warhol's mural was not the only criticism of the politics of the World's Fair in 1964. Several antiwar and antidiscrimination groups staged demonstrations at the exposition. "On opening day, three hundred civil rights demonstrators were arrested for protesting the racist nature of the fair's employment policy, which excluded minorities from all positions of power; [in addition] a group called Women's Strike for Peace, chanting 'No More Hiroshimas,' called for the immediate end to America's involvement in Vietnam." Elizabeth Bigham and Andrew Perchuk, "American Identity/American Art" in *Constructing American Identity* (New York: Whitney Museum of American Art, 1991), 16. For more on political protests at the Fair, see Morris Dickstein, "From the Thirties to the Sixties: The New York World's Fair in its Own Time" in *Remembering the Future: The New York World's Fair From 1939 to 1964* (New York: Rizzoli, 1989), 32–35.

9. Sidra Stich, "The American Dream/The American Dilemma," in *Made in U.S.A. An Americanization in Modern Art*, The 50s & 60s (Berkeley: University Art Museum, 1987), 177.

10. Andy Warhol, The Philosophy of Andy Warhol *From A to B and Back Again* (New York: Harcourt Brace Jovanovich, 1975), 85.

11. Stich, 177. To my knowledge, Stich was the first critic to link Warhol's *Thirteen Most Wanted Men* to his portraits of movie stars.

12. Thomas Crow convincingly argues that Warhol's choice of an early 1950s photograph of Monroe "measured a distance between her life and her symbolic function while avoiding the signs of aging and mental collapse." Thomas Crow, "Saturday Disasters: Trace and Reference in Early Warhol" in *Reconstructing Modernism: Art in New York, Paris, Montreal 1945–1964*, ed. Serge Guilbaut (Cambridge and London: MIT Press, 1990), 315.

    The present essay is deeply indebted to Crow's work on early Warhol and especially to the subtle connections he draws between Warhol's portraits of movie stars and his death and disaster series. Crow's discussion of the early silkscreens as "a kind of peinture noire in the sense that we apply the term to the film noir genre of the forties and early fifties—a stark, disabused, pessimistic vision of American life, produced from the knowing rearrangement of pulp materials by an artist who did not opt for the easier paths of irony or condescension" is particularly germane to *Thirteen Most Wanted Men*. See Crow in Guilbaut, 311–331, esp. 324.

13. On futurism at the 1964 World's Fair, see Rosemaire Haag Bletter, "The 'Laissez Fair,' Good Taste, and Money Trees: Architecture at the Fair" in *Remembering the Future: The New York World's Fair from 1939–1964* (New York: Rizzoli, 1989): 105–135.

14. Kenneth Silver and Neil Printz are the exceptions here. Printz's discussion of the mural appears in *Andy Warhol: Death and Disasters* (Houston: Houston Fine Arts Press, 1988). Silver's groundbreaking work on Warhol and Jasper Johns includes a brief discussion of *Thirteen Most Wanted Men*. See Silver, "Modes of Disclosure: The Construction of Gay Identity and the Rise of Pop Art" *Hand Painted Pop: American Art in Transition 1955-1962* (Los Angeles: Museum of Contemporary Art, 1992), 178–203.

15. See, for example, David Bourdon, *Warhol* (New York: Harry Abrams, 1989): 181 and Andrew Kagan, "Most Wanted Men: Andy Warhol and the Culture of Punk," *Arts Magazine* 53 (September 1978): 119–122.

16. John Tagg, *The Burden of Representation: Essays on Photographies and Histories* (Amherst: The University of Massachusetts Press, 1988), 85.

17. Judith Butler, *Gender Trouble: Feminism and the Subversion of Identity* (New York: Routledge, 1990), 29.

18. Buchloh, 54.

19. Operating under the belief that his proposal would be implemented, Warhol silkscreened twenty-five portraits of Robert Moses. The works are now in the collection of the Leo Castelli Gallery.

20. See Patrick Smith's interview with Ivan Karp in Smith, *Andy Warhol's Art and Films* (Ann Arbor, MI: UMI Research Press, 1986), 362.

21. Roland Barthes, "That Old Thing Art" in *Post-Pop Art*, ed. Paul Taylor (Cambridge: MIT Press, 1989), 239.

22. I have elsewhere discussed the way in which homosexuality may be seen to govern certain codes of Hollywood representation even as it is explicitly disavowed by those same codes. See Richard Meyer, "Rock Hudson's Body," in *Inside/Out: Lesbian Theories, Gay Theories*, ed. Diana Fuss (New York: Routledge, 1991), 258–288.

23. In *POPism: The Warhol '60s*, Warhol recalls a conversation from around 1961 in which he asked Emile De Antonio why Robert Rauschenberg and Jasper Johns disliked him. De Antonio: "Okay Andy, if you really want to hear it straight, I'll lay it out for you. You're too swish, and that upsets them" to which Andy responds, "I know plenty of painters who are more swish than me." An extended discussion of relative levels of swishness and artistic talent follows (De Antonio to Warhol: "…there are others who are more swish—and less talented [than you]—and still others who are less swish and just as talented, but the major painters try to look straight; you play up the swish—it's like armor with you.") Warhol finally determines that "as for the swish thing, I'd always had a lot of fun with that…I certainly wasn't a butch kind of guy by nature, but I must admit, I went out of my way to play up the other extreme." Andy Warhol and Pat Hackett, *POPism: The Warhol '60s* (New York: Harcourt Brace Jovanovich, 1980), 11–13. Kenneth Silver provides an insightful analysis of this passage in "Modes of Disclosure: The Construction of Gay Identity and the Rise of Pop Art" in Donna DeSalvo and Paul Schimmel eds, *Hand-Painted Pop: American Art in Transition, 1955–1962* (New York: Rizzoli, 1992), 193–197.

On the relation between Warhol's gay identity and his drawings and collages of the 1950s, see Trevor Fairbrother's extraordinary essay, "Tomorrow's Man" in "*Success Is a Job in New York...*" *The Early Art and Business of Andy Warhol* (New York: New York University Press, 1989), 55–74.

24. Andy Warhol *The Philosophy of Andy Warhol: From A to B and Back Again* (New York: Harcourt Brace Jovanovich, 1975), 53.

25. Wayne Koestenbaum, "Wilde's Hard Labor and the Birth of Gay Reading: in *Engendering Men: The Question of Male Feminist Criticism*, ed. Joseph A. Boone and Michael Cadden (New York: Routledge, 1990): 182.

26. Wayne Koestenbaum notes that the term clone "subtly derides a gay male's nonre-productive sexuality: it defines homosexuality as replication of the same." Koestenbaum in Boone and Cadden, 132.

The notion that gay men cannot (or wish not to) reproduce has long been a cornerstone of homophobic discourse in the U.S. Take, for example, the theory of homosexuality which Anita Bryant promoted during her 1977 antigay rights campaign in Dade County, Florida: "As a mother, I know that homosexuals, biologically, cannot reproduce children; therefore they must recruit our children." Cited in Frank Rose, "Trouble in Paradise," *New Times*, 15 April 1977, 48.

27. In "Will the Real Clone Please Stand Up?" (*Advocate*, 18 March 1982: 22). Randy Alfred attributes the first publication of the term "clone" to Edward Guthmann, a reporter for the *San Francisco Sentinel.*

28. Edward Guthmann,"Stars" (*San Francisco Sentinel*, 2 June 1978): 11.

29. Guthmann, 11.

30. "What is Pop Art?," Andy Warhol, interviewed by G.R. Swenson, *Artnews*, (November 1963): 26, 60–61, reprinted in *Pop Art: An International Perspective*, ed. Marco Livingstone (New York: Rizzoli, 1991), 59.

31. Edmund White, "The Political Vocabulary of Homosexuality" in *The State of the Language*, ed. Leonard Michaels and Christopher Ricks (Berkeley: University of California, 1980): 243.

32. Randy Alfred, "Will the Real Clone Please Stand Up" (*Advocate*, 18 March 1982: 22). The top-down aspect of the clone's "drag" in terms of class—the accountant as construction worker, the computer programmer as cowboy—was predicated on the relative wealth—and relative whiteness—of the so-called "gay ghetto" (i.e., the urban neighborhoods where post-Stonewall gay men settled in large numbers and where clone style first emerged). Clone style presumed a certain degree of disposable income and leisure time, the time and money to do the (right) drugs, disco, gym, and so on. The clone's masquerade of blue collar masculinity was recognizable *qua* masquerade largely because it was situated within the bars, streets, alleys, and piers already coded as gay male space.

On the history and demographic patterns of gay clone culture, see Martin P. Levine, "The Life and Death of Gay Clones" in *Gay Culture in America*, ed. Gilbert Herdt (Boston: Beacon Press, 1992), 68–88.

33. Judith Butler, "Imitation and Gender Subordination" in *Inside/Out: Lesbian*

Theories, Gay Theories, ed. Diana Fuss (New York: Routledge, 1991), 23.

34. Wayne Dynes, ed., *The Encyclopedia of Homosexuality* (New York: Garland Publications, 1990), 341.

35. In gay vernacular, "trade" refers to heterosexually-identified men who sometimes engage in sex with other men and who assume the stereotypically "dominant" or "masculine" (French passive, Greek active) positions in such encounters. In pre-Stonewall gay culture, sex with trade was typically more highly valued than sex with other gay-identified men. For a discussion of the gay epigram, "Today's trade is tomorrow's competition," see White, 240.

36. White, 243.

37. Dynes, 341.

38. On Warhol's self-image, see Bradford Collins, "The Metaphysical Nosejob: The Remaking of Warhola, 1960–1968," *Arts Magazine* 62 (February 1988): 47–59.

Frontispiece: Andy Warhol, *Thirteen Most Wanted Men,* 1964 (detail)
Courtesy, The Andy Warhol Foundation for the Visual Arts

Figure 1: Andy Warhol, *Thirteen Most Wanted Men,* 1964
Installed at the New York State Pavilion, New York World's Fair
Silkscreen ink on masonite
Courtesy, The Andy Warhol Foundation for the Visual Arts

Figure 2: Aluminum paint covering *Thirteen Most Wanted Men,*
New York State Pavilion, New York World's Fair, 1964
Courtesy, the Andy Warhol Foundation for the Visual Arts

Figure 3: Andy Warhol, *Marilyn Monroe Twenty Times,* 1962
Silkscreen ink on canvas
Courtesy, The Andy Warhol Foundation for the Visual Arts

Figure 4: FBI "Most Wanted Man" poster
used by Warhol for *Thirteen Most Wanted Men,* 1964
Courtesy, The Andy Warhol Foundation for the Visual Arts

Figure 5: Andy Warhol, *Thirteen Most Wanted Men,* 1964 (detail)
Courtesy, The Andy Warhol Foundation for the Visual Arts

Figure 6: Andy Warhol, Still from *Thirteen Most Beautiful Boys*
(Gerard Malanga), 1964
Courtesy, The Andy Warhol Foundation for the Visual Arts

Figure 7: New York State Pavilion,
New York World's Fair, 1964,
with Andy Warhol's *Thirteen Most Wanted Men*
covered in black cloth
Courtesy, The Andy Warhol Foundation for the Visual Arts

Figure 8: Andy Warhol, *Robert Moses*, 1964
silkscreen on masonite
Courtesy, The Andy Warhol Foundation for the Visual Arts

Figure 9: Andy Warhol, *Thirteen Most Wanted Men*, 1964 (detail)
Courtesy, The Andy Warhol Foundation for the Visual Arts

Figure 10: Andy Warhol, *The American Man—Watson Powell*, 1964
Silkscreen ink on synthetic polymer paint on canvas
Courtesy, The Andy Warhol Foundation for the Visual Arts

Figure 11: *Ethel Scull Thirty-six Times*, 1963
Silkscreen ink on synthetic polymer paint on canvas
Courtesy, The Andy Warhol Foundation for the Visual Arts

Figure 12: *Double Elvis*, 1963
Silkscreen ink on aluminum paint on canvas
Courtesy, The Andy Warhol Foundation for the Visual Arts

Figure 13: Installation, Ferus Gallery, Los Angeles, September 1963
Courtesy, The Andy Warhol Foundation for the Visual Arts

Figure 14: Anonymous photograph, *Drummer* magazine, 1982

Figure 15: Cover *Us* Magazine, 1978 (Village People)

Figure 16: *Elvis I*, 1964
Silkscreen ink on synthetic polymer paint on canvas
Courtesy, The Andy Warhol Foundation for the Visual Arts

Figure 17: Anonymous photograph, *Son of Drummer* magazine, 1978

Figure 18: Andy Warhol, *Thirteen Most Wanted Men*, 1964 (detail)

Figure 19: Duane Michals, *Andy Warhol*, 1958
Courtesy, Sidney Janis gallery, New York

Figure 20: Andy Warhol, *Self-Portrait*, 1964
Silkscreen ink on synthetic polymer paint on canvas
Courtesy, The Andy Warhol Foundation for the Visual Arts

7

The Trouble with "Asians"

....

Richard Fung

WHEN INVITED TO PARTICIPATE
on panels that address issues of sexuality and race, I am very rarely asked to
speak from the position of artist or video producer. Sometimes, but still quite
infrequently, I am situated as the lone gay person among other Asians or people of color. Most often, however, it is as an Asian that I am strategically
included in the lineup of speakers, whether gay or straight, and I am usually
the only Asian in a one-of-each selection of the shifting list of requisite
"minorities." In the United States this also includes African Americans,
Latinos, and sometimes Native Americans; in Canada, where I live, the register is similar, but with the addition of South as well as East or Southeast
Asians. Since the Gulf War, there is an increasing recognition of Arab
Americans and Canadians as part of the inventory of "people of color."

When I find myself in these situations, I feel a burden of representation, not
only from non-Asians who might desire an authentic account of an "other"

experience, but also from Asians in the audience, who demand that I correctly convey whatever their individual experiences and concerns happen to be. Whenever I detect this expectation—and it is often—I feel like an imposter. For one thing, I am fourth generation Trinidadian Chinese and my claim to Asian authenticity is very tenuous: I grew up with carnival, calypso, and Cat Woman,[1] along with the broken Cantonese of my parents—my father being Hakka, my mother having never set foot in China, it was a second language for both of them. In all fairness, however, I am never simply accosted on the street and dragged against my will to represent Asians. So how and why have I come to identify myself, or at least to allow others to situate me, as a gay-Asian man? For even though I grew up with a full awareness that I was Chinese, and one of my earliest memories was of kissing a poster of Ricky Nelson in my sister's closet, it was only in my mid-twenties that I adopted this particular formulation to describe myself.

I learned that I was "gay" before I learned that I was "Asian." I must have been about fifteen at the time. One evening while performing the ritual of bringing the *Evening News* to my father in the upstairs back porch, I spotted a picture of men with placards. They were picketing in front of a statue somewhere in America; some might have been hugging each other. I quickly read the short "gay liberation" item on the staircase and, with heart pounding, delivered the paper to my father. I had seen the word and I knew that it was to me that it referred. "Gay" put a name to my previously nameless transgression. Nameless, or at least named in ways I could never *choose* to describe myself; names of violence, pain, and ridicule. Even now I type the Trinidadian slang word "buller-man"—sodomite—as a sort of challenge to myself; it carries so much shame for me I still cannot say it without blushing.

It took several years and the move to Canada before I actually uttered the word gay in describing myself. As awkward as it often felt at first, that act was both a means to, and a sign of, feeling comfortable with my sexuality. It was the result of a short period of therapy and of joining a gay liberation group—before I had ever slept with another man.

"Asian" involved a slower and quite different process. In Trinidad I was Chinese. Anyone who looked like me was also Chinese. They could be "local born" Chinese, "home" Chinese (born in China) or half-Chinese. But in Trinidad there were no Filipinos, no Koreans, no Vietnamese, and no Japanese—except in the war movies. When I arrived in Toronto, however, Trinidadians who were black or (East) Indian, or even Chinese as well, did not recognize me as their own unless I opened my mouth. At the same time, people on the street or at school, approached me speaking in Cantonese, Korean, and Vietnamese. White Canadians, assuming that I came from Asia, commented on the baffling peculiarity of my accent. They would ask me if I felt more Trinidadian or more Chinese—a question I had never been asked in the West Indies. I felt a rupture develop in my identity between my look and my voice, my "race" and my "culture." I suddenly found myself a walking contradiction, and it was my look (my visibility) which predominated in everyone's perceptions.

Whereas I had to make an effort to be included as West Indian, I found myself easily organized into groups with people whose origins were in Hong Kong, Japan, the Philippines, or Korea. These groupings seldom included people from India, Pakistan, or Bangladesh, with whom I share a significant cultural and political affinity, both because almost half of Trinidad's population is of South Asian origin, and because of the common reference point offered by British colonial culture. I also found that in Toronto my lack of facility in Cantonese put my Chinese cultural credentials in jeopardy, whereas in Trinidad most Chinese people communicate in English. What I shared with East and Southeast Asians was a similar experience of being "oriental" in white society. The passive construction of my identity as an Asian—through the way others perceive me— became inextricably tied up with an active choice—of political solidarity—to identify as such. It is in this way that I became Asian in Canada after having been Chinese in Trinidad.

When I reflect on my own process of self-naming I realize not only the political significance, but also the constructedness and fragility of "Asian" identity. Asian consciousness only displaces specific national or regional identities and allegiances under the conditions of white racism, either expressed here in the diaspora, or through Western colonialism and imperialism in Asia. The term "Asian" after all corrals together people with heterogeneous, even violently antagonistic, histories.[2] Neither is this the only contradiction the category glosses over. Let me offer an example from my video producing experience.

A couple of years ago I attended a safer sex session of the recently-founded Gay Asian AIDS Project in Toronto, of which I am a member. I went with a friend, an Asian immigrant who had recently found out that he was HIV positive. He was looking for support from people who shared his culture and language. But while the men in the room intellectually recognized that Asians were susceptible to HIV infection, it was clear that having not had any "proof"—either through people they knew, or in any of the representations of PWAs that were in common circulation—they had not taken that fact to heart. The unspoken consensus was that no one in the room could be HIV positive, making it impossible for my friend to find the support he needed.

To address this problem, and the lack of any explicit reference to gay sexuality in audiovisual AIDS material geared toward Asian communities, I decided to produce a videotape about and for gay Asian men living with HIV and AIDS. In doing so, I was impressed with the necessity of actually showing the faces of Asian men whose presence declares "I am gay, I have HIV." I wanted to break that cycle of denial. Yet, precisely because of this criterion of visibility, the men who appear in the tape—men who were willing to go public as people with AIDS or HIV—were relatively secure in terms of economic and immigration status, as well as in their facility with English. They were also engaged in AIDS activism and were therefore hooked into the informational and personal support that accompanies that involvement. The tape does not, therefore, directly express the issues of Asian PWHIVs who are isolated, confused, illegal, closeted, or non-English speaking. All the men in the tape are unquestionably Asian, but that visible "Asianness," while necessary to counteract the invisibility of Asian PWHIVs, also serves to obscure the issues of other Asians. Because the men are Asian PWHIVs they can be seen to speak for all Asian PWHIVs, and their concerns can be read as *the* issues for Asian PWHIVs. In the voice-over introduction to the tape I explicitly indicate these limitations of my selection of interviews. Nevertheless, I do not believe this gesture of signalling absence is sufficiently powerful to disrupt the regime of presence at work in such a piece.

An unspecified Asianness can serve to generalize Asian cultures into an amalgam not unlike the mishmash of Hollywood orientalism. It can also conflate the realities of Asians in the diaspora with those living in Asian countries. In North America, our condition of living as "visible minorities" in a society in which whiteness is normative, means that a sensitivity to racism is always at the forefront in the agenda of politically-aware Asians. Living in Asian countries, however, where gender, class, regional, ethnic, or linguistic differences contribute more directly to one's chances of success and to the regulation of daily life, white racism has little of that urgency. At gatherings of "third world" filmmakers and filmmakers "of color," I have seen the tension level rise as the "continentals" view the "diasporics" as unproductively obsessed with the single issue of racism, and the "diasporics" see the "continentals" as naive and unpoliticized because they collaborate with inappropriate individuals or institutions in their bid to have their work produced and distributed. North Americans of color may use the term "third world" to describe ourselves only in a metaphorical sense; if not, we risk appropriating other people's struggles. For in spite of the barriers of racism and the mere crumbs we might receive, we benefit indirectly from imperialism: there are more films produced by West Indians abroad than are able to be made in the West Indies itself, for example. And of course not all Asian countries are part of the so-called third world.

It is possible to romanticize the East—the third world—only when we are far from it. Many of our ancestors left their homelands to escape political repression, male domination, stifling class structures, as well as poverty. Many of the same reasons (in addition to homophobia and heterosexism) propel people to leave Asia today. It may be true that sexism, homophobia, class exploitation, and political repression are all present in North American society as well. It may also be true that many of these oppressive social forces are maintained in Asian and other third world countries because of the imperialist foreign and economic policies of the United States, and to a lesser extent, Canada. Nevertheless, our experience of racism in North America and the racist devaluation of who we are cannot allow us to fix and romanticize Asia. When third or fourth generation Canadians and Americans of Asian ancestry embrace "Asian" culture, it is often with a self-conscious nostalgia that distorts history, ignores regional differences, romanticizes and essentializes. So I ask myself, what do stories of emperors sharing peaches with their beloved pages really have to do with me, the descendent of peasants? Or what does it mean for me to wear Chinese clothes or take up my Chinese name when I cannot pronounce the tones correctly? There are many problems with the born-again-Asian project.

On the other hand, if I concentrate solely on the appropriateness of my (re)appropriation of things Asian; if I scrutinize the use of Asian motifs in my work but take the rest for granted, am I endorsing the notion of the Western as normal and universal? In denying the "oriental" do I, by default, perpetuate Eurocentrism and white supremacy? There is a thin line between refusing the constriction of the stereotype and denying difference. The liberal declaration that Asians (or other people of color) are just like everyone else is as erroneous as the overtly racist precept that we are *fundamentally* different—for "everyone" is undoubtedly the white subject by another name. Yet if we look at North American history we can detect why some Asians might not want to emphasize their difference from the "mainstream." The internment of Japanese Americans and Canadians during the Second World War was justified by their assumed allegiance to the Japanese government, their untrustworthiness as true Americans and Canadians. Similarly, one of the grounds for excluding the Chinese from immigrating to this continent in the latter half of the last century was the impossibility of their assimilation. Witness a piece of testimony by John W. Dwinelle, "lawyer, and a resident of California since 1849." It was taken in 1884 by Canada's Royal Commission on Chinese Immigration, which led to the institution of a Head Tax on immigrating Chinese:

> I do not consider it desirable to have the Chinese here. They are not capable of assimilating with us. They do not come here with the intention of grow-ing up with the country, but only acquire a certain amount of money and return to their own country. They have no desire to acquire our language, or assimilate with our institutions, as they are incapable of doing so.[3]

During a conversation about the seventeenth-century invention of racial cat-egories as we know them in the West, a friend of mine stated recently, "there is no race beyond racism." An antiracist politic, she suggested, could only develop through the negation of race; to celebrate racial identity entails the perpetua-tion of racism. I disagree. First, I do not experience my Asian identity only as racism; neither is my homosexuality only apparent to me in the face of hetero-sexism. Our identities are sources of pleasure as well as oppression. Second, "pride" in ourselves as Asian, gay or gay-Asian does not preclude a political awareness. It is often, in fact, an important feature of political development.

The problem arises when we take the categories of race or sexuality for grant-ed as real and as natural, and when we slip into smug nationalisms, from which people like me are inevitably excluded. And it is not because my identity is any more "multiple" than that of a straight white man, who is also raced, classed, gendered, and sexually oriented. It is that the burden of "identity" falls on the socially devalued half of the binaries white/colored, male/female, hetero/homo, abled/disabled, and so on. Thus the identity of a middle class, gay, white man is seen as gay, but my race, culture, and sexual orientation are seen to compete with each other. The affirmation of identity through organizing as gay Asians is therefore necessary because that description exists for much of society as an oxymoron, this being particularly so for Asian lesbians. Of course, the notion of the binary is only a crude model for conceptualizing the mess of social rela-tions, and the reality of anyone's life is far more complicated and fluid. It is this space between politically useful categories such as class, race, gender, and sex-uality, and the shifting, contradictory ways in which these social forces are played out in the everyday, that I am interested in exploring in my video work.

I have found that the significance of speaking as a gay-Asian man shifts, depending on whether my audience is primarily defined by the venue as gay, Asian, or neither. Lesbian and gay audiences are far more receptive than those at (non-gay) Asian-oriented events. This is possibly because the lesbian, gay, and bisexual movements need to show that we cover the spectrum of society; straight Asians feel no such pressure to include queers. Audiences primarily defined by the venue as "mainstream" or "general," that is, primarily straight and white—at a large public gallery, for example—seem merely baffled by what I or my tapes have to say. I have referred to the venue as gay, heterosexual, or white, but I am aware that the audience as viewing, listening, or reading subject is always more complex, varied, and nomadic than this may imply. People in a particular setting, no matter how superficially homogeneous, will therefore intersect with my words, my tapes —the text—in a multitude of ways, as they will bring different histories, experiences, political priorities, and tastes to the interaction.

So speaking as gay, as Asian, or as a gay-Asian man is a tricky proposition. For one thing, speaking as any one thing too often implies not being listened to on any other terms. As Gayatri Spivak observes: "The question of 'speaking as' involves a distancing from oneself. The moment I have to think of ways in which I will speak as a woman, what I am doing is trying to generalize myself, make myself a representative, trying to distance myself from some kind of inchoate speaking as such."[4]

In making a videotape or speaking on a panel I cannot escape the burden of representation; it is already inside the accumulated knowledge that allows an audience to make sense of my work or of my words. This burden, which accumulates over the history of representation, cannot be transcended any more than the socially defined categories of race or gender can—they affect our lives whether we recognize them or not. Nevertheless, in foregrounding the burden of representation and in making its dilemmas explicit, we have the opportunity to clear a space where we might tentatively begin to close that distance between our socially mediated lives as "minorities," and the dominant privilege of speaking "as such."

NOTES

Thanks, as always, to Tim McCaskell for words and wisdom.

1. Almost all television programming in Trinidad was and still is American. See Richard Fung, "Breaking the Network: Grassroots Images Transform Trinidadian TV," *Fuse,* vol 13, no. 5, (June-July, 1990): 12–15.
2. I explore this question more fully in "Seeing Yellow: Asian Identities in Film and Video," in *The State of Asian America,* ed. Karin Aguilar-San Juan, (Boston: South End Press, forthcoming).
3. "Report of the Royal Commission on Chinese Immigration," reprint (New York: Arno Press, 1978), 355.
4. Gayatri Chakravorty Spivak, *The Post-Colonial Critic: Interviews, Strategies, Dialogues,* ed. Sarah Harasym (New York and London: Routledge, 1990), 60.

8

Inside Henry James

Toward A Lexicon for
The Art of the Novel

....

Eve Kosofsky Sedgwick

ANY READER INTERESTED IN
Henry James's bowels is, as it turns out, in fine company. "I blush to say,"
William James writes to Henry in 1869, "that detailed bulletins of your bowels...are of the most enthralling interest to me."[1] Maybe it seems—to some—
an odd site for such captivation, but I nonetheless want to argue that to
attend passionately or well to much of James's strongest writing is necessarily,
as it were already, to be in thrall to what had long been his painful, fussy,
immensely productive focus on the sensations, actions, and paralyses, accu-
mulations and probings and expulsions of his own lower digestive tract. The
recent publication of the two brothers' early correspondence, including pages
upon pages about Henry's constipation ("what you term so happily my moving intestinal drama" [C 138]), begins to offer an objective correlative—startling in its detail and intimacy, if not in its substance—for what had before
been inferential readings of the centrality of an anal preoccupation in James's

sense of his body, his production, and his pleasure.[2]

Even from these early letters, it is evident that there is no such thing as the *simple* fact of James's constipation: it informs not only his eating, exercise, and medical attendance but also his travel destinations (during a part of his life defined by travel), his reading, his family relations, and the composition and circulation of his writing. The need to discuss his condition with the brother at home, for instance, mobilizes a drama of secret complicity (William: "It makes me sick to think of your life being blighted by this hideous affliction. I will say nothing to the family about it, as they can do you no good, and it will only give them pain" [C113] that both mimics Henry's internal blockage and seemingly invokes the atmosphere of a sexual secret. William advises Henry, for instance:

> A good plan is for you to write such on separate slips of paper marked private, so that I may then give freely the rest of the letter to Alice to carry about & re-read…. If you put it in the midst of other matter it prevents the whole letter from circulation. *Sur ce, Dieu vous garde.* (C84)

The organizing question in the brothers' long consultation is: what available technology (chemical, electrical, thermal, hydraulic, manual) can best be mobilized to reach into and disimpact Henry's bowel? William advises:

> Inject…as large & hot an enema as you can bear (not get it, *more tuo*, scalding) of soap suds & oil….—Electricity sometimes has a wonderful effect, applied not in the piddling way you recollect last winter but by a strong galvanic current from the spine to the abdominal muscles, or if the rectum be paralysed one pole put inside the rectum. If I were you I wd. resort to it. (C 113)

And from Henry:

> The diet here is good—both simple & palatable. But the only treatment for my complaint is the sitzbath. I was disappointed not to find here some such mechanism (i.e. that injection-douche) as you found at Divonnee. (C63)

> I may actually say that I can't get a passage. My "little squirt" has ceased to have more than a nominal use. The water either remains altogether or comes out as innocent as it entered. For the past ten days I have become quite demoralized & have been frantically dosing myself with pills. But they too are almost useless & I may take a dozen & hardly hear of them…. Somehow or other I must take the thing in hand. (C105)

What I have called the "crisis" was brought on by taking 2 so-called "anti-bilious" pills, recommended me at the English druggist's. They failed to relieve me & completely disagreed with me—bringing on a species of abortive diarrhoea. That is I felt the most reiterated & most violent inclination to stool, without being able to effect anything save the passage of a little blood.... Of course I sent for the...Irish physician.... [H]e made me take an injection, of some unknown elements, which completely failed to move me. I repeated it largely—wholly in vain. He left me late in the evening, apparently quite in despair.... Several days have now passed. I have seen the doctor repeatedly, as he seems inclined (to what extent as a friend & to what as a doctor & [c] I ignore) to keep me in hand.... He examined [my bowels] (as far as he could) by the insertion of his finger (horrid tale!) & says there is no palpable obstruction.... I find it hard to make him (as I should anyone who hadn't observed it) at all understand the stubbornness & extent—the length & breadth & depth, of my trouble. (C108)

From this intense, acutely unhappy relation of a young writer to a part of his body were also to emerge, however, pleasures and riches. In particular, the valences attaching to digestive accumulation and to manual penetration were to undergo a profound change. Let thirty years elapse, and more, in the career of this deeply imagined erotic and writerly thematic. The early letters' accounts give particular point (the point of distance and imaginative transmutation, as much as the point of similarity) to a passage like the 1905 notebook entry, from a visit to California, that I quoted in a footnote to a previous essay on James—a passage that still seems to me the best condensation of the later James's most characteristic and fecund relation to his own anal eroticism.

I sit here after long weeks, at any rate, in front of my arrears, with an inward accumulation of material of which I feel the wealth, and as to which I can only invoke my familiar demon of patience, who always comes, doesn't he?, when I call. He is here with me in front of this cool green Pacific—he sits close and I feel his soft breath, which cools and steadies and inspires, on my cheek. Everything sinks in: nothing is lost; everything abides and fertilizes and renews its golden promise, making me think with closed eyes of deep and grateful longing when, in the full summer days of L[amb] H[ouse], my long dusty adventure over, I shall be able to [plunge] my hand, my arm, *in*, deep and far, up to the shoulder—into the heavy bag of remembrance—of suggestion—of imagination—of art—and fish out every little figure and felicity, every little fact and fancy that can be to my purpose. These things are all packed away, now, thicker than I can penetrate, deeper than I can fathom, and there let them rest for the present, in their

> sacred cool darkness, till I shall let in upon them the mild still light of dear
> old L[amb] H[ouse]—in which they will begin to gleam and glitter and
> take form like the gold and jewels of a mine.[3]

At the time, I quoted this as a description of "fisting-as-écriture." I am sure it is that. But to read it, as I now propose to do, in the context of *The Art of the Novel*, the collected prefaces from the New York Edition of James's novels, brings out two other saliences of this scene of bowel penetration equally strongly—saliences related to each other and, of course, also to the writing process. These involve, first, wealth, and second, parturition. One of the most audible literary intertexts in the passage is surely "Full fathom five thy father lies"—with the emphasis, perhaps, on "five," the five of fingers. The other important intertext seems to be from Book IV of *The Dunciad*, the passage where Annius describes the Greek coins he has swallowed to protect them from robbers, and anticipates their being delivered, in the course of nature, from "the living shrine" of his gut to the man who has bought them from him:

> ...this our paunch before
> Still bears them, faithful; and that thus I eat,
> Is to refund the Medals with the meat.
> To prove me, Goddess! clear of all design,
> Bid me with Pollio sup, as well as dine:
> There all the Learn'd shall at the labour stand,
> And Douglas lend his soft, obstetric hand.[4]

In the context of *The Dunciad*, the obstetric hand feeling for wealth in the rectum seems meant to represent the ultimate in abjection, but under the pressure of James's decades of brooding it has clearly undergone a sea-change to become a virtually absolute symbol of imaginative value.

The obstetric hand, the fisted bowel in James's prefaces materializes as if holographically in the convergence of two incongruent spatialities: the spatiality of inside and outside on (as it were) the one hand, and on the other the spatiality of aspects ("aspects—uncanny as the little term might sound")[5], of presented and averted, of face and back. They go together like recto and rectum.

The condensation of the two spatialities, frontal and interior, adheres insistently to invocations of the medal or medallion, perhaps through an association with *The Dunciad* passage just quoted above. In the Preface to *The Wings of the Dove*, for instance, James suggests that the novel's two plots are the sides of an engraved and fingered coin:

> [C]ould I but make my medal hang free, its obverse and its reverse, its face
> and its back, would beautifully become optional for the spectator. I some-
> how wanted them correspondingly embossed, wanted them inscribed and
> figured with an equal salience; yet it was none the less visibly my "key," as
> I have said, that though my regenerate young New Yorker [Milly], and what
> might depend on her, should form my centre, my circumference was every
> whit as treatable…Preparatively and, as it were, yearningly—given the
> whole ground—one began, in the event, with the outer ring, approaching
> the centre thus by narrowing circumvallations…(40)

To make any sense of how a geography of the concentric, involving a "key" and
the penetration of rings inner and outer, supervenes in this passage on a flat,
two-sided geography of obverse and reverse, virtually requires that obverse and
reverse be read as recto and verso—and that "recto" as the (depthless) frontal
face be understood as opening freely onto "rectum" as the (penetrable) rear.
James writes about *What Maisie Knew* of "that bright hard medal, of so strange
an alloy, one face of which is somebody's right and ease and the other somebody's pain and wrong" (143). If indeed "face" and "back" "beautifully become
optional for the spectator," that is because recto and verso, the straight or "right"
and the "turned" or perverted or "wrong," converge so narrowly onto what is
not a mere punning syllable, but rather an anatomical *double entendre* whose
interest and desirability James (and I can only join him in this) appears by this
time to have experienced as inexhaustible.

Hard to overstate the importance of "right" and some other words (direct,
erect) from the Latin /rect/, in mediating for James between, as it were, recto
and verso of the presented and enjoyed body.

> For the dramatist always, by the very law of his genius, believes not only in
> a possible right issue from the rightly-conceived tight place; he does much
> more than this—he believes, irresistibly, in the necessary, the precious
> "tightness" of the place (whatever the issue) so that the point is not in the
> least what to make of it, but only, very delightfully and very damnably,
> where to put one's hand on it. (311–12)

"A possible right issue from the rightly-conceived tight place": a phrase like this
one can refer to the "straight" (proper or conventional) avenue of issue from
the "straight" place of conception—yet also at the same time to the rectal issue

from the rectal place of conception, "strait" only in the sense of pleasurably "tight." *Whatever* the "issue," "nothing is right save as we rightly imagine it…"

This family of words, insisted on as in these constructions, positively swarm in James's late writing (the novels as well as the prefaces), as if such syllables enjoyed some privileged access to "the raw essence of fantasy":

> This is the charming, the tormenting, the eternal little matter *to be made right*, in all the weaving of silver threads and tapping on golden nails; and I should take perhaps too fantastic a comfort—I mean were not the comforts of the artist just of the raw essence of fantasy—in any glimpse of such achieved rightnesses…(69)

Nor, as we'll see, is the associated invocation of the hand at all less frequent.

Considering that *The Art of the Novel* is taken (when discussed at all) as the purest manifesto for the possibility of organic form and the power of the organizing center of consciousness in fiction, it is striking how much of it constitutes a memorandum of misplaced middles. There is nothing unproblematic about centers or circumferences in any of the prefaces. James speaks of

> a particular vice of the artistic spirit, against which vigilance had been destined from the first to exert itself in vain, and the effect of which was that again and again, perversely, incurably, the center of my structure would insist on placing itself *not*, so to speak, in the middle…. I urge myself to the candid confession that in very few of my productions, to my eye, *has* the organic center succeeded in getting into proper position.
>
> Time after time, then, has the precious waistband or girdle, studded and buckled and placed for brave outward show, practically worked itself, and in spite of desperate remonstrance, or in other words essential counter-plotting, to a point perilously near the knees…. These productions have in fact, if I may be so bold about it, specious and spurious centres altogether, to make up for the failure of the true. (85–6)

"Center" is clearly being used in a multivalent way in passages like these, as much as when it had conjured the impossible orifice by which a flat round medallion opens out into depth. Here it offers a pretext for the comically explicit anthropomorphization of the novel as a body, a body celebrated for its way of being always more than at risk of "perverse" reorganization around a "perilously" displaced and low-down zone. But, confusingly, these spatial metaphors refer to the interrelation among characters' points of view (e.g., as "centers of consciousness"), but also (and quite incommensurably) to the relation between the first half and the latter (or, anthropomorphically, the lower and/or back) half of each novel. As when James in the preface to *The Wings of the Dove* diagnostically probes "the latter half, that is the false and deformed half" of the novel, maintaining his "free hand" for "the preliminary cunning quest for the spot where deformity has begun" (302–3). Incoherent as it is, however, the relation between the halves is one whose very perils can be pleasures, and whose pleasures have the rhythm of climax: James celebrates in *The Tragic Muse*

> a compactness into which the imagination may cut thick, as into the rich density of wedding-cake. The moral of all which indeed, I fear, is, perhaps too trivially, but that the "thick," the false, the dissembling second half of the work before me…presents that effort as at the very last a quite convulsive, yet in its way highly agreeable, spasm. (88)

And over the anthropomorphic mapping of these relations there constantly hovers the even more incommensurable image of the theater. "The first half of a fiction insists ever on figuring to me as the stage or theatre for the second half," James writes, for instance, "and I have in general given so much space to making the theatre propitious that my halves have too often proved strangely unequal" (86). Or, in a very different kind of mapping:

> The novel, as largely practised in English, is the perfect paradise of the loose end. The play consents to the logic of but one way, mathematically right, and with the loose end [a] gross…impertinence on its surface. (114)

To trace the ramifications of these images through the prefaces would involve quoting from (literally) every single page of them. A more efficient approach would be, perhaps, to offer something brief in the way of a lexicon of a few of the main words and semantic clusters through which the fisting image works in these prefaces—since the accumulated and digested redolence of particular signifiers is one of the delights James most boasts of enjoying in "my struggle to keep compression rich, if not, better still, to keep accretions compressed" (232).

But in advance of offering this lexicon, I suppose I should say something about what it is to hear these richly accreted, almost alchemically imbued signifiers in this highly sexualized way—and more generally, about the kinds of resistance that the reading I suggest here may offer to a psychoanalytic interpretive project. In her psychoanalytic essay on James, Kaja Silverman declares herself (for one particular passage in one particular preface) willing to "risk…violating a fundamental tenet of James criticism—the tenet that no matter how luridly suggestive the Master's language, it cannot have a sexual import."[6] I'm certainly with her on that one—except that Silverman's readiness to hear how very openly sexy James's prefaces are is made possible only by her strange insistence that he couldn't have *known* they were. James's eroticized relation to his writings and characters, in her reading, is governed by "unconscious desire rather than an organizing consciousness"; and "armored against unwanted self-knowledge," James is diagnosed by Silverman as having his "defenses" "securely in place against such an unwelcome discovery" (149). I am very eager that James's sexual language be heard, but that it not be heard with this insulting presumption of the hearer's epistemological privilege—a privilege attached, furthermore, to Silverman's uncritical insistence on viewing sexuality exclusively in terms of repression and self-ignorance. When we tune in to James's language on these frequencies, it is not as superior, privileged eavesdroppers on a sexual narrative hidden from himself; rather, it is as an audience offered the privilege of sharing in his exhibitionistic enjoyment and performance of a sexuality organized, as I have argued elsewhere, around shame. Indeed, it is as an audience desired to do so—which is also happily to say, as an audience desired.

The terms that particularly clamor for inclusion in this little lexicon—though there could be many more, and indeed, any reader of even these few brief passages is likely to be able to generate a list of other repeated, magnetic and often enigmatic signifiers that would need to be added—are: FOND/FOUNDATION, ISSUE, ASSIST, FRAGRANT/FLAGRANT, GLOVE or GAGE, HALF, and, as we have already seen, RIGHT and a group of words around /rect/, CENTER/CIRCUMFERENCE, ASPECT, MEDAL. I pick these words out not because they are commonplace "Freudian" signifiers in the conventional phallic mode, a mode that was scarcely James's, but instead because each underwent for him

> that mystic, that "chemical" change…the felt fermentation, ever interesting, but flagrantly so in the example before us, that enables the sense originally communicated to make fresh and possibly quite different terms for the employment there awaiting it. (249)

Each opens onto—as it condenses—a juncture between the erotic fantasy-localization per se, and some aspect of its performative dimension.

FOND, for example, is one of James's most cherished words, especially when used self-descriptively: whether applied to the young author's "first fond good faith of composition" (13), to the older "fond fabulist" (318), or to the "fond…complacency" (21) of a personified fiction. It marks the place of the author's pleasure in dramatizing himself as all but flooded with self-absorbed delusion and embarrassment, but equally with pleasure. When he speaks of himself as having had a "fond idea," you don't know whether you're therefore meant to see it as having been a *bad* idea or whether you're hearing, in James's phrase, the still-current "exhibit" of "an elation possibly presumptuous" (30). But the self-absorbing "fond" marks him, by the same token, as all but flooded with transitive, *cathectic* energy, the energy of interest, fond of…someone—in particular as lovingly and interestedly inclining toward the other, usually younger male figurations in this inter/intrapersonal drama, loving and interested "all sublimely and perhaps a little fatuously" (29). The fatuous "fond" notation of delight and self-delight already notable in the California journal passage is, as you'll hear, warp and woof of the fabric of the prefaces. "Inclined to retrospect, he fondly takes, under this backward view, his whole unfolding, his process of production, for a thrilling tale" (4).

Or, with a different use of emphasis: "Inclined to *retro*spect, he fondly takes, *under* this *backward* view, his whole unfolding, his process of production, for a thrilling tale." That *fond* is also the French world for bottom may explain its affinity with the "retrospect," the "backward view," even with the "thrilling tale." The fondness of the artist, as James paraphrases it in one preface, may lie in his "willingness to pass mainly for an ass" (83).

The association between fondness and the fundamental extends, as well, to James's interest in the FOUNDATION, in the highly (and always anthropomorphically) architectural image with which he describes his ambitions for the structure of his works:

> Amusement deeply abides, I think, in any artistic attempt the basis and groundwork of which are conscious of a particular firmness.…It is the difficulty produced by the loose foundation…that breaks the heart…. [T]he dramatist strong in the sense of his postulate…has verily to build, is committed to architecture, to construction at any cost; to driving in deep his vertical supports and laying across and firmly fixing his horizontal, his resting pieces—at the risk of no matter what vibration from the tap of his master-hammer. This makes the active value of his basis immense, enabling him, with his flanks protected, to advance. (109)

Fond, then, is a node where the theatrics of shame, affection, and display are brought together with a compositional principle and at the same time lodged firmly, at the level of the signifier, in a particular zone of the eroticized body. (See also—if this were a more complete lexicon—James's quasi-architectural, quasi-anthropomorphic use of the terms ARCH, BRACE, PRESSURE, WEIGHT.) Another thing it makes sense to me to speculate about *fond*: that this syllable provides the vibratory bass note in the " 'fun' " that James was so fond of putting in flirtatious scare-quotes. "For the infatuated artist, how many copious springs of our never-to-be-sighted 'fun' " (324)! "It all comes back to that, to my and your 'fun' " (345). *Au fond*.

ISSUE and ASSIST are an important pair of pivot words in the prefaces. Each is significantly charged by allusion to the obstetric scene, as when the injunction " 'Hands off altogether on the nurse's part!' " (though "strictly conceivable") is said to render impossible "any fair and stately...re-issue of anything" (337–8). Each, too—like BROOD and CONCEIVE, which deserve separate lexicon entries but won't get them just here—is also specific to the compositional or dramatic scene. I've remarked on how the re-issue cum revision of the books and the, so to speak, reparenting process of the prefaces seem to come together in the signifier *issue*. The "issue" is not only the edition and the child or other emitted matter but the birth canal, the channel by which the issue issues, the "possible right issue from the rightly-conceived tight place" (311). And as with the "backward view" of the fond "retrospect," as also with the novels' "latter" halves, the temporal can be mapped anthropomorphically as the spatial, the past issue becoming the posterior issue:

> When it shall come to fitting, historically, anything like *all* my many small children of fancy with their pair of progenitors, and all my reproductive unions with their inevitable fruit, I shall seem to offer my backward consciousness in the image of a shell charged and recharged by the Fates with some patent and infallible explosive. (178)

Assist, like *issue*, seems to begin by alluding to the scene of birthing; it links the obstetric hand with the applauding one, the childbed with—not publication—but the theater. In the preface to *The Wings of the Dove*, James seems both to assume the attending position of the novel's master physician Sir Luke Strett, and at the same time through a chain of suggestive semantic choices, to rewrite Milly Theale's fatal illness as a pregnancy at which "one would have quiet honestly to assist": her illness is designated as "the interesting state," with intensities that "quicken" and then "crown"; her part in the matter is "the unsurpassable activity of passionate, of inspired resistance. This last fact was the real issue, for the way grew straight…" (289).

But it is less easy to say which sense of "assist," the obstetric or the theatrical, is operative in this account of the play of point of view in *The American*:

> At the window of Newman's wide, quite sufficiently wide, consciousness we are seated, from that admirable position we "assist." He therefore supremely matters; all the rest matters only as he feels it, treats it, meets it. A beautiful infatuation this, always, I think, the intensity of the creative effort to get into the skin of the creature; the act of personal possession of one being by another as its completest…[S]o much remains true then on behalf of my instinct of multiplying the fine touches by which Newman should live and communicate life…(38)

"Assist" is in scare-quotes here, and it's not easy (it hardly ever is in James) to see why—unless to point to the word's double meaning (obstetric/theatrical); or unless to signal flickeringly, as the scare-quotes around the " 'fun' " do, that a not quite legitimate French pun is slipping about in the background—in this case the association between being seated at the window and, "from that admirable position," *assisting*. *Assister* (attending, as at childbed or theatre) and *s'asseoir* (to sit) aren't actually related, even in French, but they do sound alike via the resonant syllable *ass-*. And firm though it may be with an architectural firmness, the unexpectedly dramatic associations of the seat, in particular of the relished ample seat, the "immense" "basis," "wide, quite sufficiently wide," are well attested in the prefaces. At one of the windows, for instance, at which James has done his writing,

> a "great house"…gloomed, in dusky brick, as the extent of my view, but with a vast convenient neutrality which I found, soon enough, protective and not inquisitive, so that whatever there was of my sedentary life and regular habits took a sort of local wealth of colour from the special greyish-brown tone of the surface always before me. This surface hung there like the most voluminous of curtains—it masked the very stage of the great theatre of the town. To sit for certain hours at one's desk before it was somehow to occupy in the most suitable way in the world the proportionately ample interest of the mightiest of dramas. (212)[7]

One set of associations for all this seated labor has of course to do with the process of digestion and its products; no feasible amount of quotation could offer a sense of how fully these perfume the language of the prefaces.

> [Art] plucks its material…in the garden of life—which material elsewhere grown is stale and uneatable. But it has no sooner done this than it has to take account of a *process*…that of the expression, the literal squeezing-out, of value…This is precisely the infusion that, as I submit, completes the strong mixtures…It's all a sedentary part. (312)

The most available language for digestion is that more or less ostensibly of cooking, each "thinkable…—so far as thinkable at all— in chemical, almost in mystical terms":

> We can surely account for nothing in the novelist's work that has n't passed through the crucible of his imagination, has n't, in that perpetually simmering cauldron his intellectual *pot-au-feu*, been reduced to savoury fusion. We here figure the morsel, of course, not as boiled to nothing, but as exposed, in return for the taste it gives out, to a new and richer saturation. In this state it is in due course picked out and served, and a meagre esteem will await…if it does n't speak most of its late genial medium, the good, the wonderful company it has, as I hint, aesthetically kept. It has entered, in fine, into new relations, it emerges for new ones. Its final savour has been constituted, but its prime identity destroyed…Thus it has become a different and, thanks to a rare alchemy, a better thing. (230)

The products of cooking and of digestion seem interchangeable—and equally irresistible—because each is the result of a process of recirculation described as if it could go on endlessly, only adding to the richness of (what James usually calls) the "residuum," the thing "picked," "plucked" (155) or, as in the California passage and many others, "fished" out. ("The long pole of memory stirs and rummages the bottom, and we fish up such fragments and relics of the submerged life and the extinct consciousness as tempt us to piece them together" [26].) In the artist's intellectual life, James says,

> The "old" matter is there, re-accepted, re-tasted, exquisitely re-assimilated and re-enjoyed…the whole growth of one's "taste," as our fathers used to say: a blessed comprehensive name for many of the things deepest in us. The "taste" of the poet is, at bottom and so far as the poet in him prevails over everything else, his active sense of life: in accordance with which truth to keep one's hand on it is to hold the silver clue to the whole labyrinth of his consciousness. He feels this himself, good man. (339–40)

To trace the career of the word FRAGRANT (possibly including its more explicit, indeed flamingly performative variant FLAGRANT) through the prefaces would be to get at least somewhere with the digestive plot. One culminating usage:

> The further analysis is for that matter almost always the torch of rapture
> and victory, as the artist's firm hand grasps and plays it—I mean, naturally,
> of the smothered rapture and the obscure victory, enjoyed and celebrated
> not in the street but before some innermost shrine; the odds being a hun-
> dred to one, in almost any connexion, that it doesn't arrive by any easy first
> process at the best residuum of truth. That was the charm, sensibly, of the
> picture...; the elements so couldn't but flush, to their very surface, with
> some deeper depth of irony than the mere obvious. It lurked in the crude
> postulate like a buried scent; the more the attention hovered the more
> aware it became of the fragrance. To which I may add that the more I
> scratched the surface and penetrated, the more potent, to the intellectual
> nostril, became this virtue. At last, accordingly, the residuum, as I have
> called it, reached, I was in presence of the red dramatic spark that glowed at
> the core of my vision and that, as I gently blew upon it, burned higher and
> clearer. (142)

I don't want to make *The Art of the Novel* sound too much like *The Silence of
the Lambs*, but James does have a very graphic way of figuring authorial relations in terms of dermal habitation. As we've seen, he considers "the intensity
of the creative effort to get into the skin of the creature" to be "a beautiful infat-
uation," indeed "the act of personal possession of one being by another at its
completest" (38). All the blushing/flushing that marks the skin as the primary
organ for both the generation and the contagion of affect seems linked to a fantasy of the skin's being entered—entered specifically by a hand, a hand that
touches. Some words James favors for this relation are GLOVE, GAGE, French
gageure.

> That was my problem, so to speak, and my *gageure*—to play the small
> handful of values really for all they were worth—and to work my...partic-
> ular degree of pressure on the spring of interest...(331)

Indeed the glove or gage is, for James, the prime image of *engagement*, of interest, motivation, and cathexis *tout simple*—of the writerly "charm that grows in
proportion as the appeal to it tests and stretches and strains it, puts it powerfully to the touch" (111). Even more powerfully, it offers a durable image for the
creation (which is to say: the entering of the skin) of personified characters. As
when James sees "a tall quiet slim studious young man, of admirable type," who

offers habitation to a character whom James had before barely so much as imagined: "Owen Wingrave, nebulous and fluid, may only, *at the touch*, have found *himself* in this gentleman; found, that is, a figure and a habit, a form, a face, a fate" (259–60; first emphasis added).

And, of course, the animation of character by reaching a hand up its backside has a theatre of its own: in this case the puppet theatre.

> No privilege of the teller of tales and the handler of puppets is more delightful, or has more of the suspense and the thrill of a game of difficulty breathlessly played, than just this business of looking for the unseen and the occult, in a scheme half-grasped, by the light or, so to speak, by the clinging scent, of the gage already in hand. (311)

The scent that clings to glove, to hand, to puppet may not seem particularly inexplicable by this time. It is the smell of shit even as it is the smell of shame. It is the smell of a cherished identity performed through a process of turning-inside-out.[8]

Clearly, there are more lexicon entries that could be shown to work in comparable ways in the prefaces; I'd mention only BRISTLE, INTEREST, USE, BASIS, UNCANNY, TREATMENT, STRAIN, EXPRESS, ELASTIC, the HIGH/FREE HAND, HANDSOME, BEAR (v.), CONCEIVE, TOUCHING (adj.), RICH, SPRING (n. and v.), WASTE/WAIST, POSTULATE, PREPOSTEROUS, TURN (n.), PASSAGE, and FORESHORTEN. The variety of these signifiers answers to, among other things, the range of sexual aims, objects, body parts, and bodily fantasies and pleasures clustering however loosely around the fisting phantasmatic: there are flickers of the phallus, the womb, the prostate, as well as the bowel and anus; flickers between steady and climactic rhythms, between insertive and receptive, between accumulation and release, between the allo- and the autoerotic. I hope it's evident enough that the prefaces do respond to this way of reading, "whenever the mind is, as I have said, accessible—accessible, that is, to the finer appeal of accumulated 'good stuff' and to the interest of taking it in hand at all":

> For myself, I am prompted to note, the "taking" has been to my consciousness, through the whole procession of this re-issue, the least part of the affair: under the first touch of the spring my hands were to feel themselves full; so much more did it become a question, on the part of the accumulated good stuff, of seeming insistently to give and give. (341)[9]

> [T]he simplest truth about a human entity, a situation, a relation...on

behalf of which the claim to charmed attention is made, strains ever, under one's hand, more intensely, *most* intensely, to justify that claim; strains ever, as it were, toward the uttermost end or aim of one's meaning or of its own numerous connexions; struggles at each step, and in defiance of one's raised admonitory finger, fully and completely to express itself (278).

Yet however richly the text responds to it, this cumulative and accumulative, lexicon-driven reading remains a particular, hence a partial *kind* of reading—not so much because it is organized around "sexuality," but because it is organized around the semantic unit. To say that it is tethered to the semantic and thematic is perhaps also to say that it is unsublimatably (however unstably) tethered to the intensively zoned human body. Hardly the worse for that. Yet, obviously enough, the argumentational momentum of the prefaces is impeded as much as facilitated by a reading that indulges or honors James's investment in the absorptive or (as he generally puts it) the "rich" (or strange) signifier. The clumsy, "fond" rhythm of reading enforced by any semantic absorption or adhesion seems necessarily to constitute a theoretical deviance.

NOTES:

1. Ignas K. Skrupskelis and Elizabeth M. Berkeley, eds., *The Correspondence of William James*, vol. 1, *William and Henry: 1861–1884* (Charlottesville: University Press of Virginia, 1992), 73. Further quotations from this volume will be identified as "C."
2. Other essays in which I have broached this material include "Queer Performativity: Henry James's *The Art of the Novel*" (written in tandem with the present essay), in *GLQ*, vol.1, no.1 (Summer 1993); and "Is the Rectum Straight?: Identification and Identity in *The Wings of the Dove*," in my collection *Tendencies* (Durham, N.C.: Duke University Press, 1994).
3. Henry James, *Notebooks of Henry James*, ed. F.O. Matthiessen and Kenneth B. Murdock (New York: Oxford University Press, 1947), 318. Quoted in my *Epistemology of the Closet* (Berkeley: University of California Press, 1990), 208.
4. *The Poems of Alexander Pope*, ed. John Butt (New Haven: Yale University Press, 1963), 787 (Book IV, 11. 387–394).
5. Henry James, *The Art of the Novel*, Foreword by R.W.B. Lewis, Introduction by R.P. Blackmur (Boston: Northeastern University Press, 1984), 110. Further page numbers incorporated in the text refer to this edition.
6. Kaja Silverman, "Too Early/Too Late: Subjectivity and the Primal Scene in Henry

James," *Novel*, vol. 21; nos. 2–3 (Winter/Spring 1988): 147–73, quoted from 165.

7. Or again, on going back to the magazine where an old story had been published:

> I recently had the chance to 'look up' [and note *these* scare-quotes!], for old sake's sake, that momentary seat of the good-humoured satiric muse—the seats of the muses, even when the merest flutter of one of their robes has been involved, losing no scrap of sanctity for me, I profess, by the accident of my having myself had the honour to offer the visitant the chair (214).

8. That it is thus also the smell of excitement can seem to involve grotesquely inappropriate affect—as the passage I've just quoted from continues:

> No dreadful old pursuit of the hidden slave with bloodhounds and the rag of association can ever, for "excitement," I judge, have bettered it at its best.

It is nauseatingly unclear in this sentence whether the " 'excitement' " (note the scare-quotes) attaches to the subject position of the escaping slave or of the enslaving pursuer. The way I'm inclined to read this sentence—though I could be quite wrong—ties it back up with the matter of puppetry: James's ostensible reference, I think, with the flippant phrase "*dreadful old* pursuit of the hidden slave," is not to slavery itself but to the popular forms of theatrical melodrama and audience interpellation based on (for instance) *Uncle Tom's Cabin.* But condensed in the flippancy of this citation are two occasions of shame that were enduring ones for James: first, that he did not enlist to fight in the Civil War, what he describes in another preface as the "deluge of fire and blood and tears" needed to "correct" slavery (215); and second, the unattenuated but often fiercely disavowed dependence of his own, rarefied art on popular melodramatic forms and traditions.

9. I'd call attention, in this connection, to the characteristic ingenuousness of J. Hillis Miller's reading of "the blest good stuff, sitting up, in its myriad forms so touchingly responsive…": "Here," Miller remarks, James "speaks of re-reading as a care for his books almost like combing or grooming a domestic animal or pet." (J. Hillis Miller, *The Ethics of Reading* [New York: Columbia University Press, 1987] 109.) Well…*almost.*

MATT STERLING PRESENTS
A GAY NIGHT
AT **WALT DISNEY** PICTURES

Aladdin

Plus a Live
on stage Pre-Show

Wednesday, December 23rd
7:45 p.m.
El Capitan Theatre
6838 Hollywood Blvd.
Easy Parking Directly Behind Theatre
Tickets at Sporting Club, Prime Cuts, The Abbey
For further information call 213-654-9909
All proceeds donated to PROJECT ANGEL FOOD
Suggested Donation $15

Figure 1: Publicity flyer. Exposing Aladdin to the gay gaze.

9

Rubbing Aladdin's Lamp

....

Joseph A. Boone

GAY MALE VIDEO PORN AND
Walt Disney family entertainment may not seem the most likely or compan-
ionable of subjects, regardless of those of us who spent inordinate childhood
hours humming bars from Disney's *Sleeping Beauty* and fantasizing that we
were Hayley Mills's Boston twin in *The Parent Trap*. But gay sexuality and
Disney sensibility—or, better, gay sensibility and Disney sexuality—came
together in a unique encounter during the 1992 Christmas season, under the
auspices of Matt Sterling Productions. Best known for its extensive video collection of gay male porn, as well as sponsorship of numerous exotic theme parties on the Los Angeles gay club scene, Sterling's company announced it would
be teaming up with Disney on December 23, 1993, for an exclusive "Matt
Sterling Presents a Gay Night at *Aladdin*," Disney's latest in animated family
entertainment; the special screening was a benefit for Project Angel Food, a
Los Angeles-based AIDS organization. That Howard Ashman, the Academy

Award-winning lyricist of the film's songs, had died of complications of AIDS while the movie was in production perhaps helped the Disney corporation legitimize its participation in the event, despite the fact that it meant being verbally linked on the publicity flyer with the king of West Coast gay porn (see figure 1). Yet even the Ashman connection could not entirely naturalize the sheer queerness of the unlikely liaison between "gay" event and "family" spectacle that occurred that evening.

As the seats of Hollywood's El Capitan theater, lavishly restored by Disney, filled to capacity with a virtually all gay male audience, the effects of so many gay gazes turned in unison upon the Disney screen not only gave new meaning to the "G" in G-rated entertainment, but brought into play a homoerotic undercurrent that has always lurked, I want to suggest, in the West's fantasies of an eroticized, decadent Arabic world whose perverse pleasures are matched only by its pansexual acrobatics. As Edward Said observes in *Orientalism*, the Western viewer has tended to idealize the Near East as "a place where one could look for sexual experience unobtainable in Europe" ever since the Napoleonic conquest of Egypt reopened the East to the Occidental imagination two centuries ago (190). Indeed, I will be arguing that the historical possibility of sexual contact among males within Arabic Muslim culture has often covertly underwritten the appeal of "orientalism," or the pursuit of things Eastern, as a Western mode of male perception, appropriation, and control.

As the controversies over the racist implications of several of *Aladdin*'s lyrics have attested, Disney's film is living testimony to the fact that the legacy of "orientalism" is still with us, wielding considerable power in popular culture's political unconscious.[1] While my focus here will be to examine a range of other film texts, most notably Korda's *Thief of Baghdad* (1940) and Pasolini's *Il Fiore delle mille e una notte* (1974), in which projections of homoerotic fantasy and homophobia, the politics of race and colonialism, and the constructions of foreign "otherness" intertwine, I would like to return briefly to that uncanny "Gay Night" at the El Capitan theater. At the level of the legible—which is to say, on the stage and screen beyond the proscenium—what unfolded before the audience's gay gaze was a spectacle of sheer *hetero*sexuality. The evening began with a "Live On-Stage Pre-Show" that featured a cast of male and female performers costumed as favorite Disney animated characters, cheerily dancing and singing to memorable Disney tunes in heterosexually coded pairings: Mickey and Minnie, Sleeping Beauty and Prince Charming, Beauty and the Beast. The Pre-Show was followed by the screening of the film, where the hetero emphasis continued in the story of the love-struck Aladdin's ultimately successful bid to win the Princess Jasmin's hand in marriage. But the camp response of the audience quickly made apparent a gay sensibility *already* incipient in the spectacle before us. This queerness began with the Pre-Show itself, in the audience's shared recognition of the likely *non*-heterosexuality of several of the men performing as straight Prince Charmings on stage, some of whom were singled out by friends in the audience—"Look, its xxx!" Prince Charming did not have to do a turn with Beauty's Beast in order to underline the fact that this spectacle of heterosexuality—whatever the sexual orientation of the cast members—was simply an act, a pose.

Likewise, during the screening of the film, the palpable gayness of the room made all the more overt certain gay inflections that, in a non-gay-dominant viewing context, might have been overlooked (and that the Disney corporation might well disavow). These include, for instance, the intense male bondings between Aladdin and his pet monkey Abu, whose jealousy when displaced by a *girl* in Aladdin's affections is tantamount to lover's pique, and between the villain Jaffar and his pet parrot Iago, a Paul Lynde–like "screaming queen" if ever there were one. (The fact that both of these examples of intense "male" affection occur between man and beast serves to defuse the sexual threat even as, I suspect, it enacts a certain racial anxiety.) But the prime example of the way in which the audience's readiness to interact with the screen helped bring gay subtexts to the surface involved the polymorphously perverse vocal performance of Robin Williams as the camped-up genie of Aladdin's lamp—a genie whose mind-boggling series of transformations, imitations, and comic roles included at least seven turns in female drag (harem girl, stewardess, baton twirler, prostitute, female news commentator, etc.) and one in "fag-drag" as an over-the-top fashion consultant (Aladdin and Abu also do brief turns in female drag). Never before had "family entertainment" suddenly appeared so liable to "alternative" readings, nor animation so full of, as it were, "pornographic" possibility.

I will return to *Aladdin*'s gay inflections at the end of this essay, but now I would like to consider the broader context of orientalist discourse and appropriation of Near Eastern artifacts from which this film emerges. For like Korda's *The Thief of Baghdad* from which Disney's film borrows its characters and plotline, *Aladdin* is itself a rather free appropriation of various episodes culled from the medieval Arabic classic, *Alf laila wa laila* or *Thousand Nights and A Night*. Despite its popular representation as children's fare, this work has served, since its transmission to the West in 1704, as one of the subliminal conduits through which the myth of a homoerotic Near East has entered Western consciousness. The matter-of-fact tolerance of sexual relations between males that punctuates this work occurs, to be sure, within a heterosexual framework, but the presence of same sex relations—however obscured by reticent translators before Sir Richard Burton—has inspired the imaginative *and* actual journeys of a countless number of adept gay or bisexual readers-between-the-lines such as William Beckford, Lord Byron, and Pierre Loti, for whom these tales, like the Arabic Orient itself, has always promised an outlet for sexual energies suppressed within homophobic European culture. I will be focusing at length on one such imaginative "journeyer" to the Near East, Pier Paulo Pasolini, whose filmic adaptation of *Thousand Nights and A Night* strategically plays upon the relation of screen to spectator, of hetero to homo, of West to East, and of ethnicity to erotic identification, in order to restore to these tales the homoerotic frisson that is nearly but not quite erased in big studio adaptations like those of Disney and Korda. Whether or not Pasolini's textual erotics manage to escape the colonizing erotics that typify most Western appropriations of Near Eastern exoticism, however, remains to be seen.

Before I proceed further, two brief caveats are in order. First, in speaking of "homosexual" desire among Arabs and within the cultural milieu that produced the *Nights*, terminology becomes, if not a problem, a crucial reminder that defining and categorizing "the homosexual" as such is very much a Western enterprise. While the presence and practice of male sexual relations may be an appreciable aspect of Muslim culture, the fact that there is no Arabic word equivalent to "homosexuality" (the closest approximation is the classical Arabic *liwāt*, which designates an act of sodomy performed on, or by means of—not "with"—a male youth) points to the differing social and psychological constructions that various cultures lend to sexuality itself.[2] Second, I should note that the very idea that *Thousand Nights and A Night* constitutes a *unified* work is (rather like modern conceptions of "the homosexual") a European construction. Indeed, the scholarly effort to codify a diverse collection of Egyptian, Persian, and Indian folk tales dating from the eleventh to fifteenth centuries forms a striking instance of that process of intellectual and imaginative appropriation of things Eastern that Said calls "orientalism."[3] Despite some critiques of the ways in which Said's work unintentionally participates in the production of the myth of a singular "Orient" all the more easily dominated by Western intellectuals (see Mani and Frankenberg; Bhahba; Sharpe), his groundbreaking study has proved invaluable in helping scholars to uncover the discursive paths whereby the Arabic Orient has come to represent "one [of the West's] deepest and most recurring images of the Other" (1). The threatening excess of this otherness, Said argues, has most often been gendered as "feminine" and hence sexually available, so that it can be penetrated, cataloged, and therefore contained by the "superior" rationality of the Western mind.

Said's metaphors for the West's appropriation of the East, as may be apparent, are implicitly heterosexual. But as a close analysis of the Westerner's experience and representations of the Near East *also* reveal, that which appears alluringly "feminine" and sexually objectified is not necessarily "female." A case in point is the story of Ala al-Din in *Nights* itself: it is unlikely that any of the versions most of us read as children clued us in to the fact that Ala al-Din is a beautiful fourteen-year-old boy, "handsome as a drunken angel" (Matthews and Mardrus 2:137), who is the object of a notorious pederast's extended pursuit, inspired by the way in which Ala al-Din's crystalline thighs, marked by a prized star-like mole on his buttocks, keep peeking out from his robes.

Westerners, too, have been pursuing the Ala al-Dins of the Arabic Orient for countless years, both in reality and in fiction. Representative is the rhapsody expressed by Major Scobie, a self-proclaimed pederast in Lawrence Durrell's *Alexandria Quartet*, to convey his delight in Egypt's sexual bounty: "Looking from east to west over this fertile delta what do I see?…Mile upon mile of angelic little black bottoms!" (Durrell 108). Nothing more brazenly articulates the ambiguous sexual politics underlying colonialist narrative than Scobie's wording: beneath the sexual allure of the colonized Orient's "fertile Delta"— age-old symbol of *female* fecundity—there also lurks a not-too-hidden penchant for the racially marked "bottoms" of *boys*.[4] And I might add that what the Western spectator sees—or wants to imagine he sees—when the possessors of those bottoms turn around is not only *not* female, but, in many instances, hardly "feminine," as the Western obsession with Arabic penis size that runs throughout much orientalist literature reveals. A typical example of this obsession occurs in *L'amour aux colonies* (1893) by "Dr. Jacobus X" (alias Jacob Sutor), which collapses race, genital endowment, and sodomy in its assertion that the Arab "is provided with a genital organ which, for size and length, rivals that of the Negro," and then links this "fact" to his sexual proclivities (298, 300). If, to paraphrase Wordsworth's "Intimations Ode," the son is the father of the man, within the West's homoerotic fantasy of the East the aggressively virile, mythically endowed Sheik is already immanent in the beautiful Arab youth (see figures 2 and 3 for Western artistic representations of Arab

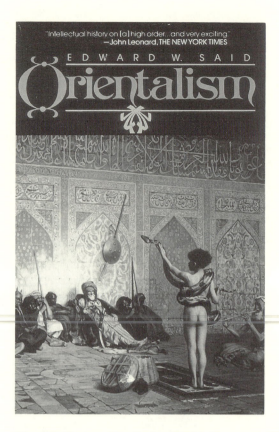

Figure 2: Representing the homoerotic in
Orientalist art: the romantic vision.
Jean-Leon Gerome's "The Snake Charmer,"
as it appears on the cover of *Orientalism*.

male sexuality as alternately pederastic and phallic).[5]

I will be suggesting that Pasolini, in his representations of the male nude in his filmic version of *Thousand Nights and A Night*, appropriates and transforms the fixation with and narrative framing of the "dark other's" phallus that runs throughout orientalist narratives by Western men. However, what for Pasolini serves as a *deliberate*, if highly idiosyncratic and partial, disruption of heterosexist ideology becomes, in many other narratives of the Near East, the site of an involuntary, uncontrollable expression of homosexual possibility that destabilizes the certitude and authority of the subject position occupied by the heterosexual Western spectator. Heterosexual masculinity, after all, is founded on a kind of obsession with and worship of the phallus that, if carried too far,

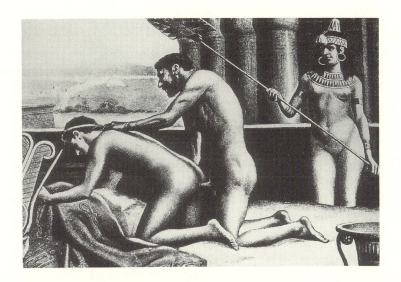

Figure 3: Representing the homoerotic in Orientalist art:
the pornographic vision. A drawing from Friedrick Karl Forberg's
De Figuris Veneris, reprinted in Cecile Beurdeley, *L'Amour Blue: Die
Homosexuelle Liebe in Kunst und Literatur des Abendlandes* (Berlin: Bruno
Gmunder Verlag, 1988), 132.

raises questions about its actual object of desire.

Indeed, several of the most blatantly heterosexual instances of orientalist propaganda betray an undue fascination with the homoerotic, even when it incites their homophobic reactions. From turn-of-the-century travelogues to pseudo-sociological studies of Eastern "sexual habits," texts abound in which the revelation of the homosexual and sodomitical penchant of Arab men forms the prurient "climax" of their narrative trajectories.[6] A relevant example is a strictly B-quality "adult" film from the 1970s that I first spied on the late night cable television circuit, evocatively if predictably titled *Sahara Heat,* a film whose "soft-core" sex scenes are presumably geared for a "straight" audience's viewing pleasure. Its blonde, buxom heroine has gone to an unspecified location in the African Mahgreb with her husband employed in the oil industry; while he drills the dunes for one kind of profit, she undergoes a sexual awakening in the mysterious streets of the Casbah, finding herself irresistibly drawn to the anonymous, dark virility of the male "foreign other." (Indeed, the unrelenting gazes of the Arab men among whom she necessarily moves on the streets so insistently sexualize her body that her sexual transformation is rendered a *fait accompli* well before the fact.) A series of clandestine encounters culminates in an increasingly kinky affair with the owner of an Arab café, which moves through various levels of "perversion" until, during the climactic tryst, the bar owner signals his "native" bar-boy to join the two of them in a *menage à trois*. Significantly, it is only as the bar-boy strips that we get our sole instance of full frontal male nudity in the film, the sight of which is followed by (and intrinsically linked to) another "first": the shock that registers on the woman's face as the two men reach over her body and begin kissing each other with knowing familiarity. This, I took it, was not standard or comfortable fare for the straight male spectator toward which this movie seemed to be pitching its soft-focus, *Penthouse*-like aesthetic. Such an intuition was, upon a second viewing, confirmed when, having taped the film from a pay-per-view station, I fast-forwarded to the climactic threesome. Imagine my consternation to find that both the frontal nudity and the kiss establishing the men's sexual relationship had been edited out of the segment. Now the men could be read as "sharing," in homosocial rather than homosexual fashion, their sexual conquest. For many men, it appears the act of imagining an eroticized Near East, much less viewing it on the screen, is coterminous with unlocking a fantasmatic realm of hitherto taboo desires whose propensity to spread without check threatens to undermine the heterosexual assumptions of Occidental male subjectivity and spectatorship—a threat that, as the editing of *Sahara Heat* evinces, hence stands in need of the constant policing mechanisms that homophobia (now you see it, now you don't) so readily provides.[7]

The Western myth of an eroticized Arabic world that respects no bounds is, as I have already noted, one by-product of the translation and reception of *Thousand Nights and A Night* over the past two hundred years, and I would like now to evaluate what happens to that work's homoerotic elements when its tales are adapted to both popular and avant-garde cinema. Given the appeal that *Nights* (in its expurgated versions) has always had for children, it is not surprising that its fantasy elements have often been mined by filmmakers in their search for family entertainment. I would argue, however, that at least one in this genre—Korda's remake of *The Thief of Baghdad*, aptly subtitled *An Arabian Fantasy in Technicolor*—reveals an unconscious kinship to the homoerotics of orientalism this essay has been tracing.[8] Overtly the story of the adventures of a handsome young prince who has been cheated of his throne, and of Abu, an adolescent street urchin and "thief" of the title who saves the Prince's life and helps him win his Princess, the film is also the story of Abu's adolescent crush on his companion and his despair at being displaced in the Prince's affections by the Princess. (Here, the resemblance to Disney's *Aladdin* is apparent, except that the Aladdin-like character rather than his sidekick monkey plays the role of "unrequited lover.") "You want someone to look after you," Abu says as he kneels abjectly at the Prince's feet in worshipful adoration. Such sentimental love between two males, of course, is an acceptable, even beloved, Hollywood staple, as long as it remains couched in a kind of Huck Finnish or Kiplingesque "innocence." In contrast to this benign topos, however, the actual *filmic image* of man and youth encoded in this "Arabian Fantasy in Technicolor" simultaneously speaks (to) another story, particularly for the gay viewer familiar with the sexual exploits of Western writers (from Gide and Wilde to Orton and Barthes) with adolescent boys.[9]

What *visually* stands out, then, when Ahmed and Abu share the screen is not simply the affection they share, but the fact that a *white Western man* is playing the part of the Prince and a *brown Eastern boy*, as-it-were authentic "other," is playing the part of Abu. The fact that this "other" is the Indian child-star Sabu, playing a Persian lad, only underlines the degree to which one "brown" actor serves as well as another in the racist homogenization of "otherness" pervading the West's mainstream film industry. The overt hierarchies of age and economic status inscribed into the film—man/boy, prince/beggar—are thus underwritten by the racial and geographical hierarchies—white/brown, West/East—that have made possible the colonial trade in boys inspiring many gay Westerners' visits to the Near East. This interpenetration of filmic and cultural texts is only heightened by the fact that the loinclothed Abu is cinematically represented as something akin to pederastic fantasy material: indeed, we watch the actor undergo puberty during the course of the film. Given that this film is family entertainment, one may well ask what it has to offer in the way of the "phallic framing" that I have been arguing is present is so much of this literature. I would suggest, not entirely facetiously, that a candidate exists in the scene in which shipwrecked Abu wakes up alone on the beach of a strange island. Unable to find his Prince, heartbroken Abu finds instead a corked bottle, which he places between his legs and starts rubbing until a towering one hundred foot tall genie—the avatar of Robin Williams in Disney's film—erupts forth, literally rising from between Abu's widely splayed legs as the astonished youth, in a series of intercut shots, leans back on his elbows. The fact that the genie has been dressed to look like an overgrown infant (an apt representation of the polymorphously perverse) whose tantrums Abu can barely control, only confirms my suspicion that what we have here, intended or not, is an image of adolescent

fear and delight over the discovery of masturbation, as well as an image of anar-
chic sexual desires that may travel in *any* direction. It is perhaps, then, inevitable
that the wish Abu asks his phallic genie to grant him is to be reunited with his
beloved Prince.

What happens to the sublimated homoeroticism underlying such a fantasy
when *Thousand Nights and A Night* is adapted *not* by the studio system but by a
highly iconoclastic auteur such as Pasolini who is himself homosexual? How
does the overlap of the visual and textual in his adaptation negotiate the sexual-
racial politics of orientalist fantasies of Near Eastern eroticism? Is the result yet
another, only perhaps more explicit, appropriation of Eastern otherness? On
the surface, the contrast is glaring: Pier Paulo Pasolini's 1974 adaptation of
Thousand Nights and A Night is striking for its attempted fidelity both to the
medieval Arabic text and to the cultural milieu that produced it. This representational "authenticity" is apparent on several fronts. First, Pasolini quite
brilliantly captures within his film's narrative structure the layered effect of the
written text, in which the seemingly endless regress of framed, inset, and inter-
rupted tales, creates, in Pasolini's phrase, the possibility of "limitless narration"
(Greene 189). Second, he deliberately positions his camera as an avowedly neutral recorder of events, rather than as an inquisitive, prying eye that attempts to
impose an interpretation on what it sees. "I have increased the passivity of the
camera," Pasolini explains. "Except for a few panning shots...I let the profilmic
world flow, just as dreams and reality flow" (Pasolini 76). Third, Pasolini
attempts to remain as "authentic" as possible by filming entirely on location in
Third World countries, peopling his frames, as he puts it, with the "dust and
faces of the poor" (76), and relying largely, as in his early sub-proletariat films,
"on popular milieus, nonprofessional actors, and regional dialects" as the back-
drop for his adaptation (Greene 184). Through his trademark techniques of the
single shot, repudiation of the traditional matching shot, and immobile camera, Pasolini thus creates an image of a remote world of medieval popular culture
that simply exists "as given fact," without elucidation, just as the enigmatically
laughing faces of the anonymous peasants that fill the screen remain "just faces,"
without assignable meaning—faces that the spectator must simultaneously
respect for their complete but indecipherable "presence" as well as for their
inevitable "otherness," or, as Nowell-Smith puts it, as images "up there, outside," on the screen (9–11).[10]

The result was what Pasolini called his most "radically ideological" film
(Pasolini 77), his most successful "polemic...against [a] dominant Eurocentric

culture"[11]—a culture the outspoken Marxist director frequently equated with heterosexual, bourgeois capitalism under modernity. Given this equation, one might logically ask where Pasolini's sense of his own sexual marginality fits into this "polemic" against "Eurocentric," heterosexist "culture." How, in other words, does his filmic text capitalize on, create a reverse discourse out of, the homoerotic strands of the written *Thousand Nights and A Night?* First, it is necessary to understand the conflicted nature of Pasolini's attitudes toward his homosexuality and toward the politics of homosexuality in general, as well as the impact of these ambivalences on his encoding of male homoeroticism within his filmic text. Although brazenly uncloseted about his homosexual orientation and his numerous liaisons with Rome's sub-proletariat *ragazzi di vita*, Pasolini also manifested an internalized homophobia[12] that mitigated against his championing of the Italian sexual liberation movement, whose creeds of permissiveness he only saw as another bourgeois symptom of the decline of modern Western culture (and, perversely, as the potential death of homosexuality). Indeed, for Pasolini, the appeal of the erotic universe of the medieval *Nights* lay in its remoteness and feudal class structure, the latter of which paradoxically made possible, in Pasolini's nostalgic fantasy of the past, a "real" sub-proletariat or peasant class capable of enjoying fully, and without (modern bourgeois) guilt, a joyful, exalting, protean Eros (Pasolini 76).[13] Thus, the act of making Near Eastern "homosexuality" part of his polemic against "Eurocentric culture" was for Pasolini less an activist gesture made in the name of contemporary "gay rights" than a strike against the joint institutions of heterosexuality and the nuclear family supporting the middle-class hegemony of modern culture.

Second, it is important to note that as part of his attempt at representational authenticity Pasolini does not simply seize upon and amplify the more explicitly homoerotic moments in the tales, which might have been a possible, indeed tempting, tactic. Rather, he chooses to honor, on the level of plot, the dominant *heterosexuality* of the original: the film is thus framed by the saga of the youth Nur al-Din's quest for his abducted slave-girl Zumurrud,[14] an adventure complemented by three extended inset fables motivated by heterosexual desire. Nonetheless, as even its first audiences and reviewers sometimes uneasily intuited, the film pulsates with a "gay" sensibility that ultimately emanates from Pasolini's manipulation of the cinematic apparatus; his strategy is to inflect the predominantly heterosexual erotics of the film's superstructure with a subtle homotextuality that exists as much within the *mise-en-scène* and between spectator and screen as in the narrative proper. As such, the heterosexual negotiation of the homoerotic characterizing so many Western accounts of Arabic exoticism gives way, in Pasolini's vision of *Nights*, to a homoerotic negotiation of the heterosexual.

These filmic strategies are threefold. The first, and most simple, is the thematic incorporation of two of the more frankly homoerotic tales in the written text into the film's diegesis, both of which are shot with full frontal male nudity. Thus, twelve minutes into the film we are presented with the story of how the Caliph Harun al-Raschid's court poet Sium (the historical Abu Nuwas in the written text) uses lines of verse to entice three handsome youths into his tent to give each other and himself pleasure.[15] The fact that the vehicle of seduction is art, and that the camera's eye enters the poet's tent where the seduction unfolds as if through the parting curtain of a theater, reinforces the spectator's impression that the homosexual poet is an intradiegetic vehicle for inserting the director's homosexual point of view. The second direct transcription of an explicitly gay discourse from the tales into the filmic text—the last of the film's inset narratives—lyrically evokes the tragic love affair between young Prince Yunan and the fifteen-year-old jeweller's son who has been hidden in an underground chamber on the remote island where the shipwrecked Yunan (who has providentially lost all of his clothes!) discovers him. Except for the fact of Yunan's nudity, which is Pasolini's addition, the episode is taken nearly verbatim from the "Tale of the Third Kalandar."[16] Yet, however well both scenes may work as cinematic and erotic moments, their ideological effect is limited by the fact that their homoerotic content is presented at once as 1) structurally *detachable* from the rest of the film and 2) thematically *self-enclosed*. The latter is registered in the remote, enclosed settings in which each occurs—the darkened interior of the tent, the underground chamber.

This equivocal structuring of homosexual behavior as a potentially isolatable anomaly within the film's episodic superstructure is only partially allayed by Pasolini's second mode of destabilizing the overt straightness of the filmic text. This strategy involves capitalizing on the elements of gender disguise and bisexuality in the original, imbuing the film with a playfully protean Eros in which the blurring of the boundaries of gender and/or sexual orientation allows for the momentary emergence of same-sex desire. Two examples clarify this strategic interpolation of homosexuality, under the guise of pansexuality, into the film. First, the frame story of Nur al-Din and Zumurrud ends in a cross-dressing episode where Zumurrud, disguised as a Prince, orders Nur al-Din to drop his trousers and prepare to be sodomized: she quotes Arabic homosexual verse to ease his fears before revealing herself at the last moment to be his long-lost and faithful slave-girl. This momentary illusion of imminent "male-male" sex is ultimately, as in Shakespeare's comedies, at best a playful tease, and at worst—given Nur al-Din's distress—discomfitingly homophobic.[17] A more complex example of Pasolini's attempt to capitalize on the myth of Arabic pansexuality, transpiring about seventeen minutes into the film, involves the inset story of the Caliph Harun al-Raschid and his Queen Zubaydah, each of whom argues that his/her own sex is most beautiful and desirable. The sequence focuses on the King and Queen watching a boy and girl, whom each believes is most beautiful, make love. Fondling each other they voyeuristically look on from a raised balcony that makes their tent uncannily resemble a theater (reminding the extrafilmic audience of its analogous voyeurism). What we have, then, is a scenario in which a male-female couple gets off by putting their "same-sex" object choices into heterosexual play with each other. And because the bisexuality of the episode remains safely encased within a duplication of *heterosexual* couplings—King/Queen, boy/girl—the effect is that the episode's homoeroticism merely ends up "adding spice" to what remains heterosexual love-play. It is thus curious that many film critics who mention the film's encoding of homosexuality point to this scene as its most complete realization (see, for example, Nowell-Smith 18), whereas what we in fact get is a kind of politically suspect androgyny that mitigates against a more radical intervention of homosexuality in critiquing the heterosexism of the dominant culture.[18]

This, however, is not to say that other aspects of the film's homoerotic subtexts are without transgressive effect. For Pasolini's third strategy for disrupting heterosexual norms is at once his most subtle, his most "radically ideological," and yet, as I will ultimately suggest, his most complicit in the colonial ethos that his desire for "authenticity" otherwise counters. Involving neither the overtly homosexual nor the pansexual elements of his narrative, this strategy rests upon his calculated representation of those insistently heterosexual moments of male and female coupling that fill the screen. For in filming these scenes Pasolini repeatedly uses the cinematic apparatus—including scenic composition, camera angles, lighting effects, cutting and cropping—to focus the spectator's gaze *not on the two bodies involved, but specifically on the male body of the couple.* It is the nude male, and even more specifically, through its repeated cinematic framing, the focalized close-up of his penis, that is made symbolically, iconographically, and ideologically resonant in these scenes. Hence Pasolini's comment to those Marxist critics who criticized the film for its apparent social irrelevance: "ideology [is] really there, above [your] heads, in the enormous cock on the screen."[19]

But *whose* ideology? On the one hand, Pasolini's statement underlines the problematics inherent in all masculine subjectivities, gay or straight, constructed under the sign of the phallus in patriarchal culture: cock remains king, representationally speaking—and indeed, in Pasolini's boast, larger than life. On the other hand, the sheer iterativeness of projecting that "enormous cock on the screen," if only for a few seconds at a time, also works importantly to undermine the heterosexism of phallocentric ideology on at least two levels, whether or not Pasolini fully perceived their consequences. First, this focusing on the phallus potentially "undoes" the position of the heterosexually identified male viewer, forcing him to engage in a homoeroticizing aesthetic that, in de-emphasizing the objectification of the female of the couple and in forcing an uneasy *identification with* the homoeroticized male icon, destabilizes the overtly heterosexual trajectory of such scenes—a trajectory in which, according to Freudian logic, the objects of desire and identification are supposed to remain separate and oppositely gendered. Second, these phallic still lifes serve as an "in" for non-straight male viewers, giving us, quite literally, something else, something more interesting, to look at in those heterosexual love stories unfolding on the screen. Within such a liminal gay viewing space—which Earl Jackson, Jr., has called, in terms of Almodovar's cinema, the intersubjective (74–77), and which Diana Fuss has, in the context of fashion advertisements, theorized as the homospectatorial (730–36)—audience and artifact participate in a parlay of identification and desire, of subject and object positions, that prevent Pasolini's visual text from merely repeating, only now from a gay point of view, the oppressive regime of the "male gaze," substituting an objectified male body for the traditionally oppressed female one. For it is crucial to recognize that the naked male bodies upon which Pasolini's camera lingers are not, as Richard Dyer asserts (62), male "pin-ups" in a hyperbolic or homogenized sense of "masculine beauty."[20] Rather, these torsos, of varying shapes and conditions, are constantly presented in various states of repose and openness. Likewise, the frequent close-ups of male genitalia most often depict the penis, represented in various states of arousal and flaccidity, as a vulnerable rather than aggressive extension of the male body. Even the editing of the body shots to focus on the penis, cropping the actor's head or limbs from the frame, works less as an objectifying *blazon* of the male body than as the creation of a contestatory position for the male spectator.

At this point, I would like to summarize some of the methods by which these phallic framings invite and direct the spectator's gaze, deferring for a few moments a consideration of the third-world contexts of these spectacles. First, Pasolini presents the repeated scenario of a passive male body being disrobed by a female agent. In the framing sequence, for instance, Nur al-Din does not seduce Zumurrud but waits, laughing, as she takes charge, first stripping him of his waist-skirt and then unwinding his loin cloth. Such moments, analogous to the Barthesian erotics of the textual striptease, force the spectator to wait and watch to see how long the camera will hold the image before cutting to a less explicit shot; however, against our Hollywood expectation, it rarely does.

Second, often accompanying these scenes of disrobing, Pasolini uses hands as on-screen markers to direct our gaze within the wider frame to the gradually focalized crotch of the male torso; hands extended toward, brushed across, or molded about the penis become a means of creating a "sensationalization," in D.A. Miller's term (146–48), of the *offscreen as well as onscreen body*, thereby implicating the perhaps interested, perhaps uneasy, male spectator even further in the image and "ideology" of "the enormous cock" unfolding above his head "on the screen."

Third, Pasolini strategically uses lighting, shading, and blocking to highlight the male body while blocking out the female participant, even when both sexes occupy equal screen space. One notable example occurs in the inset tale of Aziz and Azizah, in which Aziz is waylaid by a widow who throws him to the floor and deftly hikes his djellaba, his stiffening erection springing to sight and grasped by the hand of the offscreen woman. In the close-up of the prone Aziz, the clearly lit shaft of his penis, extending horizontally across his belly, seems to take up the whole frame. Only a closer look reveals that the woman's genitalia are *also* on screen, in the upper left hand corner, but so shadowed as to seem invisible. Such moments encode, of course, the unequal power dynamic between the sexes in the film and attest to the misogyny that frequently accompanies Pasolini's homoeroticizing aesthetic, wherein the latter gains attention at the expense of the female agent working to make all this male flesh available for our delectation.[21]

This framing of Aziz's body also illustrates a fourth technique in the film which I call the "phallic still life"; here the penis occupies the exact center of the screen and is presented in extreme close-up, forming the momentarily static object around which the entire frame composes itself. Seen on the theater's large screen, in technicolor, the impact is truly startling.[22] Examples of this technique abound, but perhaps the most dramatic occurs when Prince Taji, during the film's fourth inset tale, falls asleep on his back after having successfully wooed and bedded the previously man-hating Princess Dunya. Dunya places a golden robe over Taji's upper torso, stopping just short of his pubic hair; she then rests her head, eyes closed, on Taji's thighs, so that her profile points at Taji's penis (see figure 4). Framed on the left by the golden fabric, on the right by Dunya's sightless gaze, Taji's cock dominates the screen. Pasolini repeats the shot without any time lapse from a slightly different angle to reiterate the framing. One of

Figure 4: Framing the phallic "still life" in Pasolini's *Arabian Nights.*

the ironies of this cinematic framing of the "phallic still life" is the degree to which it can make even a dead body or body in pain the occasion for homo-erotic display; thus, as a cord is placed and tightened around Aziz's genitals prior to his castration by Delilah's female retainers (for his infidelities) the repeated close-ups not only evoke horror but may provide the gay viewer (who might not feel much sympathy for this heterosexist cad anyway) an opportunity to derive a modicum of titillation from the exposure of yet more usually-censored male flesh.

A fifth technique—to which I have already indirectly alluded—is that of the repeated shot of the same nude male torso from more than one angle, without any time lapse. In such cases, I would argue that what is generally celebrated in the Pasolini canon as a mode of breaking filmic linearity or sequentiality here seems to serve an altogether different "theoretical" agenda, that of providing the knowing gay viewer with a "second glimpse."

A final technique that Pasolini employs has to do with the overall compositional effects achieved in these scenes of heterosexual coupling that force our attention to the eroticized male body. In such examples, the penis need not be seen in close-up to make its, as it were, phallic point. For example, in the next to last inset narrative, adapted from the "Tale of the Second Kalandar," Shahzaman falls in love with a princess he has found imprisoned in an underground chamber by an evil genie. Shahzaman and the princess proceed to make love on a bed with gigantic phallic pillars, three of which are in view (and one of which virtually eclipses the princess's body). As Shahzaman rolls off the princess and into our angle of vision, his hand can be seen holding his erect penis. By the time he lies flat on his back, his erection, held upright by his hand, figuratively becomes the fourth bedpost missing from the camera's view and thus literally completes the "composition" of the frame.

The cumulatively transgressive power of all these strategies for focusing the spectatorial gaze on the "forbidden" male body—however overdetermined the ideological meanings of that body in our culture—should not be underestimated. Just as for many Western readers *Thousand Nights and A Night* has traditionally served as a conduit for imagining "forbidden" sexual possibilities left unspoken in Western culture, so this text becomes Pasolini's vehicle for intervening in heterosexist ideology as he immerses his audience in a subtextual homoeroticism that cannot be ignored. Thus Pasolini argues that the "trauma" incited by the shock of viewing such sexually explicit images is political by nature: it has the positive value "of a rupture, [the] value of liberation both on the right and the left" (Greene 181). But there are degrees and kinds of politics, and it is crucial to note that Pasolini's "rupture" of heterosexist modes of representation occurs at a certain expense, not only (and most overtly) the elision of women, but also one that returns us to the legacy of colonialism inherent in even the *gay* occidental tourist's encounters with homosexuality abroad. If according to Pasolini "a body is always revolutionary because it represents what cannot be codified,"[23] we still need to ask ourselves, in the context of the film, *whose* male bodies are we talking about. In terms of the way in which the homoerotic presentation of these corporeal images may well incite a destabilization of masculine authority in the uneasy straight Western viewer, the ideological work done by these screened bodies and phallic still lifes is perhaps "revolutionary." But in terms of the nationality and race of the bodily parts being viewed, a rather different ideological project is being advanced, one in which Pasolini's claim of the *universality* of the body's resistance to codification, its revolutionary potential, elides the fact that not all "bodies" in all contexts are the same or equal.

For instance, despite his avowed intention to make the film a record *of*, rather than an orientalizing commentary *on* "otherness," Pasolini uses the camera—as the nuances of his various framing techniques illustrate—in ways that are anything but neutral or, as he claims, "passive" in his self-conscious framing and arrangement of the male body. Indeed, the very framing techniques that make possible a gay subtextual reading participate in a colonization of the Arabic male *as* "foreign other." Pasolini's comments in an interview during the making of the film are telling:

> May I say, a bit tautologically, that for me eroticism is the beauty of the boys of the Third World. It is this type of sexual relation—violent, exalting, happy—that still survives in the Third World and that I have depicted almost completely in *Il fiore delle mille e una notte* although I have purified it, that is, stripped it of mechanics and movement [by] arranging it frontally, almost arresting it.[24]

Transforming the "beauty of the boys of the Third World" into still lifes for the delectation of Western viewers is, as Pasolini's wording betrays, to "arrest" these figures and frontally "arrange" them, in more ways than one. Pasolini's camera has become, in effect, a stand-in for the eye of the all-seeing Western observer, objectifying for the occidental audience the allure of an exotic East rendered synonymous with "pure" sensuality and bodily surfeit. As such, these boys are not only denuded of their clothing and movement but of their own stories of desire. For what Pasolini also erases in his "purified" vision of third-world eros is the fact that, for generations of gay Western men drawn like himself to the colonized third world, the availability of "exalting and happy" sex depends on an *economics* of boys as objects of Western consumption: you get what you pay for, and pay for what you get, a tautological truth that overwrites the tautology (beautiful boys = third-world sex) that Pasolini attempts to claim is self-evident.[25]

There is, moreover, one final twist to Pasolini's complicity with a colonializing ethos. Despite Pasolini's claim to present the Arabic Muslim world as itself, many of the principal nude torsos used to "frame" the Arabic phallus are actually those of *Italian* actors, a visual "cheat" that replicates the Western penchant

of projecting fantasized images onto an East that primarily exists in the spectator's eyes. There are two indicators that should have alerted me to this fact, but it
took obtaining the cast lists to realize how off-target my initial viewing experience had been. First, when I saw the film in its English rather than subtitled
Italian version, the effect of the dubbing into English was to amplify my illusion
of watching a truly "foreign" world unfold. Only upon seeing the subtitled
Italian version did I realize how many of the actors whom I had assumed were
Arabic were speaking fluent Italian. When third-world actors speak, moreover,
their voices are the ones dubbed over in Italian, providing an ironic demon-
stration of the film's silencing of the "other" to whom it is purporting to give
voice.[26]

The other indication, which has been paraded in front of the audience's eyes
the entire time, is the simple fact that the majority of the framed penises to
which I have been alluding are *uncircumcised*; that is, given the prevalence of
the Muslim law of circumcision throughout the Near and Middle East, these are
not, despite the occidental fantasy, necessarily "Arabic" cocks. Seeking to celebrate the eroticism of "the boys of the Third World," Pasolini instead substitutes
"beauties" gleaned from his own backyard, demonstrating the degree to which,
once again, the exotic, eroticized "East" has become an imaginative projection of
Western fantasy.[27]

Where "authenticity" ends and "appropriation" begins, in gay as well as
straight discourses on a (homo)eroticized East, is a story towards which the
screening of the "framed" phallus can only begin to gesture. It is one that also
returns us, crucially, to theorizations of the position(s) of gay male spectators
in and of Western popular culture. Earlier, I suggested that the liminal cinematic
space created between gay viewer and gay spectacle, in which the male subject's
gaze identifies with the equally male object of his desire, subverts psychoanalytic paradigms of heterosexual masculinity as well as qualifies those oedipalized
theories of film spectatorship (such as Laura Mulvey's) predicated on the mutually exclusive options of identifying with the camera's gaze (male scopophilia)
or identifying with the passive object being viewed (female narcissism). In contrast, as Jackson notes, "the gay male spectator's options for identification
among camera, profilmic gazing male, and object of the gaze are multiple and
mobile," creating an "ego-erotic" subjectivity that, in its difference from hegemonic masculinity, is necessarily, and valuably, "political" (75, 77). It must be
added, however, that this gay capacity to move seamlessly among positions of
identification and desire, of subject and object, maintains its descriptive power

only insofar as it universalizes the "sexual" apart from the national and racial constituents of subjectivity and desire that a consideration of the homospectatorial erotics of orientalism necessitates. For the Western gay subject who desires Arabic men, that is, his object of desire remains simultaneously same *and* other, a source of troubling identification *and* differentiation. As long as the economics of colonialism and its attendant hierarchies of race remain part of our political unconscious, the same unresolved oscillation must hold true for the gay spectator when he finds himself temporarily occupying a similar position— as for instance, when he views those nude homoerotic icons of Pasolini's film who are also "coded" as racially other. In the final count, the *psychosexual issues* of desire/identification that emanate from Pasolini's visual text and become constitutive of its gay spectatorship cannot be isolated from those *sociocultural issues* of authenticity/appropriation that, as we have seen, problematize the thematics of Pasolini's text on *both* narrative and visual levels.

If for all its intellectual ambitions, Pasolini's film ends up domesticating the homoeroticized "foreign other," finding its third-world "beauties" in its own backyard, what finally might be said of the fate of the foreign other in a product of orientalist fantasy designed for popular mass consumption like Disney's *Aladdin*? Not surprisingly, this animated feature does everything possible to Americanize its Eastern exoticism in order to sell it to a public used to seeing its national image emblazoned everywhere, especially where it does not exist. Thus, the dubbing over of Pasolini's third-world actors with Italian speakers more than finds its match in the voice assigned Aladdin, which lacks even a hint of an accent to signify "foreignness"—on some profound level Aladdin is simply an all-American boy with a good tan, Huck and Jim rolled into one.[28] Likewise, the "character types" signified by the proto-feminist, independent-minded Jasmin and her lovable but crack-brained father, like the coy, family-oriented love plot that they bring to the narrative, come right out of Hollywood, not Baghdad. And even the genie's magic—along with flying carpets, *the* embodiment of exotic otherness—is transformed, via the image and voice of Robin Williams, into the razzle-dazzle of American stand-up comedy.

None of these appropriations of foreign otherness are particularly surprising. But what *is* unexpected is the way in which even the "homoerotics" of the film manifest a similar "at homeness," rather than a further distancing as "other." One might hypothesize that, given the degree to which the "Orient" is always a projection of Occidental fantasies and anxieties, even those taboo fantasies that have been projected onto the foreign other precisely to make them articulable will, sooner or later, come home to roost. In *Aladdin*, it is symptomatic that such a return of the repressed most dramatically occurs at what is simultaneously its most uncloseted moment when Robin Williams's ever hyperbolic, often downright campy genie and the youthful Aladdin find themselves in an unexpected embrace. They just as instantaneously spring apart, as the genie cracks a gay joke—the film's only overtly gay reference—in order to dispel the very tension that he is in the process of articulating: "Gee kid, I'm growing fond of you too, but I'm not about to start choosing curtains or anything!" In the simultaneous avowal and disavowal of the homoerotic possibility (here, of man-boy love) to which the film's Near Eastern setting gives historical credence, the punch line refigures that possibility in terms that are quintessentially all-American—the domestic act of "choosing curtains" being shorthand for shacking up or getting married, just as "kid" is, as Humphrey Bogart would remind us, slang for "girlfriend"—and that are far removed from the realities of sexual encounters among Near Eastern males or between Western and Eastern men.

The homoerotics of this orientalist narrative indeed have "come home," in ways that, however subtly, keep open the possibilities that they are meant to contain within the realm of the familiar. What the big-screen spectacle of the exoticized Arabic world of *Aladdin* makes tangible in such moments, moreover, has had its small-screen correlative, most notably in television coverage of the Persian Gulf War, the media event immediately preceding and to a significant degree framing the release of the Disney film. It is not coincidental that the pro-war, anti-Arab sentiment fueling American patriotic machismo was often expressed as the warning not to let our nation be "Saddam-ized." Yet if the effort to create a public menace repulsive enough to trigger "our" manly desire for an all-out frontal assault necessitated the naming of a sexual act that to most Americans connotes male "homosexuality," such a naming serves, once again, to bring that act home, firmly lodging it in the American imagination not only as a source of anxiety but as a potent possibility; the homophobic pun on Saddam's name reveals more than it intends about the sexual fantasies that Western male culture *needs* to project onto the foreign "other." Hence, as with Pasolini's attempts to "frame" the Arabic phallus in the name of an ideological radicalness that redounds upon itself, rubbing Aladdin's lamp may yield "movie magic" that exceeds one's sanitizing intentions. It may in fact unleash a disruptive energy that, like Williams's double-edged campiness, makes the appropriation of foreign otherness, along with its homoerotic connotations, a never quite completed task.

NOTES

An earlier, and different, version of the Pasolini section of this essay appears in "Framing the Phallus," listed below. My thanks to the participants at the "Homotextualities" Conference in Buffalo, New York, in October 1991 for their comments and suggestions on the first draft of this essay, as well as to audiences at UC-Santa Barbara, UC-Davis, USC, and the Fifth Annual Lesbian and Gay Studies Conference. Thanks also to David Román, Elizabeth Young, Leo Braudy, and Earl Jackson, Jr. for their helpful criticism of this project.

1. See for example, Shaheen's critique of the stereotypical association of barbarism and Arab culture in the lyrics of the movie's opening number. The latest report is that Disney has bowed to public pressure and will alter a few of the most offensive lyrics before the movie is released on videocassette.
2. For more on the specific practice of sexuality among males in the Near East, see Bouhdiba, Daniel, and the essays in Schmitt and Sofer, eds. As Daniel sums up the distinction between Islamic and Christian customs, "It is not the frequency of homosexuality [in Muslim culture] that is noteworthy; it is the frequency of all forms of sexual pleasure" (42). One product of this ethos, Bouhdiba writes, is the sharp divergence between condemnations of *liwat* in traditional doctrine and the flexibility of attitudes towards its presence on the level of social practice (Bouhdiba 103–4, 119, 141–2). It is precisely this diversity that confutes Western attempts to impose categories (like "the homosexual") on Near Eastern culture that are more relevant to Occidental constructions of sexual identity. Abetting the tolerance of sex between men in Arabic cultures is the much stricter separation of male and female worlds and tendency to measure sexuality in terms of activity or passivity, rather than in terms of gender. This understanding of sexuality along the axis of role rather than gender means, for instance, that a man can penetrate a male youth without fearing the compromise of his own "masculinity." As long as discretion is maintained, Schmitt asserts, what everyone knows is going on can be ignored; the most important criteria is that the relationship not disturb existing social relation-ships (7). This is not to say taboos and prohibitions do not exist, but that the mechanisms of social regulation operate according to social-communal rather than moral-ethical codes.
3. Kabbani (23) also clarifies this point. On general backgrounds of the translation of *Nights* into English, see Caracciolo.
4. I comment at greater length on the way in which Durrell's novel participates in a "homoerotic negotiation" of Near Eastern sexuality in "Mappings of Male Desire."
5. It strikes me as rather ironic that the first of these illustrations, Jean-Leon Gérôme's *The Snake Charmer*, was chosen for the cover of Said's *Orientalism*, given Said's omission from his discussion of any mention of the homoerotic element in orien-

talist discourse. For despite its aura of "innocence," all the lines of vision encoded *within* the composition point toward the boy's nude front (where his unseen penis is more than amply signified by the snake that rises from his body); meanwhile the lines of vision that solicit the *external* spectator's gaze direct us to the boy's backside, inscribing thereupon a specifically pederastic fantasy in which the hierarchies of East/West, object-gazed-upon/subject-doing-the-gazing are reinforced by a hierarchy of age. The second illustration, an example of early nineteenth-century gay "pornography" included in Friedrick Karl Forberg's *De Figuris Veneris*, makes graphic the homoerotic element that Said's account of the "sexual promise (and threat)" of the Orient (188) glosses over. Set within an explicitly Egyptian context (the three great pyramids are in the background), this fantasized scene of sodomitical coupling between the swarthy (read Arabic-Semitic), hyper-masculine penetrator and coroneted youth forms the exact visual center of the drawing; note the central positioning and lighting of the penis, underlining the phallic power of the penetrating Arab, as well as the way in which the bed upon which the sex occurs serves as a kind of stage, reminding us that if we are looking at this spectacle of male intercourse, it's probably for good reason.

6. A fascinating example is Hector France's collection of vignettes of his experiences in the French Algerian army (*Musk*, 1900), which climaxes in the depiction of a group of transvestite male prostitutes dancing for an appreciative all-male audience; while the narrator feigns horror, he cannot help but return to the subject of Arabic male sexuality at the end of his text, in a coy appendix that betrays a fascination with the "uncommon dimensions" of the genital endowments of the "Arab race" (443) that is excessive, releasing an extraneous homoerotic charge into this otherwise unremittingly heterosexual example of orientalist propaganda. I comment more extensively on the sexual/textual dynamics of France's text in "Framing the Phallus" (24–5). Allen Edwardes's supposedly scholarly account of Near Eastern sexual cultures, *Jewel* (1960), follows a similar pattern of saving the "best" for last: he ends with a long chapter on Eastern male homosexual practices where serious informational content is subordinated to increasingly prurient excitations—which has to be read to be believed.

7. Even the serious orientalist like Sir Richard Burton falls prey to this imagined threat of unchecked proliferation when, in the famous Terminal Essay of his translation of *Nights*, he attempts to establish the prevalence of the vice of sodomy in the Arab Muslim world; beginning with the premise that sexuality among men is contained within what he calls the "Sotadic zone," his definition of this geographic area keeps spreading as he moves eastward from the Mediterranean belt, so that, by the conclusion of the essay, it encompasses *all* the East, the entire continents of precolonized America, and, as East spins back into West, the major European capitals, proving the *uncontainability* of his own definition. I analyze these and other instabilities in Burton in "Framing the Phallus" (25–6).

8. Korda's film is an adaptation of the silent film version starring Douglas Fairbanks, a veritable showpiece for displaying Fairbanks's physique and acrobatic skill. This

display, however, strikes me as less an example of homoerotic spectacle than one of (in this case heterosexual) male narcissism; hence the embarrassed feeling one gets watching this clearly adult man attempting to act and cavort like an adolescent. Other filmic adaptations of the Aladdin story include *Aladdin's Lamp* (1907), *Aladdin and his Wonderful Lamp* (1917), and *The Wonders of Aladdin* (1961).

9. Gide comments on his sexual initiation in Algeria (267–68) and on the role Wilde played as his procurer (303) in his memoir; Orton records his gay exploits with Tangier youth in his diaries (174–87ff); Barthes meditates on his North African tricks in a series of posthumously published fragments (23–61).

10. Here one can see Pasolini's divergence from the Neorealist movement in Italian cinema. While he shares with his predecessors a concern with "authenticity" and commitment to sub-proletarian representation, his deliberately stylized use of the camera, fetishizing "things" as "things," slowing the camera to break spatial/temporal continuity, isolating shots from each other, and so forth, create an ultimately poetic, static vision that goes against the Marxist dictate for change that underlies the Neorealist commitment to representing the "reality" of the working class (Greene 21–23, 40, 44).

11. Pasolini, *Il cinema in forma de poesia*, 162, quoted in Greene, 185.

12. An instructive example of Pasolini's internal conflicts over his homosexuality are his comments to Silvana Mauri, in a letter written upon his arrival in Rome: "my homosexuality was something extra, it was outside, it had nothing to do with me. I always saw it beside me like an enemy, I never felt it within me" (quoted in Greene 16).

13. Pasolini's attraction to the remote medievalism of *Nights* was also tied to his belief that feudal society had fostered a common cultural aesthetic shared by rich and poor alike, a culture in which homosexuality, like the belief in magic, the celebration of the body, and popular entertainments like *Nights* themselves, provided a unifying link between rulers and subjects (Pasolini 75–76). Paradoxically, Pasolini's love of the peasantry's capacity for enjoying culture and the body to its fullest led him to lament the passing of feudal conditions—and more particularly, feudal *oppressions*—that created a peasant class in the first place: hence his love of the Third World, particularly the underdeveloped countries of North Africa, as the last stronghold of the "real" proletariat (76).

14. In the written text, the analogue is the tale of "Ali Shar and Zumurrud"; Pasolini has—for reasons undetermined—changed Ali Shar's name to that of another, unrelated character in the tales. See Burton, vol. 4, 191ff.

15. See "Abu Nuwas with the Three Boys and the Caliph Harun Al-Raschid," Burton 5, 64–67.

16. It is instructive to compare Burton's translation (1, 139–49) to that of Matthews and Mardrus (1, 121–29). Despite his claim of producing the first unexpurgated version of *Nights*, Burton goes out of his way to obfuscate the sexual nature of Yunan's relationship to the boy. For example, the narrator's highly specific, sensual reaction to the boy's beauty ("he bewitched the heart out of *my bosom* and made

all the texture of *my flesh* tremble in love" [Matthews and Mardrus 1, 126] becomes, in Burton's paraphrase, a general effect ("[he] ravished *every heart* with his loveliness and subdu[ed] *every soul* with his coquetry and amorous ways" [1,144]) that denudes the statement of its erotic specificity. Burton also manipulates the text to imply no sexual contact takes place the first night, *pace* Matthews and Mardrus's rendition ("Afterwards I proved the greatness of my love for his charms, and then we lay down and slept all night"[128]). Even in the one reference to sexual contact that remains in Burton's version of the tale ("we played and ate sweetmeats and we played again and took our pleasure till nightfall" [1:147]), the parallel, doubled syntax works to veil what those stated "pleasure[s]" might be.

17. Similarly mixed messages emanate from a cross-dressing sequence shot for but deleted from the film. In this outtake (shown at a Pasolini festival at UCLA in November 1991), Prince Taji is saved by a masked soldier (his beloved, Princess Dunya, in disguise), who after demonstrating "his" prowess on the battlefield, takes Taji to "his" tent and attempts to seduce the unnerved prince, taunting him, "Why do you fear the forbidden, you have not reached the age of discretion; after tonight there will be nothing to repel you." And of course there isn't, since Dunya immediately reveals her sex, saving Taji from any further awkward confrontations with the "forbidden" or "repulsive." The homosexual possibility introduced by such gender confusion is again reduced to heterosexual foreplay.

18. This is the one major sequence in the film for which I have found no corresponding analogue in the written text, attesting to its emblematic significance in Pasolini's imagination as his creative approximation of the tales' spirit of sexuality.

19. Pasolini, "Tetis," *Erotismo, eversione, merce*, 100–1, quoted in Greene, 183.

20. So Dyer suggests in an essay that draws upon Laura Mulvey's feminist-psychoanalytic reading of the male gaze (57–62); while I would agree with Dyer that Pasolini's images are more imbued in ideology than he might think, Dyer's dovetailing of gay looks into heterosexual ones, rendering the former equally oppressive and phallocentric as the latter, causes him to overlook the very different "work" that Pasolini's images of naked men accomplish for gay and straight spectators. Likewise, a crucial distinction must be made between the visual economy whereby Pasolini represents naked men and that of, say, Matt Sterling's gay porn. For the trajectory of gay male porn, as Dyer himself astutely notes in "Coming to Terms," is geared toward the visible coming of the actors (293), a very different scenario than the repeated, static close-up of the male nude characteristic of Pasolini, which de-emphasizes the temporality, or movement through time toward ejaculation, that Dyer sees as intrinsic to male pornography, gay or straight.

21. Although such instances of misogyny pervade the film, especially on the visual level, Pasolini's thematic representation of women is much more complex than immediately meets the eye. Zumurrud, for instance, may be Nur al-Din's slave-girl, but the fact is that her former master's will has given her the right to choose her next master (thus she opts for an impressionable youth whose beauty she can enjoy), and she even gives Nur al-Din the money to "buy" her. Throughout the film, women seem

much more actively in control than the hapless Nur al-Din, who has repeatedly to be saved from his various scrapes by their knowledge. Women, moreover, become the agents of the film's trajectory of narrative desire in one very significant regard: they are the possessors of the books and knowledge of reading in this world. The frame-tale is punctuated with lulls in lovemaking (usually initiated by these women) during which they read to Nur al-Din, as if to transpose their sexual pleasure into another medium of desire, one whose open-ended structure might be said to mirror female orgasmic potential; and the stories they tell become the launching points for the visualized inset stories underlying the film's Chinese box-like structure. Even female vengeance against men seems to be partially valorized; the story of Delilah's castration of the faithless Aziz—graphically filmed in close-up—implies that Aziz gets what he deserves. Finally, if Pasolini's strategic highlighting of the male nude occurs at the expense of a female participant, it seems important to note that the camera's most extended depiction of female nudity occurs when Zumurrud, disguised as a man, strips in front of the princess she's just married. Rather than the dismay that cross-dressing occasions for men (see pages 160–161 above and note 17), Zumurrud's "mate" shares merrily in the secret. Zumurrud's stripping to "unveil" for another woman "man's" lack of a phallus thus becomes the perfect joke on phallocentric culture.

22. I was reminded of this anew when I had the chance to see a beautifully restored, wide-screen print of *Nights* at a Pasolini film festival in 1991, "The Eyes of a Poet," sponsored by the UCLA Film and Television Archives: you could have heard a pin drop in the audience when shots like this one of Aziz's erection lit up the screen. While it is true that few of these "phallic still lifes" last longer than a few seconds to a half-minute, the constant repetition of such moments throughout the film has an important cumulative effect, I would argue, creating a kind of subliminal "freeze-frame" image in the mind of the viewer. The full force of this iterative technique, I should add, cannot be fully appreciated watching the film on video—particularly the dubbed Italian version, whose interior shots are unnaturally darkened.

23. Quoted in Tommaso Anzoino in *Pasolini, Il Castoro* 51 (Feb. 1974): 7–8; cited in Greene, 183.

24. Pasolini, "Eros e cultura: Interview with Massimo Fino," *Europeo* (19 October, 1974), quoted in Greene, 194.

25. I write extensively on the colonial "trade in boys" in North Africa in a forthcoming essay, "Vacation Cruises."

26. I have since found this discovery confirmed by a footnote in Greene, where she notes that even "the black Africans and Arabs of *Il fiore delle mille e una notte* are dubbed by speakers from the south of Italy" (184). As for the practice of dubbing, it turns out that all major Italian studios regularly post-synchronized their films, relying on standard studio voices, not necessarily those of the actors, in order to simulate a "pure" or national Italian dialect. I have not yet learned whether Pasolini's independence of the studio system and advocacy of dialects inspired him to break with this homogenizing tendency; but even assuming that all the actors in *Nights* are

dubbed with voices not their own, the subliminal overall effect is that of Italian actors speaking Italian, whereas the non-congruence between the lip movements of the Arabic speakers and the soundtrack only emphasizes the degree to which the film *speaks for* the third world "others" to whom it is purportedly giving voice.

27. The backyard reference is not entirely figurative, given Pasolini's tendency to find his sexual partners among the working class *ragazzi* of Rome. Finding the "other" at home, Pasolini proceeded to give many of these youths employment as his actors, some of whom appear as the Arabic "others" of *Nights*. The implications for the film's representation of the "foreign other" is highly complex and ultimately indeterminate, given the fact that much of Rome's sub-proletariat derives from southern Italy, whose mixture of Italian, Arabic, and African heritages is proportionally greater than in the rest of Italy. Who, that is, is to say that some of these "Italian" actors featured in the film as "Arabs" are not also of North African Arabic descent, despite the fact they speak Italian and are not uncircumcised? See also note 26 above.

28. Thanks to Robert Vorlicky and Elizabeth Young for these insights.

BIBLIOGRAPHY

Barthes, Roland. *Incidents*. Paris: Editions DuSeuil, 1987, 23–61.

Bhabha, Homi K. "The Other Question…Homi K. Bhabha Reconsiders the Stereotype and Colonial Discourse." *Screen* 24 (1983): 18–36.

Boone, Joseph A. "Framing the Phallus in the *Arabian Nights*: Pansexuality, Pederasty, Pasolini." In *Translations/Transformations: Gender and Culture in Film and Literature East and West*, eds. Cornelia Moore and Valerie Wayne. Honolulu: University of Hawaii Press, 1993, 23–33.

_____. "Mappings of Male Desire in Durrell's *Alexandria Quartet*: Homoerotic Negotiations in the Colonial Narrative." In *Out of Bounds: Male Writers and Gender(ed) Criticism*, ed. Laura Claridge and Elizabeth Langland. Amherst, Mass.: University of Amherst Press, 1990, 316–44.

_____. "Vacation Cruises, or the Homoerotics of Orientalism." *PMLA* 110 (January 1995).

Bouhdiba, Abdelwahab. *Sexuality in Islam*. London: Routledge, 1985.

Burton, Sir Richard, trans. and ed. *The Book of the Thousand Nights and a Night: A Plain and Literal Translation of the Arabian Nights Entertainments*. 10 vols. London: Burton Club edition, n.d. [1885–86].

Caracciolo, Peter L. *The Arabian Nights in English Literature: Studies in the Reception of the Thousand and One Nights*. London: Macmillan, 1988.

Daniel, Marc. "Arab Civilization and Male Love." 1975–76; rpt. in *Gay Roots: Twenty Years of Gay Sunshine: An Anthology of Gay History, Sex, Politics, and Culture*, ed. Winston Leyland. San Francisco: Gay Sunshine Press, 1991, 33–75.

Durrell, Lawrence. *Justine* (vol. 1 of the *Alexandria Quartet*). 1957; rpt. New York: Pocket Editions, 1961.

Dyer, Richard. "Pasolini and Homosexuality." In *Pier Paulo Pasolini*, ed. Paul Willeman. London: British Film Institute, 1977, 57–62.

_____. "Coming to Terms." In *Now You See It: Studies on Lesbian and Gay Film*. New York and London: Routledge, 1990, 289–98.

Edwardes, Allen. *The Jewel in the Lotus: A Historical Survey of the Sexual Culture of the East*. New York: Julian Press, 1960.

France, Hector. *Musk, Hashish, and Blood*. London and Paris: Printed for Subscribers Only, 1900.

Fuss, Diana. "Fashion and the Homospectatorial Look." *Critical Inquiry* 18 (Summer 1992): 713–37.

Gide, André. *If It Die…An Autobiography* (*Si le grain ne meurt*). Trans. Dorothy Bussy. New York: Random House, 1935.

Greene, Naomi. *Pier Paulo Pasolini: Cinema as Heresy*. Princeton, NJ: Princeton University Press, 1990.

Jackson, Earl, Jr. "Graphic Spectacularity: Pornography, Almodovar and the Gay Male Subject of Cinema." In *Translations/Transformations: Gender and Culture in Film and Literature East and West*, eds. Cornelia Moore and Valerie Wayne. Honolulu: University of Hawaii Press, 1993, 63–81.

Kabbani, Rana. *Europe's Myths of the Orient: Devise and Rule*. London: Macmillan, 1986.

Mani, Lata and Ruth Frankenburg. "The Challenge of *Orientalism*." *Economy and Society* 14 (May 1985): 174–92.

Matthews, Powys, trans. from the French trans. of J. C. Mardrus. *The Book of the Thousand Nights and One Night*, 2 vols. London: Routledge & Kegan Paul, 1951.

Miller, D. A. *The Novel and the Police*. Berkeley and Los Angeles: University of California Press, 1988.

Nowell-Smith, Geoffrey. "Pasolini's Originality." In *Pier Paulo Pasolini*, ed. Willeman. London: British Film Institute, 1977.

Orton, Joe. *The Orton Diaries*, ed. John Lahr. New York: Perennial, 1986.

Pasolini, Pier Paulo. "Interview with Paul Willeman." In *Pier Paulo Pasolini*, ed. Willeman. London: British Film Institute, 1977.

Said, Edward. *Orientalism*. New York: Vintage, 1979.

Schmitt, Arno and Jehoeda Sofers, eds. *Sexuality and Eroticism Among Males in Moslem Societies*. New York: Harrington Park, 1992.

Schmitt, Arno. "Different Approaches to Male-Male Sexuality/Eroticism from Morocco to Uzbekistan." In *Sexuality and Eroticism Among Males in Moslem Societies*, ed Arno Schmitt and Jehoeda Sofers. New York: Harrington Park, 1992, 1–24.

Shaheen, Jack G. "Arab Caricatures Deface Disney's 'Aladdin.'" Counterpunch column, *Los Angeles Times*, 21 Dec. 1992: F, 3.

Sharpe, Jenny. "Figures of Colonial Resistance." *Modern Fiction Studies* 35 (Spring 1989): 137–55.

Sutor, Jacob (Dr. Jacobus X). *Untrodden Fields of Anthropology: Observations on the*

Esoteric Manner and Customs of Semi-Civilized Peoples (orig. *L'Amour aux Colonies*). 2 vol. Paris: Librairie de Medecine, Folklore et Anthropologie, 1898.

Willeman, Paul, ed. *Pier Paulo Pasolini*. London: British Film Institute, 1977.

10

Anxieties of Identity

Coming Out and
Coming Undone

....

Julia Creet

COMING OUT

....

I met Maureen and Martha one spring day in the park playing football. They were both in university and I was a precocious fourteen year old. They lived across the street from the park around the corner from my parents' house in a grand Bagot Street building that had been chopped up into apartments. Nothing has changed much since then; the park, the houses, and the back alley that almost connected them are all still there. They invited me home after our game, offered me beer or coffee and were surprised that I was too young to drink either.

We began a great friendship that day, one that I passionately pursued and they generously tolerated. I went to visit them almost every day, often climbing up the fire escape and through their living-room window. After several months of this, I came in the fire escape as usual one morning, wandered through to the front of the apartment and found Maureen lying in Martha's bed. Why they allowed me into the bedroom I don't know, but I remember very clearly my thoughts as I pulled a chair up beside the bed. How I wanted a "roommate" like this.

A few days or perhaps a week later, I once again climbed into my friends' apartment, this time getting no farther than the living room. I sat on the pea-green couch and Martha sat across from me; she had a conversation in mind.

"I have something to tell you," she said with some nervousness, "Maureen and I are 'gay.'"

"What does that mean?" I sat clutching a pillow to my chest for protection.

"If you don't know then maybe I shouldn't tell you."

"If you don't tell me then I'm going to think the worst," thinking they were lesbians even though I only had a vague idea of what that meant.

"We're lesbians," said Martha.

I remember only fragments of conversation after that, my promising her that it wouldn't make a difference in our friendship, her telling me they were worried that I had seen too much and would say something at home—I was 'jail-bait' after all. We walked to the apartment door, her arm around me. She hugged me goodbye, but when she tried to kiss me I turned my head away. I had always had a sense of watching myself, spectator and performer both, and on that day I know that I performed shock. I left the apartment shaken and pale, down the dimly lit front stairs shadowed by red flock walls.

I left town shortly afterwards on summer holidays to my family's farmhouse which was near a lake I had swum in all my life. Water was my element; in it all was possible with bodies, they floated and dove, you could touch them almost anywhere. One day the water was cool and the sky slightly overcast. As I waded slowly towards shore, I noticed a rash on my legs. By the time I reached the shore it had spread noticeably and as my father came up I collapsed. Welts covered my body, the blood drained from my extremities and I lost all feeling in the arm my father held on to as we walked home. He carried me over the fence, his concern as deep as I have ever felt before or since. Clinically, I was on the verge of shock.

The next three weeks I remember as a series of physical nightmares and sexual daydreams. Each time I swam my body broke out in hives and started to display signs of shock. This extended dream—aided by several doses of strong antihistamines—replayed my last minutes with Martha endlessly until my only wish was that I had not averted my lips. After I returned home, I went to see Martha and announced, "I now know what I am — I'm gay." "No" she said, "you're not. You don't want to be."

This narrative of my coming out, begun in the summer of 1974, was swept along by momentum of two movements, feminism and gay liberation. I arrived on the scene on the brink of a shifting consciousness. Whereas Martha's "You don't want to be" resonated with the depression and fear of a group less than a decade older than me, Sidney Abbott and Barbara Love's *Sappho Was A Right-On Woman* offered me a better vision of the near future. My identity, as a woman (not yet consciously marked as white or Jewish at this point) and as a lesbian, quickly became the center of my interaction and struggle with the world. I was not usually dogmatic, but the defense of the integrity of my identity (in both the moral and structural sense) provided me with emotional stability and political vision.

Since "coming out" to Martha I have proudly been "gay," "lesbian," a "dyke," a "lesbian-feminist," and now, a "queer theorist." But lately the incidents which had brought me to this point, and the emotional and physical shock that were part of them, have given me pause for thought. How much have my pride, my twenty years of dedication to the cause of lesbian and gay liberation, my successive identities, my intellectual obsession with this thing called identity, and my retelling of this story in many variations (and only recently with the scene by the lake), actually obscured the trauma, the shock, and the many teenaged years of depression that followed? Has some part of my need to repeat the story of the actions which secured my identity been an attempt to master a situation that in the first instance was deeply threatening—so much so that it may have produced a histological reaction? (For years I kept adrenaline and a syringe for quick administration at the onset of shock.) And, perhaps most importantly, are those anxieties and my techniques for mastering them re-emerging in this current climate of contesting the singularity and stability of identity categories?

As Kobena Mercer has pointed out in his discussion of the construction of "/black/" in England in the eighties, "whatever it is, identity becomes an issue when it is in crisis" (424). "Lesbian identity" like other kinds of identities is in a crisis of representation, entangled in the need for political and emotional stability, and subject to the radical destabilizing of post-structuralist theories, as well as challenges to boundaries by cross-currents with other categories. This essay explores the notion of identity "crisis" as a psychic crisis which is fully grounded in historical and political contexts and explicable, in part, in theory. That is, the shocking acquisition of my label "lesbian," says something about what I fear, and resist, faced with the possibility of its change — whether it be the loss of "lesbian" or the unpredictability of its transformation (i.e., I could always go "straight," I should probably more accurately call myself "bisexual," it is all just parody anyway). Although the story of a crisis of lesbian signification, this essay also examines what the stakes are in the defense of many kinds of identities, particularly those that one has come into or that can be lost.

Homosexual, gay, lesbian "identities," formulated as identities rather than strictly as behavior, have been predicated on a speech act: "coming out."[1] This act often describes a process of signification, of naming or categorizing feelings that had previously existed. A single utterance will not suffice, for new situations demanding the revelation of identity are encountered constantly. The story of coming out is itself a narrative of development—a kind of voyage usually—and the repetitive act of coming out (or "being out") is performative, that is, it (re)creates and maintains identity, not just discloses it.

I will examine a story of lesbian signification (which in post-structuralist thought is also inevitably a moment of loss) for its modes and meanings of repetition. Notions of fixed identity have been recently charged with upholding regulatory regimes—the laws of sexual difference and the stability of heterosexuality—while concepts of masquerade and performance have become popular as figures of the embodiment of mutability.[2] If the narrative replay of the coming out story can be seen as both a constitutive and a repetitive moment in the formation and maintenance of a (political) lesbian identity, how then does its retelling work within and against this framework of mutability? And, more specifically, how does its retelling and the identity it substantiates work in the light of two currently theorized modes of repetition: parody and compulsion? Does this story represent anything that might be specific to lesbianism, or as Judith Butler argues, does it demarcate a lesbian specificity by its inevitable exclusions? Further, how do I understand the anxieties associated with "coming out" which have surfaced again with the specter of "coming undone"? And finally, is there a constant pull to give up identity, to let it lapse, to give up on this difference?

To address these questions I will refer to Freud's discussion of the compulsion to repeat in *Beyond the Pleasure Principle*, and to Michel Foucault's commitment to the dissipation of identity. Further, since I have emphasized the narrative expression of identity in the form of the story that opens this essay, the form and function of narrative repetition will also be considered. My main argument, however, will be with Judith Butler's *Gender Trouble: Feminism and the Subversion of Identity* and her essay that quickly followed it, "Imitation and Gender Insubordination."

Butler's writing provokes a contradictory response in me. On the one hand, I agree with her insistence on the political potential of the "subversion" of identities; on the other, I am anxious about championing the psychic instability that characterizes this theoretical subversion and what seems to be a loss of memory and location that accompanies it. The result is that "lesbian" identity retains its position as a kind of singular identity in her work, seldom marked in any way other than by sexuality and by the "fiction of gender" (a phrase of Monique Wittig's). This essay does not take her to task on this front, but in its resistances demonstrates my own psychic stakes in "identity." As such it should prompt the question: What are the psychic stakes in claiming any strong individual and collective identity—sexual, racial, national or otherwise?

At the end of *Gender Trouble*, Judith Butler focuses on the theme that organizes her book and necessarily reappears in her subsequent writings: repetition and parody as strategies for the insubordination of gender and identity. Repetition, Butler is careful to point out, is not a decision one makes but is a performative act one is compelled to carry out: "In a sense all signification takes place within the orbit of the compulsion to repeat; 'agency,' then, is to be located within the possibility of a variation on that repetition" (145). It is between the compulsion to repeat the same theme over and over (Freud—repetition as mastery) and the compulsion to repeat variations on a theme (Foucault—repetition as movement or parody) that Butler locates the available field of change for gendered and erotic identities.

Butler amalgamates a Lacanian concept of the constitution of the linguistic and split self with a Foucauldian understanding of identity as a category of regulation. Since feminists have reworked Lacan to demonstrate the failure of identity, and since Foucault theorizes identity "as an effect of a repetition that is regulated by given power regimes," then "how," asks Butler, "do we work these two dimensions of gender performativity together?" ("Lana's Imitation" 3). Her aim is to unsettle the opposition of male and female that undergirds Western thought, "to center on—and decenter…phallogocentrism and compulsory heterosexuality" (xi). Following Derrida and the insights of deconstruction, "woman" as the binary opposite of "man" fixes the place of both. And "woman" as a primary identity for feminist politics precludes, Butler argues, a "radical inquiry into the political construction and regulation of identity itself" (xi).

Analyzing gender practices within gay and lesbian cultures which "often thematize 'the natural' in parodic contexts…bring[ing] into relief the performative construction of an original and true sex" (*Gender Trouble*, x), Butler further interrogates presumptive heterosexuality and the ontology of sex—the given "truth" of sex, the "natural" distinction between men and women, "masculine" and "feminine." Charges of mimicry are a staple of homophobes: a butch really wants to be a man, a gay or lesbian couple really want to be heterosexual. Butler inverts/subverts this charge by pointing to the hollowness of the "original." Like Frederic Jameson's idea of pastiche, Butler argues that "gay is to straight *not* as copy is to original, but, rather, as copy is to copy" (31). Parodic repetition "reveals the original to be nothing other than a parody of the *idea* of the natural and the original" (31). The parodies of gender in gay cultures (drag, butch/femme) perform the "natural" whereas heterosexuality naturalizes what is performance.

Crucial to Butler's invocation of parody as inspired politics is the denaturalization of all sexuality and accompanying gender roles. Thus, what begins as a critique of the centrality of the figure of "woman" for feminist theory and politics carries through to the identity politics foundation of gay and lesbian politics. The radical subversion of sexual difference and heterosexuality enacted by (some) performances of gayness and lesbianism must also be brought to bear on the sacredness of the notion of fixed identity for homosexual activism. Sexual identity appears as a symptom of the Foucauldian paradox: that is, as both a vehicle of creativity and a category of constraint.

What Butler seems able to accomplish with confidence (and a good bit of hyperbole) in her subversion of gender becomes more complicated when it comes to her own identity as a lesbian. In an essay published after *Gender Trouble*, "Imitation and Gender Insubordination" (Fuss, 1991), Butler considers her participation in the 1989 Conference on Homosexuality. She tells friends that she is "off to Yale to be a lesbian" (18), a statement that is not just humorous but resonates, as she notes, with "anxiety and discomfort."

> How is that I can both "be" one [a lesbian], and yet endeavor to be one at the same time?...This is not a performance from which I can take radical distance, for this is deep-seated play, psychically entrenched play, *and this "I" does not play its lesbianism as a role.* (emphasis in the original, 18)

It is the "I," says Butler, that produces the effect of continuity between moments of repetition, yet it is also the "string of performances that...contest the coherence of that 'I' " (18). Earlier in her paper, Butler points to the "troubled" instability of identity categories as a place of pleasure also: "In fact if the category were to offer no trouble, it would cease to be interesting to me: it is precisely the *pleasure* produced by the instability of those categories…that makes me a candidate for the category to begin with" (14). The instability of homosexuality may in fact be necessary if it is to continue to create trouble, since the "homosexual," as Eve Sedgwick has pointed out, as an identifiable and abnormal other only helps to secure and sustain heterosexuality.[3]

Butler delights in figures of double trouble, and the pleasure of her text is quite irresistible, but the words that catch my eye are not so much words of pleasure but those of anxiety and compulsion. The strength of her analysis lies in her insight into parodic possibilities of sexed and gendered categories. Yet I find the anxiety of the text surfaces most when Butler approaches questions of her own lesbian identity: her will to dismantle it and her compulsion to repeat it are psychic and philosophical explorations seemingly isolated from very specific social, political, and personal contexts.

I want to focus on that constitutive moment that Butler alludes to in her essay, that moment in which she sees herself to be a candidate for the category: "Since I was sixteen, being a lesbian is what I've been" (18). Butler admits to early anxieties about being a lesbian—a poor copy of a heterosexual man. Her comfort comes in the form of Esther Newton's *Mother Camp* which argued, as early as 1972, that "drag enacts the very structure of impersonation by which *any gender* is assumed" (quoted by Butler, "Imitation," 21). One could read Butler's subsequent thinking and writing, particularly *Gender Trouble* and this essay on "imitation," as a continued working through of that teenage anxiety that her desire is an imitation of masculine desire. And in many ways Butler masterfully "suspends and resolves," even if only provisionally, her anxieties. If "being" a lesbian is seen as a kind of mimicry, its failure is inevitable in the context of the "phantasmatic plentitude of naturalized heterosexuality" (21).

Yet the invocation of the specifically lesbian signifier draws fire from Butler, for she says that "its signification is always to some degree out of one's control…[and] its *specificity* can only be demarcated by exclusions that return and disrupt its coherency" (5). Butler implies different stakes for the maintenance of heterosexual identity and for the maintenance of gay/lesbian identity as distinct, comprehensible categories. She asks what the "outness" of a lesbian or gay identity represses.

> It is not something like heterosexuality or bisexuality that is disavowed by the category, but a set of identificatory and practical crossings between these categories that renders the discreteness of each equally suspect. (17)

Whereas,

> heterosexuality's *panicked* imitation of its own naturalization…'knows' its
> own possibility of becoming undone: hence, its compulsion to repeat which
> is a foreclosure of that which threatens its coherence (23).

But in spite of the kind of neurotic/psychotic divide that characterizes the difference between homosexuality and heterosexuality in Butler's scheme, these descriptions are hardly mutually exclusive, and might, in fact, be interchangeable. For my need for a lesbian identity could possibly be described as a compulsion to repeat. I "know" the possibility of "coming" undone (the opposite of coming out?) and though I don't disavow that which threatens my coherence—which is precisely that attraction to heterosexuality with all of its social stabilizers—I do defend myself against it. The narrative of coming out marks exactly a point of "crossing" from one category to another. Further, the insistence on the distinctness of homosexual identity functions politically as a defense against re-incorporation into heterosexuality or into the categorization of what more accurately might be bisexuality.

It is in this "crossing" that I sense Butler at her most troubled, and perhaps not enjoying herself. Can lesbian specificity only be demarcated by sexual exclusions, and by those that return and sound ominously like the return of the repressed? Do the exclusions that demarcate its specificity run only along the axis of sexuality? Ekua Omosupe points out that "[t]he term 'lesbian' without racial specificity, focuses on and refers to white lesbian culture. White lesbian culture, or the white lesbian, has become the quintessential representation of lesbian experience, of the very concept 'lesbian'" ("Black/Lesbian/Bulldagger" 108). Are those of "us" who have spent the last twenty years defining the category "lesbian" still defending (consciously or unconsciously) the singularity of the term even as we try to examine its categorical qualities?

COMING UNDONE

Identity and its repetitions can be viewed at once in an individual context and a social context, so that to speak of the return of exclusions can mean a return of repressed material for an individual, or the reintroduction by individuals of experiences which challenge the unity of the group or category. Such is the tone of some of the writing on bisexuality which points to the narrowing definitions of sexual/political categories—lesbian feminism in particular—as sites of repression and therefore also as targets for disruption. In spite of Butler's claim that "it is not something like heterosexuality or bisexuality that is disavowed," the panic and general flap that followed Jan Clausen's article "My Interesting Condition" in *OUT/LOOK* in which she describes her process of falling in love with a man after years as a dedicated lesbian, indicated to me that bisexuality is very much seen as a threat to lesbian identity and, perhaps more importantly, to lesbian politics.[4] "In choosing to love a man, it was, on some level, chaos itself I needed to invoke" (19), writes Clausen. For her,

> bisexuality is not a sexual identity at all, but a sort of anti-identity, a refusal (not, of course, conscious) to be limited to one object of desire, one way of loving.... British feminist Jacqueline Rose has argued for recognition of a "*resistance to identity* which lies at the very heart of psychic life." (italics added by Clausen, 19)[5]

Clausen again:

> I decide that this difficulty in devising appropriate labels is merely the most obvious symptom of an underlying process marked by many layers of ambiguity, which might aptly be termed *identity loss*. I amuse myself by inventing ironic self-descriptions, metaphors for my non-identity: Stateless Person of the Sexual World. Tragic Mulatto of the Sexual World. Lesbian-feminist Emeritus. Twilight Girl. In conversations with myself, I make reference to "my interesting condition"—that old-fashioned euphemism for pregnancy which seems to me to convey not only the thinly veiled, at times intrusive, curiosity with which others regard me, but my own hopes for extracting meaning from the mess. (17)

Whether or not she derives "meaning from the mess," Clausen's ironic self-descriptions succeed in distancing her from her loss of identity. Although she herself claims she had less trouble accepting and being accepted for her lesbianism than for her consequent hetero- or bi-sexuality, she quotes a friend who

> gave voice to a poignant moment of insecurity which perhaps crystallizes the terror behind this issue: "You get the feeling maybe pretty soon you'll be the only [lesbian] left."...I record it here precisely because it is a feeling, and, as such, in some absolute sense unanswerable, except by a social transformation which could remove the need for anyone to experience dread or loneliness because of sexual choices. (21)

It is precisely this melancholy moment that I think needs closer inspection.

The unanswerablity of feelings in contrast to the possibility of deriving meaning from mess seems a handy way to invoke the psychic in aid of the political, only to let the psychic drop out again because of the intellectual and emotional difficulty of its exploration. Resistance to identity is a crucial psychic concept at this juncture, but not without also acknowledging the specter of loss. Clausen addresses this identity loss in political and social terms—the loss of a righteous platform, and the loss of a label—but her friend's poignant moment is left in its lonely place to await social transformation. I would argue also that Judith Butler's work, though a much more sophisticated argument against the constraints of identity categories than Clausen's, also veers away from the questions of loss in both constitutional and deconstructive moments in identity narratives.

Though Butler addresses a scene of loss in *Gender Trouble*, it is that loss usually associated with identification, incorporation, and the constitution of the split-subject—a loss that Freud describes in "Mourning and Melancholia" (1914) as one which results in an identification with the lost object and its subsequent incorporation. But whereas Freud's description of incorporation of the lost object revolves around the actual death of a parent or a loved one, Butler takes up Lacan's reworking of melancholia as a fundamental process in the formation of a notion of self and identity:

> In my view, the self only becomes a self on the condition that it has suffered a separation (grammar fails us here, for the "it" only becomes differentiated through that separation), a loss which is suspended and provisionally resolved through a melancholic incorporation of some "Other."…[T]he disruption of the Other at the heart of the self is the very condition of that self's possibility. (27)

Thus for Butler, following Lacan, loss is a condition of signification. Loss of an/other (which in Lacan's formulation of the "mirror stage" is an idealized part of the self) allows for the differentiation of the self. But these are processes of an early age, of infancy and early childhood, and though they may be good descriptions of the beginnings of the idea of a self, they do not get at the formulation of adolescent and adult sexual identities that are necessarily *political* and historical as well as psychic.

For myself, for Butler, and for many others, coming out as a moment in the signification of lesbian identity was an adolescent experience.[6] This moment

which marks the age/date of attainment of a specifically articulated sexual identity, seems to me to have a different constitution from the Lacanian split which
initiates the comprehension of self and language. The split self with its post-
structuralist heart (suffering "a loss suspended and provisionally resolved"
[*Gender Trouble*, 28]), may very well be a good description of the mimetic
momentum of a kind of primary identity. But I wonder if we can separate to
some degree a secondary identity, a lesbian one, and its social and psychic signification at the moment of, and through repeated retellings of coming out. To
speculate on this is not to try to create an "origin story" specific to lesbian or
gay or any other kind of identity, but to examine a representation of an experience that serves to configure a physical and psychical relationship to oneself and
others. That it is often located in adolescence may have some significance.

In a footnote to "The Psychogenesis of a Case of Homosexuality in a Woman"
(1920) Freud, referring to the overcompensation for his analysand's hostility
towards her mother, and the search for a substitute mother to whom she could
become passionately attached, notes that

> the displacements of the libido here described are doubtless familiar to
> every analyst from investigation of the anamneses of neurotics. With the
> latter, however, they occur in early childhood, at the time of the early efflo-
> rescence of erotic life; with our patient, who was in no way neurotic
> [though she was "perverse"][7] they took place in the first years following
> puberty, though, incidentally, they were just as completely unconscious.
> Perhaps one day this temporal factor may turn out to be of great impor-
> tance. (158)

This "Oedipus attitude at puberty," as Freud calls it, could then be more than
just a manifestation of early childhood psycho-sexual development.[8] It may very
well constitute an originary moment for homosexuality, not in the sense of cause
but in the realm of signification (conscious recognition) and loss.

Adolescent sexuality is undertheorized in both Freudian and Lacanian psychoanalysis. Although Freud devotes the third of his "Three Essays on Sexuality"
(1905) to pubescent sexuality, his main arguments can be summed up in his
observations that in adolescence sexual instinct, which had been dominantly
auto-erotic, finds a sexual object, and that sexual development between boys
and girls begins to diverge greatly. He writes,

> Puberty, which brings about so great an accession of libido in boys, is

> marked in girls by a fresh wave of *repression,* in which it is precisely clitoral sexuality that is affected. What is thus overtaken by repression is a piece of masculine sexuality. (*SE* 7)

Thus Freud sees puberty not as a time of the instantiation of lesbian desire, but a time when girls must turn away from it.[9] Rather than postulate an infantile female desire that is in the first case lesbian—a girl's love for her mother—he masculinizes her desire, turning her, in effect, into a little boy.

I am not primarily concerned here, however, with the unconscious desires of children or the oedipal configuration at puberty, but rather, I want to argue that coming out for the adolescent lesbian marks a coming into consciousness of the incongruity of her sexual object choice with her social role. Identity is thus formed as a defense against the repression of what well may be a continuous desire. It is the externalization of desire in the form of object choice (a woman) which brings it into the social realm, and concomitant with that externalization comes social censure. Martha's warning "No you're not. You don't want to be" was sad testimony not only to the problems she had and I would face but to the costs that my claiming of this protective identity would incur. It was a moment of signification that marked discontinuity in my life. I now had a name for something I hadn't before; I was now something different than I was before. Yet I now knew it was something I should not be or feel or act upon.

In order to think about this "secondary identity"[10] then, it may be helpful to look at it both in terms of its continuities and discontinuities with childhood processes of identity formation. If, as Butler claims, the "I" is a string of performances that produces the effect of continuity between moments of repetition ("Imitation," 18), then what happens if we look at coming out as a moment of discontinuity? I do not want to over-generalize that coming out marks a radical break for all lesbians or gay men or any other sexual dissident—the processes of individual consciousness and histories are far too varied for that—but the story of coming out is often told in such a way that it recreates a kind of epiphany, a revelation that produces a different "I."

To understand the function of the repetition of the story, and the continuities and discontinuities it produces, it is first necessary to look more closely at the concept of repetition itself and its companion, in Freudian terms, compulsion. *Beyond the Pleasure Principle* is an extraordinarily complicated and ambiguous text which is seen as a turning point in Freud's thinking as well as one of the most speculative pieces of his writing. In it, he focuses on two themes that interlock: the compulsion to repeat and the instinct for mastery (also called the will to power, or the destructive instinct). "The investigation of the mental reaction to external danger" (*Beyond*, 11) is what pushes Freud to revise his earlier insistence that a singular principle—the desire for pleasure—dominated psychic functions. Two sources of observations form the foundation for the speculations of *Beyond*, first the analysis of traumatic neuroses and, second, Freud's observations of particular games played by his grandson Ernst. The common theme is that of the repetition of unpleasant experiences as a means of retroactively controlling events which were shocking and beyond one's control. Freud moves quickly from the "abnormal" functions of the adult neurotic to the "normal" activities of children's play.

Ernst's "*fort-da*" game has been repeatedly examined for its significance to the analytic situation and to the meaning of psychoanalytic interpretation as a whole. Briefly, the story goes like this: staying with his daughter's family, Freud observed a game his grandson had devised. In the absence of his mother, Ernst threw away his toys uttering "o-o-o-o," which Freud and the child's mother interpret as meaning the German word for "gone": "*fort.*" With a spool tied to a string, the game became "*fort-da,*" or "gone" and "there" as the child repeatedly threw away the spool and retrieved it. "This, then, was the complete game—disappearance and return…. He compensated himself for [his mother's disappearance] by himself staging the disappearance and return of the objects within his reach" (14).

Freud then associated the compulsion to repeat with control over the presence and absence of a loved object. The game worked to turn the child into an agent.

> At the outset he was in a *passive* situation—he was overpowered by the experience [that of his mother's departure]; but, by repeating it, unpleasurable though it was, as a game, he took an active part. These efforts might be put down to an instinct for mastery that was acting independently of whether the memory was in itself pleasurable or not. (16)

Other events which have left a strong impression are treated similarly, for as the child repeats them in play "they abreact [that is, discharge the emotion] the strength of the impression and, as one might put it, make themselves master of the situation" (16–17). To master a situation protects one against the shock of unexpected reoccurrence by the substitution of a symbol for the loved object, a symbol that can be controlled.

The coming-out story resembles the repetition of Ernst's game. Its telling is presumably pleasurable, ending as it does with triumph, usually less a story of loss than a story of discovery. Like Ernst, one throws away the symbol of the desired object (identity as the representation of desire), only to retrieve it again. One puts it in the closet in order to take it out. Perhaps a sense of awe may remain, but the story loses its emotive charge over the years. Perhaps one even puts it away for long periods, secure in the knowledge that it can be taken out. This representation of one's identity stabilizes what might be much less easily categorized, easily controlled or predictable—such as desire and behavior.

My coming-out story that opens this essay is not the same story that I have always told. It took me fifteen years to connect the first and second parts, to recognize that the emotional shock of naming might very well have written itself on my body as a physical shock. Water had been my sexual element, but for years after I came out (emerged?) I could no longer swim. If water had been a sea of sexual bliss and blissful ignorance, it now became a body of unpredictability and terror. I almost died swimming in the cold ocean off the Nova Scotian coast, but what terrified me most was the loss of control, the paralysis of my will in relation to my body.

How might this particular reworking of my coming out story, this retelling, this story of the signification of a body as a lesbian body, function within Butler's discussion of the subversion of identity? As Butler notes, "In a sense, all signification takes place within the orbit of the compulsion to repeat; 'agency,' then, is to be located within the possibility of a variation on that repetition" ("Imitation," 18). This notion of "agency" is fully cast within Lacan's re-reading of Freud's theory of the function of repetition. Lacan suggests that repetition is the inevitable structure of the ego and subjectivity itself. Butler writes (and one should keep in mind here Rose's "resistance to identity"):

> Repetition, Lacan suggests, is the inevitable structure of the subject itself, a structure that effectively resists the subject as synthesizing or mastering agency in favor of a disunified subjective field punctuated by multiple sites of agency. Repetition cannot be reduced to a recollection refused, he argues, for that formula presumes the integrity of a psyche that recollects; rather, for Lacan, repetition designates the primary splitting (*Spaltung*) of the subject. The "resistance of the subject," a phrase he insists on thematizing with inverted quotation marks, is "repetition in act," meaning that the discontinuity of the subject, enacted by repetitive acts, is a resistance to the notion of the subject as a unified and unifying agent or master. (14–15)

But one might ask, what does Lacan's—and following his, Butler's—insistence on the unconscious primary splitting of the subject have to do with much more conscious and political questions about identities that function as categories at both an individual and a communal level?

As Shoshana Felman points out, repetition in Lacan's work rewrites both history and meaning.

> [W]hat is *beyond* the wish for pleasure—the compulsion to repeat—radically displaces the conception both of history and of meaning, both of what history means and of how meaning comes to be and is historicized...Since the compulsion to repeat is, in Lacan's view, the compulsion to repeat a signifier, *Beyond the Pleasure Principle* holds the key not just to history or transference but, specifically, to the *textual functioning* of signification, that is, to the insistence of the signifier in a signifying chain (that of a text or of a life). (*Jacques Lacan and the Adventure of Insight*, 139)

That the term "lesbian" operates as an insistent signifier in my life has never been clearer to me. Implicit in its structure, the coming-out story has a moment of revelation that structures the meaning of what came before it. Perhaps it explains the feeling I had of being "different." Perhaps it explains unnamed desires or any number of dissonances, conscious and unconscious. My latest version offers an explanation for a physical affliction that for years had been a mystery to me. It now functions not just to identify me as a lesbian who came to the knowledge of her lesbianism quite early in her life, but also to reveal the anxieties associated with it, its inflections of shock and sadness. The function of this coming-out story has now doubled. Where once it was a story evoked by personal contact, told to friends and acquaintances for intimate and political reasons, now it is written down, evoked in and by a theoretical context. A story of coming into a social consciousness has also become, in its more recent psychoanalytic context, a story about possible unconscious associations and reactions. A story of revelation and discovery is now also a story of shock and loss of control, verging on death.

This story might function for me like psychoanalysis itself does for Shoshana Felman:

> What then, is psychoanalysis if not precisely a *life usage of the death instinct*—a practical, productive use of the compulsion to repeat, through a replaying of the symbolic meaning of the death that the subject has repeatedly experienced, and through a recognition and assumption of the

> meaning of this death (separation, loss) as a symbolic means of the subject's coming to terms not with death but, paradoxically, with life? (139)

Thus my coming-out story is now also about coming to terms with the possibility of coming undone, as well as coming to understand how its "insistent" presence tells of past losses. But if these are some of the psychoanalytic meanings of the story's repetition at a very individual level, how might it be understood in Foucauldian terms, as a story which participates in stabilizing a collective category?

Both a Freudian and a Foucauldian understanding of identity orbit around notions of repetition. If the compulsion to repeat and the return of the repressed are psychoanalytic concepts, repetition as parody has a different theoretical history. While Freud's formulations are based on originary moments in the past, parody is much more a creature of the present; it has closer links to Foucault. Patrick Hutton in an essay on "Foucault, Freud, and the Technologies of the Self" makes this comparison:

> Foucault argues that we discover our identity not by fathoming the original meaning of behaviour precedents, as Freud taught, but rather by deconstructing the formalities through which we endlessly examine, evaluate, and classify our experiences…. Freud's concern about the past emphasizes recollection. Foucault, in contrast, stresses repetition, which reinforces his central proposition about the paradox of the human condition: We are beings that create forms which ironically imprison our creativity. This pattern of creation and constraint is ceaselessly repeated. Past experiences, Foucault argues, do not shape us irrevocably, as Freud believed. Rather, we continually reshape our past creations to conform to our present creative needs. (Martin, 136–137)

Hutton's generalization about Freud is correct: the compulsion to repeat is a failure of recollection. But what is also clear is that the respective emphases on recollection and repetition on the parts of both Freud and Foucault also involve a valuation of those processes. For Freud, repetition is a symptom and recollection the cure, while for Foucault, recollection is an artifice and repetition is the generative moment. However, in a more didactic and less dialectical moment, Foucault writes, "The purpose of history…is not to discover the roots of our identity but to commit ourselves to its dissipation" (quoted in Weeks, 111). Rather than commit herself to the dissipation of identity, however, Butler argues against Foucault that non-identity is neither the goal nor a state of bliss.

Foucault, in his introduction to the memoirs of a nineteenth-century her-
maphrodite, Herculine Barbin, writes that her reminiscences shortly before her
suicide evoke "the happy limbo of a non-identity." Barbin's deprivation was not
due to the undecidability of her sex, but rather her deprivation of the "delights
she experienced in not having one, or in not entirely having the same sex as the
girls among whom she loved and desired so much" (*Herculine Barbin*, xiii).
Butler argues that Foucault's theorizing of Barbin's "non-identity" bears a strong
resemblance to female homosexuality, and further, Foucault's own "non-identity" can be seen as a parallel subtext (*Gender Trouble*, 93–106). Foucault's
antipathy to lesbianism theoretically, historically and in contemporary politics,
is made quite clear by Butler, and perhaps fuels her fight with him. For Butler,
Barbin's ambivalence about her identity tests the limits of Foucault's idealization of non-identity. One might also say that Foucault's idealization of
non-identity tests the limits of Butler's ambivalence to her identity.

Which brings me back to my coming-out story. It is certainly a story of the
production of an identity within the category of a regulatory regime. My subsequent "confessions" of my sexuality led to moral regulation at home and at
school. But the events of the story also occurred in a specific historical time and
place, when the political *need* to assert lesbian identity was perhaps at its peak.
Sidney Abbott and Barbara Love wrote in 1972:

> A Lesbian activist tries to achieve a new way of looking at herself and the
> world. She frees her ego from the crushing influences of society and con-
> siders herself the equal of men and heterosexuals. She resolves sane schiz-
> ophrenia by withdrawing ego investment from her straight-identified
> component and investing it in her new identity as a total Lesbian woman.
> At first there is considerable fear that the Lesbian identity is too small,
> too incomplete to build a life on. "I am more than a Lesbian" is a common
> statement. However, as gay women begin to think about sexuality, its place
> in a life as well its relationship to cultural and political patterns, the term
> Lesbian begins to expand in scope and meaning. (*Sappho Was A Right-On
> Woman*, 218)

Reading this passage now, one can see the structuralist sins Abbott and Love
commit.[11] Equal to men and heterosexuals, the category "Lesbian" could also
conserve the boundaries of both gender and heterosexuality. An ego that with-
draws its investment in its straight-identified component would in fact be
disavowing the role of heterosexuality. No ego is unified or masterly enough to
enact this withdrawal successfully. The effect would be repression, and ultimately

it would return to undermine the identity of the "total Lesbian woman." The expansion in scope and meaning of the term "Lesbian" can only be relative to its incorporation into regulatory regimes.

My flippancy here is not to dismiss the importance of the insights of both psychoanalytic and Foucauldian theory into the functions and failures of identities. However, in twenty years' time current configurations of the potential of identity could seem as ideologically bound as those of twenty years ago seem now. Because twenty years ago I came out, and in the process recognized that I belonged to a certain category and now, twenty years later, I also recognize the potential of coming undone, I have learned that versions of the self (to use a phrase of James Clifford's) can change dramatically through political and historical time. Rather than invoke the "chaos" of Clausen's odd metaphors— "Tragic Mulatto of the Sexual World"—or do the Butler backpedal, bodies do matter after all—I would rather try to remember the various versions of my self, what evoked them and why I might want consciously or unconsciously to defend them. My discomfort with Butler's work is in the end quite simple, and perhaps simple-minded: recollection, contextualized historically, is what gives repetition memory. That is, there may be great subversive potential in parody but we parody ourselves as much as any other "original." I am not trying to reinstate the coming-out story as an origin story for gay and lesbian identities, or argue that it cannot be dispensed with in the name of progress, but it truly does remind me, in the face of much seductive theory to the contrary, that I do not "play my lesbianism as a role." It is "psychically entrenched play," as Butler points out, but, one must insist, physically and historically entrenched play also. Identity as fantasmatic and parodic can work to both display and displace the operations of power. But even fantasies have historical contexts, and parodies can wreck permanent havoc on the body.

NOTES

1. The trope of "coming out" has recently begun to lose its specificity as a term of gay and lesbian identity as its usages have proliferated to other kinds of sexual identities—coming out as a bisexual or an incest survivor, for example—and generally to any telling of experience that breaks some code of silence. But the very nature of "coming out," whether it only applies to things that can be hidden, not obviously

marked on the body, can also be used to describe a process of coming into a consciousness and identifying and making visible to others differences which are often more obvious. Can one "come out" as racially marked, for example?

2. At the same time neuroscientists search for the germ of homosexuality to remove any of the contaminating notion of "choice." See Simon LeVay, *The Sexual Brain.*

3. A particularly interesting reading on the need for "homosexuals" by heterosexuality is given by Eve Sedgwick in her introduction to *The Epistemology of the Closet.*

4. See also Loraine Hutchins and Lani Kaahumanu eds. *Bi Any Other Name: Bisexual People Speak Out*, particularly part IV, "Politics: A Queer Among Queers" which provides strong evidence of how the gay and lesbian movement has come to be seen in some ways as a new locus for identity regulation.

5. A nodal point is emerging around the question of identity stability and the insights of psychoanalytic theory for lesbians. In her oft-cited essay, "Femininity and its Discontents" Jacqueline Rose writes that "The unconscious constantly reveals the 'failure' of identity...something that is endlessly repeated and relived moment by moment throughout our individual histories" (91). Rose argues that "Feminism's affinity with psychoanalysis rests above all...with this recognition that there is a resistance to identity at the very heart of psychic life" (ibid). See also Diane Hamer, "SIGNIFICANT OTHERS: Lesbianism and Psychoanalytic Theory." Hamer makes a good argument why this formulation of the instability of identity in psychoanalytic theory is particularly fraught for lesbians. She asks, "How do we move towards a psychoanalytic understanding of lesbian identity—and by that I mean how do we begin to think about the history of the formation of our lesbianism, as a contingent identity constructed from individual biographical details rather than as something authentic, natural or pre-given—without pathologizing it, without making it a symptom of a sickness?" (135).

6. Many women I have talked to over the years have spoken about a "second adolescence" that seemed to be part of the process of starting sexual relationships with other women at any point in adulthood. Perhaps the newness of the sexual experience, the unfamiliarity of a new set of social conventions or a new social milieu reminds one of the awkwardness of adolescence. But the change in sexual identity that is likely to accompany this change in sexual behavior might also harken back to something that is often associated with adolescence, in Freud's terms, a new awareness of sexual object choice. See "Three Essays on the Theory of Sexuality," particularly "The Transformations of Puberty" (1905, *SE,* 7).

7. See Mandy Merck "Train of Thought in Freud's Case of Homosexuality in a Woman." *m/f* 11/12 (1986): "[H]e believed that the girl 'was not in any way ill'— not neurotic, but its negative, perverse. (As early as 1905, Freud has opposed the neuroses to the perversions, arguing that neurotic symptoms are formed at the cost of abnormal sexuality...)" (36).

8. See Freud's "Dora" (*SE* 60–63) and Judith Roof "Freud Reads Lesbians" (*Lure of Knowledge*, 190–197).

9. For an excellent discussion of Freud's wavering conclusions about lesbian sexuality

and the problems it poses for his generalized theory of female sexuality see Judith Roof, *A Lure of Knowledge*, particularly chapter four, "Freud Reads Lesbians."

10. The notion of "secondary identity" then could be applied to that process by which any political identity is developed even if the physical or other characteristics on which it depends are previously present. It describes a coming into consciousness in relation to historical and social processes, much like Teresa de Lauretis's definition of identity in "Eccentric Subjects": "identity is a locus of multiple and variable positions, which are made available in the social field by historical process and which one comes to assume subjectively and discursively in the form of political consciousness" (137).

11. It is interesting to note that in 1972 Abbott and Love offered a critique of the "naturalness" of heterosexuality much like that of Butler's in *Gender Trouble*: "Heterosexuality—far from seeming effortless or natural, seems to be taught, reinforced, and rewarded from earliest childhood" (190). However, their critique is undermined by their immediate renaturalization of sexuality: "It is plausible to assume that the reason strong social controls rewarding heterosexuality and punishing homosexuality exist is exactly that homosexuality is equally natural, and is therefore a real danger to a heterosexual social system" (ibid).

BIBLIOGRAPHY

Abbott, Sidney and Barbara Love. *Sappho Was a Right-On Woman: A Liberated View of Lesbianism*. New York: Stein and Day, 1972.

Brown, Norman O. *Life Against Death: The Psychoanalytic Meaning of History*. Middletown, Conn.: Wesleyan University Press, 1985. (1959).

Butler, Judith. *Gender Trouble*. New York: Routledge, 1990.

———. "Imitation and Gender Insubordination." In *inside/out: Lesbian Theories, Gay Theories*, ed. Diana Fuss. New York and London: Routledge, 1991. 13–31.

———. "Lana's 'Imitation': Melodramatic Repetition and the Gender Performative." *Genders* 9 (Fall 1990): 1–18.

———. "The Pleasures of Repetition" In *Pleasure Beyond the Pleasure Principle*, eds. Robert Glick and Stanley Bone. New Haven and London: Yale University Press, 1990.

De Lauretis, Teresa. "Eccentric Subjects: Feminist Theory and Historical Consciousness." *Feminist Studies* vol. 16, no. 1 (1990): 115–150.

Clausen, Jan. "My Interesting Condition." *Outlook* 7 (Winter 1990): 10–21.

Derrida, Jacques. "To Speculate—On 'Freud'." Kamuf ed. 516–68.

Felman, Shoshana. *Jacques Lacan and the Adventure of Insight: Psychoanalysis in Contemporary Culture*. Cambridge, MA: Harvard University Press, 1987.

Foucault, Michel. *History of Sexuality*. Vol 1. New York: Vintage, 1980.

———. *Herculine Barbin*. Trans. Richard McDougall. New York: Pantheon, 1980.

Freud, Sigmund. "Remembering, Repeating and Working-Through." (1914). *The*

Standard Edition of the Complete Psychological Works of Sigmund Freud, trans. and ed. James Strachey. Vol 12. London: Hogarth Press. 24 vols. 1953–74. 146–56.

———. "Mourning and Melancholia." (1915). *The Standard Edition*. Vol. 14.

———. "Beyond the Pleasure Principle." (1920). *The Standard Edition*. Vol 18. 3–64.

———. "The Psychogenesis of A Case of Homosexuality in a Woman." (1920). Vol 18. 146–72.

Grosz, Elizabeth. *Jacques Lacan: A Feminist Introduction*. London and New York: Routledge, 1990.

Hamer, Diane. "SIGNIFICANT OTHERS: Lesbianism and Psychoanalytic Theory." *Feminist Review* 34 (Spring 1990): 134–51.

Hutchins, Loraine and Lani Kaahumanu, eds. *Bi Any Other Name: Bisexual People Speak Out* Boston: Allyson Publications, 1991.

Irigaray, Luce. "The gesture in psychoanalysis." Trans. Elizabeth Guild. In *Between Feminism and Psychoanalysis*, ed. Teresa Brennan. London: Routledge, 1989.

Jameson, Fredric. "Postmodernism and Consumer Society." In *The Anti-Aesthetic: Essays on Postmodern Culture*, ed. Hal Foster. Port Townsend, WA: Bay Press, 1983, 111–25.

Kamuf, Peggy. *A Derrida Reader: Between the Blinds*. New York: Columbia, 1991.

Lacan, Jacques. *Écrits*. Trans. Alan Sheridan. New York: Norton, 1977.

———. *The Four Fundamental Concepts of Psycho-Analysis*. Trans. Alan Sheridan. New York: Norton, 1981.

Laplanche, J., J.-B. Pontalis. *The Language of Psychoanalysis*. Trans. Donald Nicholson-Smith. New York: Norton, 1973.

LeVay, Simon. *The Sexual Brain*. Cambridge, Mass.: MIT Press, 1993.

Martin, Luther H., Huch Gutman, Patrick H. Hutton. *Technologies of the Self: A Seminar with Michel Foucault*. Amherst: University of Massachusetts Press, 1988.

Merck, Mandy. "The Train of Thought in Freud's 'Case of Homosexuality in a Woman.'" *m/f* 11/12 (1986): 35–46.

Mercer, Kobena. "'1968': Periodizing Postmodern Politics and Identity." In *Cultural Studies*, eds. Lawrence Grossberg, Cary Nelson and Paula Treichler. New York: Routledge, 1992, 424–49.

Newton, Esther. *Mother Camp: Female Impersonators in America*. Chicago: University of Chicago Press, 1972.

Omosupe, Ekua. "Black/Lesbian/Bulldagger." *differences* vol. 3, no. 2 (1991):101–11.

Rose, Jacqueline. *Sexuality in the Field of Vision*. London: Verso, 1986.

Sedgwick, Eve Kosofsky. *Epistemology of the Closet*. Berkeley: University Of California Press, 1990.

Weeks, Jeffrey. "Foucault for Historians." *History Workshop Journal* 14 (1982): 106–19.

Contributors

Joseph A. Boone is Associate Professor of English at University of Southern California. He is co-editor with Michael Cadden of *Engendering Men: The Question of Male Feminist Criticism* (Routledge, 1990).

Julia Creet is a doctoral student in the History of Consciousness program at UC-Santa Cruz. She has published a number of articles on lesbian representability, including "Daughter of the Movement: Psychodynamics of Lesbian S/M Fantasy" which appeared in a special queer theory issue of *differences*.

Samuel Delany is the author of the recently reissued four volume *Tales of Neveryon*. He has also written three volumes of memoirs, the latest of which is *The Motion of Light in Water*, and has a book of written interviews, *Silent Interviews*, forthcoming from Wesleyan University Press.

Monica Dorenkamp is a doctoral student in English and Film Studies at Rutgers University. She was the coordinator of the Fifth Annual Lesbian and Gay Studies Conference.

Richard Fung is a Toronto videomaker and activist. His videos include *Chinese Characters* (1986), *The Way to My Father's Village* (1988), *My Mother's Place* (1990), and *Fighting Chance* (1990). He has also published an essay, "Looking for My Penis: The Eroticized Asian in Gay Video Porn" in *How Do I Look?* (Bay Press, 1991).

Richard Henke recently received his doctorate from Rutgers University. He is currently completing a manuscript, *Passive Resistance*, on Henry James and the social construction of masculinity.

Marcia Ian is an Assistant Professor of English at Rutgers University. Her book, *Remembering the Phallic Mother: Psychoanalysis, Modernism, and the Fetish*, was published by Cornell University Press (1993).

Richard Meyer is a doctoral student in art history at the University of California, Berkeley. He has published essays on Rock Hudson and Robert Mapplethorpe.

Sylvia Molloy is Professor of Comparative Literature at New York University. She is the author of a novel, *En breve carcel* (*Certificate of Absence,* 1981), and of a book on Borges, *Las Letras de Borges* (*Signs of Borges*).

Eve Kosofsky Sedgwick is Professor of English Literature at Duke University. She is the author of *Between Men: English Literature and Male Homosocial Desire* (1985) and *Epistemology of the Closet* (1990).

Simon Watney is the Assistant Editor of the National AIDS Manual in the UK. He has been actively involved in gay politics since the early 1970s, and is the author of *Policing Desire: Pornography, AIDS and the Media* (1987), and co-editor with Erica Carter of *Taking Liberties: AIDS and Cultural Politics* (1989).